THE CASTLE
ON THE HILL

ELIZABETH GOUDGE

ELIZABETH GOUDGE

THE CASTLE
ON THE HILL

HODDER AND STOUGHTON

*The characters in this book are entirely imaginary
and have no relation to any living person*

FIRST PUBLISHED   MAY 1942
HODDER PAPERBACK EDITION 1954
SECOND IMPRESSION   1966
THIRD IMPRESSION   1967
FOURTH IMPRESSION   1968

(PUBLISHED BY ARRANGEMENT WITH THE
ORIGINAL PUBLISHERS OF THE BOOK,
GERALD DUCKWORTH & CO. LTD.)

Printed and bound in Great Britain for
Hodder and Stoughton Ltd.,
St. Paul's House, Warwick Lane,
London, E.C.4
by Hazell Watson & Viney Ltd.,
Aylesbury, Bucks

SBN 340 00396 0

HID deep in the heart of the woods, haunted and old,
The shell of a Castle still stands, a story told,
Built high on a rock in the woods, frozen and cold.

Deep are the night-dark shadows under the wall,
Breathlessly whispering downward the snowflakes fall,
Shrouding the desolate towers in a stainless pall.

Fearful within me my own heart, failing, has died,
I too in the woods am frozen, bereaved, sore tried.
Alone here . . . There in the shadows, who was it sighed?

There, in the bastioned walls where the gateway stands,
Are there shadows within its shadows, weaving the strands
Back through the loom of past sorrow with pain-worn hands?

Shadows weeping a world grown cold and stark with pain,
Mourning once more the lights put out, put out again,
The loveliness broken and lost, the young men slain.

Has sorrow alone lived here for a hundred years?
Is only hatred immortal, men's craven fears?
Only the weeping of women, their useless tears?

Not winter only reigns here in this haunted place.
As the cold clouds part, defeated, the sunbeams lace
The dark trees with their diamond light, touch the worn face

Of the frozen stone with colour, with azure fire
Of spring-times long past, yet alive, the hot desire
Of summers never forgotten, hopes that aspire

For ever, courage unbeaten, valour aflame,
The unshaken victory of the men who name
Holy things to their strength. . . . Nor fear, nor hate nor shame

Is theirs. . . . I see the flashing of arms on the wall,
Hear the deep roar of the conflict, the thrilling call
Of the silver trumpet sounding high on the tall

Towers of God's immortal fortress, that he made
Against the evil out of the love of men laid
At his feet, their sweat, their blood to the last drop paid.

For this is the rock that for all time man defends,
The rock of his soul against which all evil spends
Its fury in vain in the warfare that never ends.

And these the embattled walls that the heroes trod,
Swift-winged with flame, their feet with the gospel shod,
For this is the house of all life, the house of God.

Lift up, lift up your constant hearts, the trumpet cries,
Lift them up to the shining walls, the sun-drenched skies,
For beyond the night for ever the sun will rise.

CHAPTER I

I

VERY few people noticed the woman who was sitting in the sunshine on the seat at the top of the steps outside the Free Library, the roar of London's traffic at her back and her eyes upon the notice board with its list of vacant situations. She was not noticeable. She was one of those nondescript women to whom one may be introduced ten times but still one doesn't recognize them when one meets them in the street. There was just nothing about Miss Brown that stood out, nothing, so to speak, to catch hold of. Yet she was a pretty woman, with a neat little figure and a quiet dignity that were attractive. Her small features were clear-cut, her pale skin smooth and unwrinkled in spite of her forty-two years. Her delicate lips were sweetly and firmly folded and her beautifully shaped dark eyes beneath the pencilled eyebrows were shy and gentle as a doe's. Her straight brown hair, severely fastened in a knot in the nape of her neck, was soft and smooth and had no grey in it. She had so much freshness, so much outward serenity, that it was surprising that she was not more noticeable. But then Miss Brown had never wanted to be noticed. She was one of those people with a gift for protective colouring, like a shy white rabbit in the snow. Wherever she went she could manage to be so much a part of her background that one did not see her there.

This gift for protective colouring was partly due to Miss Brown's shyness, partly due to her invariable contentment with her background, and partly to her style of dress. She was fastidious and she liked to be neat and tidy, but she never had any money to spend on her clothes and so she had years ago adopted the tailor-made style of dressing that fits in anywhere and does not go out of fashion. She wore a dark-blue coat and skirt, shabby but well-brushed, and fitting her well, grey stockings and neatly-laced black shoes, and a severe plain straw hat was placed dead-straight upon the top of her round little head. In spite of the beauty of the day she carried a neatly-furled black umbrella, in case a thunderstorm should come on and ruin her hat, for she had to be careful of her hats, and her hands in their neatly darned grey gloves were quietly folded upon the large old-fashioned bulging black handbag in her lap.

7

She sat very still upon the seat before the Free Library, the roar of London at her back, and for almost the first time in her life she was not liking her background. Though her eyes were fixed upon the notice board with its meagre list of vacant situations that would not do at all, she was no longer seeing it. She was seeing nothing. For Miss Brown was in the grip of fear; not just apprehension or anxiety, but real fear, naked and horrible. Though she looked so serene sitting there in the sunshine her body was ice-cold and she was finding it quite difficult to breathe.

"And yet I'm not worse off than many other people," she said to herself. "I have lost my home and my livelihood, but so have lots of others. This that is happening to me, this sort of chasm opening at my feet, is happening to the whole world. I am not alone. I am not alone. I am not alone."

But what she reiterated to herself brought her no conviction. Her loss of everything she had hitherto known was making her feel as solitary as though she were the only human creature alive in the world. And what a world! It was June nineteen forty. Yesterday was gone, burnt up in the blazing inferno of its suffering. There was to-day, a tiny patch of foothold, but there was no to-morrow. The abyss at whose edge she seemed to herself to be standing was filled with swirling mist. Down below the mist were lightnings and thunders and great voices, and out beyond it presumably the sun still shone, but what shape the things below would take, and whether one would ever win out into the sunlight again, one could not know. To-day was one step at a time in the mist, a step taken quite alone because if there were other people there she could not see them, and to-morrow was so uncertain that it did not exist. Memory of the past and hope for the future are companionable things. Now that they seemed to have vanished the loneliness made her very afraid. I can't bear it, she thought abruptly, and for the first time in her life. I just can't bear it. What do I do? What do I *do*?

Such a small thing can sometimes lighten despair. In Miss Brown's case it was just a tune. A street musician was playing a violin somewhere down in the street below. Miss Brown was not particularly musical but she liked good tunes, and especially on the violin. It always seemed to her that a violin was more of a living voice than other instruments. In a great symphony it was the first violins that seemed to cry out the good news while the other instruments throbbed and murmured in assent. And it always seemed to Miss Brown that you couldn't use a violin to say mean or lying things. If you tried to it merely made revolting noises. The authentic voice was not heard unless it spoke the truth.

And she knew it was the truth that she was listening to now. She heard no words, she saw no vision, but she was slowly made aware that she was one of a multitude that went upon pilgrimage to something or other. She had no idea what the something was, or how they were to get there, all she knew was that the way was stony and painful, dreadful, terrifying; yet worth daring all the same. The pilgrims, she knew, were a motley crowd, old and young, rich and poor, brave men and cowards, kings and queens and merchants, cunning thieves and footsore ragged vagabonds, confused, quarrelsome, ignorant, even the wisest of them, their abysmal ignorance merely a question of degree; but as they journeyed they sang, and always they went on; whatever happened they went on, and sang. That was the truth about this pilgrimage. It went on, and it was a matter for rejoicing.

A small movement of relaxation was observable in Miss Brown's quiet taut figure. She was leaning back against something, not the hard wooden rail of the seat but the roar of the London traffic. She felt it suddenly as a wall behind her. Buses, lorries, cars, vans, drays, bicycles, all carrying human people, all going somewhere, and glad of it. The roar of their passing was no longer just a noise, it was the throbbing and murmuring chorus of assent to the solo voice of the violin that was still crying aloud good news somewhere down on the curb; it was the song of the pilgrims as they journeyed along to wherever it was they were going. And Miss Brown was going with them. She was not alone. She was not alone. She was not alone.

She got up, and her knees were shaking beneath her. Just as she had never in her life before experienced such fear as had lately shaken her, so she had also never experienced such a flashing moment of delight as had come to her when she had felt she was leaning back against that wall. Both moments had passed now and except for her shaking knees she was her precise and ordinary self again. She looked at her watch. It was time to be going on. That music! The man, whoever he was, was still playing away down there, though not now the music that had so moved her. Surely he was playing remarkably well for a street musician? She opened her bulging black handbag and looked thoughtfully at its contents. Could she afford to give him something? He had lifted her out of a moment of quite dreadful fear and she was grateful. Resolutely she took out a shilling. To her, at the present time, a shilling was rather a large sum of money.

She walked down the steps to the street, and along the pavement towards the tall man with a violin tucked beneath his chin whom she saw standing beside the curb. The music that he was playing now made her think, in this hot London street filled with the fumes of petrol, of cool green leaves rustling in a wood. The shadows beneath them were deep and cool, and they cried with their myriad rustling voices, "Come this way. Come this way." There was something hidden in the heart of the wood, some sort of refuge.

She reached the musician and bent to put her shilling into the battered hat he had placed upon the pavement. Then she straightened herself and looked at him, and he, seeing that she wanted to speak to him, stopped playing.

"Thank you, Miss," he said.

"It is I who should say thank-you," said Miss Brown. "Thank you for your nice music." And then she blushed, for she was one of those old-fashioned modest women who always blush when they are doing something unusual. And it was most unusual for Miss Brown to speak to a strange man in the street. She could never recollect having done such a dreadful thing before.

Then she looked into the eyes of the man before her and completely forgot herself. For this man, though he had played music that had lifted her out of her fear, was yet himself afraid. His eyes were as windows opening upon the abyss of fear. Through them she saw not only this man's fear, but the fear of the whole world. For a terrible moment, for the few seconds during which she shut her eyes and opened them, she felt it surge over her; then she looked again and saw just one of those battered human creatures who float about the shores of great cities like scum on the surface of a stream. . . . But no, he was not quite the usual poor vagabond whom one saw about these streets. When she had thanked him for his music his face had softened, as though he were suddenly sharply touched, and in that moment she had been aware of a certain style about him. He had looked—kingly was the word that occurred to her, though it was an odd word to use about a street musician. She wished it were possible for him to know the compassion that was in her heart for him. She wished it showed as clearly in her eyes as his fear had shown in his.

He was a tall bony man, a Jew by the look of him, with strong fierce bones jutting through the tightly stretched sallow skin, black eyes deeply sunken beneath bushy grey eyebrows, the fear in them quickly veiled of deliberate intent, a tight bitter mouth closed angrily upon his pain, whatever it might be, and deep lines scored from the arrogant reddened nose to the ill-shaven chin. In spite of the heat of the day he wore a threadbare overcoat buttoned over in a futile attempt to hide the dilapidation of the clothes beneath. His trousers were frayed, and the boots beneath them were broken.

"That was a nice piece you were playing," said Miss Brown, her bulging black handbag thrust under her arm and her gloved hands clasped tightly together in her nervousness. . . . For was "piece" the right word to use when speaking to a musician of a musical composition? She was not sure, though it was what she had called "The Harmonious Blacksmith" when she had played it on Sundays on the upright piano at home. . . . "That piece with whispering leaves in it," she went on shyly, "and some sort of refuge in the middle of a wood."

The musician looked startled. "Delius' 'Song of Summer,'" he said. "I've thought, too, that there is a refuge in the wood. Are you a musician?"

"No, oh no," said Miss Brown, clasping and unclasping her shy hands. "Though I used to play the piano a little once. . . . I've never heard of Delius," she added.

The musician grinned, the hard lines of his face softening again in his amusement at the naïveté of this demure, old-fashioned little woman. "It's not my usual habit to commit sacrilege by playing Delius in these streets," he said. "Those like yourself who are sensitive to musical impressions are rare in these parts. I usually play the latest tripe from the musical comedies. To-day, for some reason or other, I suddenly tried to play Delius. Only tried. My violin's as worn out as my talent. And in any case a song written for the orchestra can scarcely be captured by one voice only."

"But the first violin is the important voice," said Miss Brown. "The one that tells the truth."

Again the musician grinned, and gave her a mocking little bow. "That is a most magnanimous confession for a pianist to make," he told her.

His voice was husky and harsh, the voice of a man who has been for a long time exposed to hardship and bad weather in the streets, but something about its intonation, as well as the words that he used, startled Miss Brown into wondering if once he had been a gentleman.

"Was the other piece that you were playing Delius too?" she asked.

"Which one?" he asked, and again he was smiling. She knew

that he knew which one. He was just amusing himself by testing what he called her sensitiveness to musical impressions.

"The one that made me think of people—all of us—going on pilgrimage," she faltered, and blushed crimson.

"Yes, that was Delius," he said. "At least what I was able to reproduce of his setting of the Pilgrim's Song in Flecker's 'Hassan'."

Miss Brown was no wiser. She looked at him in mute appeal. "Where were they going?" she asked.

"They'd no more idea than the rest of us," he said. "But they had a notion that when they got there they would know why men are born."

"Beyond the veil all things will be made plain," said Miss Brown tritely, echoing a platitude she was very fond of; and then she was suddenly frightened by the look of bitter mockery that flickered over the musician's face. What had she said this time that was funny? People often smiled at her remarks, and she never knew why. And she was becoming more and more overwhelmed by the oddness of this conversation, and by the remembrance that it is most unladylike, as well as dangerous, to speak to strange men in the streets. "I must go now," she faltered. "I have a train to catch." And she moved away a little.

He bowed, gracefully and easily, as though from the concert platform, but she felt the quick hurt withdrawal in him, as though he felt she had repulsed him, and she immediately moved back. "Thank you," she said again. "I was feeling very afraid when you played that Pilgrim's Song, but when I heard it I was not afraid any more." The she really did go, quickly, lest worse befall, and so she did not see the look of amazed, incredulous delight that swept over his face.

I I

As she walked along the street to catch her bus to the station Miss Brown discovered that memory of the past and hope for the future, which in her fear and loneliness a little while ago she had felt were destroyed for ever, were with her again, and were good company.

Her thoughts moved back into the past and were at home. How absurd to think that one could lose one's past. One couldn't. It was part of one. Her father and mother, whom she had so deeply loved, James Brown the commercial traveller in hardware and Agnes his wife, were walking down the street one on each side of her, and she was holding their hands, as she had done when she was a little girl. The keen salt air of the sea-coast town that had been her home was blowing in her face and she could see the sunlight sparkling on the sea. She adored the sea, and the hard keen breath of cold winds. They were in her blood, because James Brown had once been a sailor and had always been a man who liked hardness. His boyhood had been spent in a windjammer, his early manhood as first mate of a British coaster, and when injuries received in a storm at sea drove him back to the land for good he had travelled firmly in fire-irons and coal scuttles. This he had done not from chance but from choice. He could have travelled in silk petticoats if he had wanted to, or perfume or soap, but he had preferred hardware. He was that sort of man; an ugly, brave, proud, independent, sensible little man, a stern Methodist and an adamant disciplinarian. He had most deeply loved his daughter but as he had never happened to mention the fact to her she did not know how much. Perhaps she would have been a different kind of woman if she had; the hidden adoration she had had for him might have been encouraged to creep forth into some sort of flowering. Yet if he had contributed to the stunting of her womanhood he had contributed also to the richness of her humanity; as well as his love of the sea he had given her his pride, his courage, his common-sense and his passionate love of independence.

Miss Brown's Christian name was Dolores and it did not suit her at all. It had been given her by her mother. The marriage of Agnes and James Brown had been the marriage of opposites. James's affection for fire-irons and coal scuttles had been nicely balanced by Agnes's passion for soiled blue hair ribbons and little unread dusty books of poetry bound in purple calf. Agnes had been a silly, loving, sentimental woman, never at grips with reality yet utterly single-minded in her perpetual striving after Beauty and Romance. When they had failed her in her own life, for her fluffy fragile looks had soon faded and not even she could prolong the romance of marriage to a man like James beyond the honeymoon, she had lived vicariously in her child. Dolores should be the very incarnation of Beauty and Romance, she had decided, with the beauty of Helen of Troy and the noble moral qualities of all the heroines of Miss Marie Corelli rolled into one. She should be the faithful wife of one adoring husband, though of course her path should be strewn with the corpses of rejected lovers, and she should produce six angelic little children with no difficulty at all. When she passed in the street every eye should follow her and when she died, at a ripe old age and quite painlessly, there should not be a dry eye at the graveside.

But Dolores had never at any time been in the least like that. She had not even seemed to want to be like that. Her own looks had never interested her very much and the only proposal of marriage she had ever had, from Mr. Jobson of the gents' underwear department at Smerdon and Hodges, a most respectable widower bearing a strong resemblance to the Duke of Wellington, she had immediately refused. She had seemed to be possessed of neither yearning nor ambition. Her working days spent in the haberdashery department at Smerdon and Hodges, her evenings at home playing demure little pieces on the demure upright piano, and her Sundays of chapel-going and rambling on the seashore, had seemed utterly to satisfy her. The romantic name of Dolores was a complete misfit. Once she had put up her hair no one but her mother had ever used it. . . . She had always been Miss Brown.

Life is very disappointing for the romantics and Agnes had died of bronchitis and discouragement when she was only sixty years of age, lamenting almost with her last breath that absolutely nothing of her lived on in her daughter. Yet here she had been wrong. Miss Brown's unexpressed love of natural beauty, her absorption in the white wings of the gulls beating against the blue of the sky and her hour-long watching of the waves, had been her mother's love of blue ribbon and dusty purple books purged by her father's common-sense.

It had been after her mother's death that Miss Brown had left Smerdon and Hodges and turned their house "Sea View" into a boarding house, so that she could look after her father, not so strong now as he had been, and not able to travel so far or so persuasively, and at the same time augment the rapidly diminishing income from the hardware by taking lodgers. Apart from her sorrow at his failing powers, and her grief for her mother, this had been perhaps the happiest time in her happy life. It had been very hard work, but she had increasingly loved her father, and the walls of her beloved home had been always about her and the sea had been always just outside her windows. As she had worked, polishing the beloved furniture and washing the precious cups and saucers that had been her friends from babyhood, she had heard the crying of the gulls and the murmur of the waves on the shore and had known what it was to be content.

And then her father had died and for some while her happiness had been shattered. But it had returned. She had still had her beloved "Sea View" and into it had gone all her strength and her courage, her hopes and her savings. It had been grand work to care for her lodgers who were sick or tired, rest them and feed them and make them whole again. She had stinted nothing that she had to give and though she had made new men and women and children of them she had not made much money and she had worked much too hard. But she had been happy and useful and perpetually needed, and as she grew older she had developed a taste for reading that had given new joy to her very few leisure hours. It had been pure delight to sit before the fire in her little parlour on winter evenings when she had no lodgers, with the wind roaring over the roof and the waves thundering on the shore, and read history books from the Free Library. History was her favourite reading, especially the history of the great men of her country's past. She was a hero worshipper and she had a love of tradition that had come to her from her father, whose boyhood's training had taken place beneath the panoply of towering white sails and to the music of the capstan chanties. . . . Miss Brown had had a dream that one day, when she did not have such difficulty in making both ends meet and the boarding house was on a more secure footing, she might save enough money to take a long holiday and, history book in hand, visit the Castles of England, the Cathedrals and the old ports and cities where the great deeds had been done.

But that longed-for prosperity had never come. The war had come instead, France had fallen, and with her, so inter-knit are the fortunes of the human race, had come crashing the fortunes of a little lodging-house keeper on the south coast of England. The tragedy of France had been Miss Brown's tragedy too, and Miss Brown's tragedy, though in the agonised confusion of the times no one would notice it, would not be without its effect upon the spider's web of human entities into which it would throw her.

As she walked along the street her thoughts of the past reached the last crashing weeks that had landed her, so desperately afraid, on the seat before the Free Library. Like the fall of France it had all seemed to happen so quickly. The sea view from her windows, that had always been so lovely and such an asset to her boarding-house, had suddenly, with enemy-occupied France only a few miles away across the Channel, become the very reverse of an asset, and her guests had abruptly left her. Then, almost overnight so it had seemed to Miss Brown, there had been khaki-clad heroes in tin hats swarming everywhere, guns on the cliffs and barbed wire entanglements along the beach in front of her windows, the drone of enemy planes overhead and the crashing and vibration of their bombs. Stunned and bewildered Miss Brown had listened to grim yet stirring speeches over the wireless, and gradually, in company with all her countrymen, had been dragged by the genius of the man who stood at the head of the nation from bewilderment to resolution, from horror to hope, until at last, though there was no to-morrow, to-day had given her firm ground beneath her feet and a courage in her soul like beating and ascending wings. Living on the heights, thoughtless of the morrow that did not exist, she had been suddenly ridiculously at rest, and ready to dare to the uttermost. Physical injury or death had seemed only little things. She and "Sea View" would take in military instead of civilian lodgers and see things out joyfully together till the end.

To begin with, she had thought things were going to happen as she had hoped. Those men in the tin hats who swarmed among the guns and the barbed wire had suddenly ceased to be rather nebulous heroes, at whom she peered reverently through the wire netting that protected her window panes, and became instead a couple of concrete and business-like young men standing upon her doorstep and explaining kindly but firmly that they wanted her house.

"Yes," had said Miss Brown joyfully. "Certainly. This *is* a boarding-house. I can take six."

But it had seemed that she herself was not wanted. All civilians must leave the sea-front. Her house was taken over by the government, but not her services. How soon could she pack up and go? A paper of instructions was handed to her. Good afternoon. Thank you.

There had been no help for it and she had made no fuss. She had packed away her treasures in the attic and left the beloved house where she had been born and had lived her happy and arduous life. She had even left the town, fanatical as was her love for it, for the shops were closing down as well as the boarding-houses, and there had been nothing for her to do there and nowhere to go. She had drawn her tiny stock of money out of the bank and accompanied by her tin trunk and a hat box had come to stay with Cousin Emmie in London. Cousin Emmie did not like her and did not want her but was willing to house her for a week or so while she looked about her for a job.

But she could not find a job. She was experienced in no trade except haberdashery, and no one wanted a shop assistant. No one seemed to want housekeepers or companion helps either; they could not afford them or they already had five hundred applications for the post. She could not get any war work to do; at present they wanted only strong young women and she was forty-two and looked fragile. As the days had gone by a leaden despair had grown in her. When she had heard by this morning's post that her beloved house and all her possessions had been blown sky-high she had hardly been surprised; she had said to herself that it merely meant that now there was no past as well as no future; only to-day with its fear.

But now, because of a few scraps of music played by a street musician, her fear was eased. It would come back again, probably, as recurrent pain comes back, but the fiddler had given her a blessed respite. Bombs had no power over memories; the sun-drenched days of her childhood and youth were back with her again, the carefree working days at Smerdon and Hodges, the light on the sea as she walked home at evening, her mother's cry of welcome, her father's smile, the pattering feet of little children who had been her lodgers and the gay tunes played by the band on the esplanade; she recaptured them all as she walked along the street.

And hope was hers too now because of those tunes. There had been a refuge in the whispering wood; both she and the musician had been agreed about that. And there is never a pilgrimage without somehow, somewhere, a worthy ending. Would she ever see that fiddler again? It was not very likely. But she wished him well as she stood waiting for the bus that was to take her to Paddington station; she wished him well and cried out in her heart, thank you, thank you.

She was going to spend the day with Cousin Emmie's married daughter Dorothy at Maidenhead. Cousin Emmie had suggested this visit to get her out of the way for a bit, for her fear, not unnaturally, got on Cousin Emmie's nerves till she hardly knew how to keep a civil tongue in her head. Not that Miss Brown expressed her fear, she moved through her days with Emmie calmly and proudly, and she spoke always as though the solidity of her future were a thing of which she had no doubts at all, but of all the emotions fear is the most catching, and Cousin Emmie, afraid herself, was most horribly aware of Miss Brown's. Not only was it a clammy sort of thing to live with, but for some reason or other it increased Cousin Emmie's own particular nightmare to enormous proportions; and Cousin Emmie's nightmare, not hidden like Miss Brown's but most volubly expressed from the moment she woke up in the morning till the moment when she went to bed at night, was that with the first bombs on London the tower of the church across the way would fall slap on top of her. Since Miss Brown's coming she had scarcely dared to set foot over her doorstep.

"So silly!" thought Miss Brown, waiting at the bus stop. "So dreadfully silly of Emmie. What silly things people are afraid of."

Her own fear, so she thought in company with most of the human beings alive in the world at that moment, was a sensible fear, even a respectable fear, of the type felt by sane and normal people. She was so sure about this that it never even occurred to her to take out her fear and examine it for those distinguishing marks. . . . At least not then, not yet. The time was not ripe for the supreme revelation of her senselessness.

The bus came and she climbed in and sat down with hands quietly folded. She was still in a half-dream, companioned by her memories, anæsthetised by the music she had heard, and as the bus bowled along she scarcely noticed the streets she was passing through, the war time streets of London, emptied of most of their children and sightseers, peopled only by taut figures who went quickly about their business, and by the aged and infirm and those without hope who were too tired to be bothered to run away. She did not notice anything very much and she did not think what she was doing until she had reached the station, got out of the bus, bought her ticket, asked her way of an irritable porter and found the platform where her train waited, bound for the West Country by way of Maidenhead.

And here she abruptly came alive, for if she was to get on the train immediate and violent action was required of her. There might have been few children on the streets, but here on the platform all the children in the world seemed gathered in one solid heaving mass, all bound for the West Country and what a paternal government fervently hoped would be comparative safety.

At the sight of them something like a stab of agony went through Miss Brown, for she loved children. She had not known there were so many of them still left in London. How many children were there in England? Oh for a Pied Piper of Hamelin who would with his immortal music lead them into the depths of the earth until this tyranny was overpast. The sins of the fathers shall be visited. . . . One may batter oneself to pieces against that stumbling block but the tightly-locked unity of the human race cannot be shifted. They were so good, holding tightly to the hands of teachers, or of mothers who in a moment would be parted from them, wide-eyed with apprehension, toys and gas-masks slung round their necks and packets of food bulging in their pockets. There were very few tears, very few lamentations. No time for that now. No time for anything but to get away quickly.

And no seats in the train, apparently, for any one but the children. Miss Brown searched frantically up and down the crowded platform until she was tripped up by a teddy-bear who suddenly threw its arms passionately round her left ankle. The string that had hitherto tethered it to its owner had apparently snapped, leaving it abandoned on the platform. Miss Brown picked it up. It was a very old and shabby teddy-bear, with one eye gone and a bad patch over its nose, but it had a bit of pink ribbon tied round its neck and it was borne in upon Miss Brown that the nose was bald because the fur had been kissed clean off it. Someone loved this teddy-bear. Someone was in grief because the string had snapped. Miss Brown abandoned her search for a seat and looked about her instead for the creature's owner. Good-ness knew there was enough anguish in the world at this moment without its being added to by the loss of a teddy-bear with a pink ribbon round its neck and a nose that had been kissed quite bald.

Presently she saw two little girls standing hand in hand. They seemed to have no mother or teacher to hold on to, so they held on to each other. They were perhaps six and eight years old, typical London children with straight tow-coloured hair, rag-gedly bobbed, pale blue eyes and pale pointed little faces. They came evidently from a good if poor home, for the scanty blue and pink cotton frocks and carefully darned little knitted jackets that clothed their undernourished bodies were very clean, and so were the white socks above their well-polished clod-hopping shoes. Two shabby cardboard suitcases stood beside them on the platform and their gas-masks were slung across their shoulders. The elder girl had a little book clutched firmly in one hand, and held tightly to her sister with the other. Though she kept her head well up she was yet very frightened; her small chin quivered and even her lips were white. The little one was crying; or rather bellowing; Miss Brown had never heard a small child make so much noise. Slow tears of an immense size ploughed their way through the dirt that collects on every London child's face, no matter how clean it started out, and her nose was running, but she was much too abandoned to misery to make any use of the clean cotton handkerchief pinned to her chest with a large safety pin. A broken string hung round her neck. Miss Brown pushed her way through a group of indignant teachers with the utmost rudeness and held out the teddy-bear.

She was rewarded. A smile of quite ineffable beauty lit up the wet messy little face and the teddy-bear was clutched speechlessly to his owner's bosom.

The elder girl was trying to speak, doing her best to force her words out of a throat all dried up by the terror of the unknown that had her in its grip.

"Say thank-you to the lady," she said at last in the hoarse croak that was all the voice much grief had left her.

But the little one was utterly engrossed in kissing the teddy-bear's bald nose.

"Never mind," said Miss Brown kindly. "Where are you going, dear?"

"The country," came the whisper.

"Your mother is not with you?" asked Miss Brown.

But that was a question causing so much sorrow that the child could only shake her head speechlessly, and Miss Brown turned away, cursing herself for her stupidity. There was nothing she could do. Better leave them alone.

With pain at her heart she walked blindly to the other end of the platform, and then a whistle sounded. Through a mist of tears she saw that the train was moving and she began to run, bumped into someone and then ran again. Too late. She was just turning away when the door of a first-class carriage opened and a hand was held out. "Quick!" said a voice. "In here."

"My ticket's third-class," quavered Miss Brown.

"No matter," said the voice.

It was so authoritative that she put her own hand into the hand held out and was swung with one easy movement into the now quickly moving train, and deposited, for the first time in her life, upon the soft seat of a first-class carriage.

"Forgive me for my importunity," said the voice. "But you looked so distressed."

"Distressed?" said Miss Brown, her hands pressing the cushioned seat with an unconscious gesture of childish pleasure that brought a smile to the face of the man opposite. "It was not about missing the train that I felt distressed, but about the children. There are so many of them."

"The stage is undoubtedly overcrowded," said the man. "That is going to be one of our main difficulties. Yet if overcrowded it is finely set for one of the greatest dramas in all history. Don't you think so?"

"Yes, oh yes," said Miss Brown, and then, still agonized by the thought of the children, she burst out with the question that everyone was always asking everyone else nowadays, "Shall we get through?"

And the stranger gave the usual answer.

"Dunquerque."

And they smiled at each other. One could not know . . . But there had been Dunquerque.

"I like reading the history of heroic ages," said Miss Brown, "but I don't think I like living in them very much."

Her companion laughed and Miss Brown abruptly withdrew into herself. Her cotton-gloved hands, that had been so childishly feeling the softness of the seat, were withdrawn and folded neatly upon the bag in her lap. Her compact little figure, that had been almost gracefully asprawl after the swing into the carriage, was compressed again into severity and dignity, the back straight as a ramrod, the feet placed side by side upon the floor. How dreadful of her to have burst out like that! It was both risky and unlady-like to talk to strangers of the opposite sex, and here she was doing it for the second time to-day. She flushed and looked down attentively at the shabby old bag in her lap. Presently, however, she lifted her head and peeped cautiously through her eyelashes at the man opposite her, for if it could be done without being either risky or unladylike it would be nice to get a good look at him; for he was what she most admired, but seldom got the chance of really studying except on the films, and then you could never be quite sure it was the genuine article, a Real Gentleman. It was because he was a Real Gentleman that she had asked him about England's chances like that. A Real Gentleman would surely know.

For Miss Brown admired Real Gentlemen in the same way that she admired the Royal Family, the Bank of England and the British Constitution. It had never occurred to her to test their value or enquire into their uses. She had been brought up to believe in them as admirable things and it was typical of Miss Brown's mental make-up that unless they were forcibly removed from her she should hold on very tightly to the beliefs of her youth.

She was able to observe her companion to her heart's content for he, noting how second thoughts had inclined her to gentility and silence rather than humanity and conversation, had absorbed himself in *The Times*. He was a big man, grown gallantly old, with long loose sprawling limbs that one felt might at any moment fall on him. Old age had made them a nuisance to him, one felt, and he kept them together more by mental determination than physical strength. Yet a nuisance or not he wore them with the same easy grace as he wore his loose, shabby, expensive tweed clothes, with their innumerable pockets and their faint fresh scent like the scent of heather. He had a fine old face, seamed and weather-worn, with a great jutting nose upon whose apex he wore a pair of gold pince-nez, fiery grey eyes beneath overhanging craggy brows and a large amused mouth above an exceedingly self-willed chin. His head was bald, except for a fringe of grey hair like a tonsured monk's, and tanned copper colour by many suns. His possessions, suitcases labelled with his name and destination—Birley, Torhaven—papers, hat and stick and gloves, were cast about the carriage in kingly disorder. Although there was no "Reserved" notice upon the window it was unlikely, Miss Brown thought, that any one would have dared to enter upon him without his express assistance and permission.

Yet presently the man from the refreshment car dared to enter.

"Nothing, thank-you," said Miss Brown sadly. Her economic situation did not admit of unlimited cups of tea. Yet how she longed for them! They were her chief bulwark against the lowering effects of war.

"This lady will have a cup of tea," said the old gentleman firmly, and fished up a shabby hog-skin purse from one of his many pockets.

"No thank-you," said Miss Brown, her customary shy demureness suddenly extinguished beneath the flashing of her pride. "I am perfectly able, should I want a cup of tea——"

"You entered this carriage at my express invitation," interrupted the old gentleman. "You are therefore my guest." His voice was surprisingly gentle for a man with so obviously forceful a character, but it had a commanding edge to it against which even Miss Brown's pride was not proof.

"Thank-you," she murmured, but she was not pleased, and as she withdrew once more into herself her disapproval saturated the very atmosphere. So pained was it that after she had drunk her tea the old gentleman found it impossible to accede to her obvious wishes and return to their former condition of silent gentility. He flung *The Times* upon the floor, where there already lay *The Observer, The Times Literary Supplement,* the *Daily Telegraph,* and *Punch,* cast his pince-nez adrift upon their gold chain and leaned towards her, his big veined old hands hanging loosely between his knees, fixing her with a piercing grey eye.

"Old age has its privileges," he told her. "And you like reading history."

Miss Brown looked up, surprise banishing disapproval. It astonished her that he should have gone in at one end of *The Times*' leading article, in war time, and come out the other end still remembering her chance remark.

"I too like history," he said. "Both reading it and writing it. I think it is the greatest delight I have in life."

Miss Brown suddenly remembered the name on his suitcases, Birley, and recollection came to her. Birley's *History of England*, Birley's *History of Our Times*, Birley's *Seamen of England*. Out of a dozen of his books she had tackled these three. The first two had defeated her but the third had thrilled her as no book had ever thrilled her before. She had breathed more deeply because of it, she had grown in strength and courage and well-being.

"Did you write *Seamen of England*?" she asked him shyly.

"I plead guilty," he said.

"I read it," Miss Brown informed him. "I got it out of the Free Library. I thought it was very nice. My father was a sailor and I like the sea."

The inadequacy of her remarks hit Miss Brown like a blow in the face. Very nice? Was that the way to speak of a book that had made one grow? She blushed and looked down at her hands. The little private school that she had attended before she went to Smerdon and Hodges had not educated her very well. It had not taught her to express herself. Her enthusiasms and her thoughts were fresh and deep and strong but they had no outlet. They did not show. No one, talking to or looking at Miss Brown, ever saw even a shadow of them.

Except upon this occasion, Charles Birley the historian. For an old man and a writer he had astonishing powers of observation. Old age, for him, had not meant a return to the self-absorption of childhood, and even a lifelong devotion to the writer's craft had not succeeded in making him think that the life of his own mind and spirit, out of whose reactions to external events he fashioned his books, was the most important life there was. He was as much of an *externe* as Miss Brown herself, and something of a paradox to those who did not know his history. Those who did know it understood him. For Charles Birley had become a man of letters only through chance, not through heredity or inclination. The men of his family had always been men of action, soldiers, seamen, sportsmen and administrators, and he would have been one of them but for a hunting accident in his boyhood that had kept him an invalid through the best years of his life. Shut out from active comradeship with men of his own kind he had set himself instead to be their chronicler. A total lack of aptitude and a temperament most unsuited to a writer had not discouraged him. He had fought with them as with wild beasts at Ephesus, and at last, after many heart-breaking failures, had learned to wield his pen with as masterly a power as his forbears had used their lances at Agincourt and their swords at Waterloo. But he remained utterly free of the taint of self-absorption and most deeply and sensitively aware of the life about him.

And so in this case Miss Brown's total lack of the power of self-expression was no hindrance to understanding. Her enthusiasm for the sea and its heroisms touched and interested him just as she herself had touched and interested him when he had watched her searching for a seat in the crowded train, so controlled, neat and unflustered, but yet so mortally afraid.

"No doubt you know that famous phrase, 'History is the cordial of drooping spirits'?" he asked her.

Miss Brown shook her head.

"A true saying," he said. "It's consoling to turn the pages of a history book and note how valiantly that man dared death and this woman endured persecution. They were of the same flesh and blood as you and I, and their dislike of living in history was probably just as great. What they can do we can do. We shall conquer fear as they did. Never doubt that."

Miss Brown raised her head and looked at him. "Did you see that I was afraid?" she asked him. There was a challenging note in her voice. Some people probed too deep. It was not fair. One had a right to one's privacy.

"I am sorry," he said. "I could not help it. I have lived for many years in this world and fear is a thing I cannot help but recognize. However well controlled it shows in the eyes."

"I am not afraid of what I expect you think I am afraid of," said Miss Brown belligerently. "Not of death."

"Of course not," he said. "Few of us are. It is the way that we must tread to get there that is inclined to put us off."

"Nor of that either," said Miss Brown with increasing belligerency, for what right had this old man to sit there smiling at her, asking no direct questions but yet somehow drawing her out of her natural element of reserve as inexorably as though she were a minnow hooked on a string. "Physical things have never frightened me."

"To many natures economic uncertainty is much more trying," he agreed. "Though I think it is not so much poverty in itself that frightens people as what poverty so often stands for; loss of work seems like loss of one's place in the world."

Miss Brown gave it up. She supposed he had noticed her shabby handbag and her darned gloves. She supposed those terrible piercing eyes of his saw most things. But yet they were kind eyes. As he sat there opposite her, leaning back so easily with one long leg crossed over the other, so relaxed, yet so observant, his kindness radiated from him like warmth from a fire.

"Yes," she said, looking unseeingly out of the window. "To lose one's niche. To feel, so to speak, thrown away out of the pattern of things."

"It is not possible to be thrown out of the pattern of things," he said quietly.

"Not even," asked Miss Brown, "when, as now, the pattern itself is lost, sane living just blown away into fragments?"

"The pattern is never lost," said the historian. "Nor the place of individuals in it."

Miss Brown smiled at him tolerantly. His academic way of speaking, rather as though she were an audience he was lecturing to, was new to her and amused her. But she thought he was absurdly optimistic; but then he looked as though comfortable circumstances had always been his lot in life. Probably he still had a background, old, rich and cultured. Probably, though his future might hold a depleted bank balance, it would not hold utter ruin.

"Personal experience and the study of history have both taught me to believe in a pattern," he said. "And in spite of all that has befallen the world I still believe that the threads of it, ourselves, are held securely in the scheme of things by some great unconquerable spiritual power. Call it what you will—destiny, fate, the first cause, the life-stream, God—it does not lose hold of a single thread. In wanton wickedness we may tangle the pattern into what looks like hopeless confusion, but in unwearied patience that power unravels the tangle, reforms the pattern, keeps it moving along to some great goal of order whose nature we cannot even guess at yet. If the threads are not lost there can be no lasting chaos."

Miss Brown smiled. She had held tenaciously to the Methodist faith in which she had been bred until just lately, but during the last week or two her faith had shown signs of collapsing beneath her. She still believed in Real Gentlemen and the British Constitution.

"Put it another way," lectured Mr. Birley. "Imagine God and Man set down together to play that game of chess that we call life. The one player is a master, the other a bungling amateur, so the outcome of the game cannot be in question. The amateur has free will, he does what he pleases, for it was he who chose to set up his will against that of the master in the first place, he throws the whole board into confusion time and again and by his foolishness delays the orderly ending of it all for countless generations, and every stupid move of his is dealt with by a masterly counter-stroke and slowly but inexorably the game sweeps on to the master's victory. But, mind you, the game could not move on at all without the full complement of pieces; Kings, Queens, Bishops, Knights, Pawns, the master does not lose sight of a single one of them."

"I wonder why it all started?" said Miss Brown.

Mr. Birley laughed. "Even a historian cannot tell you that," he said. "Every bit of reasoning has as its foundation-stone just one fact which must be accepted without question. Life exists. Accept it, in spite of all, with gratitude, and forgive, if you can, my prosing. It grows on me with age."

"Oh, but I have been most interested," Miss Brown hastened to assure him. "I don't usually talk to people like you—I mean—I don't go by train very often, you see, and even when I do I don't usually——"

"Gossip with perfect strangers." Mr. Birley finished her sentence for her with a twinkle in his eye. "Nor as a matter of fact do I. The shock of this war seems to have cracked our English reserve. Not altogether a bad thing, either. That being so I suppose you couldn't tell an old man whose besetting sin is curiosity where your home is, what your work is, where you are travelling now and to what future you look forward?"

"I have no home," said Miss Brown. "It was blown up. So was my work. I'm going now to spend the day with my cousin at Maidenhead. As for the future, I don't know. There doesn't seem to be one." She smiled. "The only certain thing about me is that I am to spend the day with my cousin at Maidenhead."

"One positive fact among three negatives," said Mr. Birley. "And that one not very positive, either, considering that we passed through Maidenhead a long while back."

Miss Brown gasped, clutched her bag, got up and sat down again.

"I think you must have been misinformed at the station," said Mr. Birley. "The authorities are very confused these days, and no wonder. We passed through but we did not stop there. This is the West Country express."

In her overwrought condition this mistake affected Miss Brown as though it had been a disaster of the first magnitude. Though she had had no future, to-day, with its visit to Maidenhead, had been firm ground beneath her feet. Now that had gone too and she felt as though she was falling through space. She looked speechlessly at Mr. Birley and the fear in her eyes was naked.

"I think," he said gently, "that the time has come for our English reserve to be not only cracked but smashed up altogether. I think you must tell me all about it in order that we may consult together as to what it would be best for you to do."

Miss Brown was too shattered to resist. She was silent a moment, gathering mind and body up again into their usual condition of compact neatness, and then she told him all about it. Only the bare facts, of course. She left her feelings out of it altogether.

Yet even so the bare facts affected Mr. Birley painfully. "Dear me," he said, and became absorbed in twisting the heavy gold signet ring round and round upon the little finger of his left hand. "Dear me." He realized that this little woman was only one of a great multitude. "Thrown away out of the pattern of things," she had said. All over Europe spread this multitude, homeless, workless, despairing, trekking they knew not where. Only a short while ago he had felt a little sorry for himself, facing the probable bereavements and losses of the war in an old age robbed of its hoped-for serenity. Now, contrasting his lot with that of others, he was ashamed of his good fortune. His roots were still firm in the land of his birth. His home was still his home and, as far as anything could be foreseen, likely to remain so. Though the pattern of things reformed painfully about him his was at present merely the pain of the onlooker.

"Did you ever read a book called *The Bridge of San Luis Rey*?" he asked Miss Brown.

"No," she said. His abrupt return to the world of books struck her as perhaps just a little heartless.

"The scene was set in Peru," said Mr. Birley. "In the story there was a bridge, and the bridge broke just as five travellers were crossing it, hurling them to their end. On the surface of things there seemed no point in it, it seemed just a senseless tragedy causing nothing but pain and death. But the author of the book looked below the surface. He had the power, as have all historians of a tale either real or imagined, of seeing its unseen reverberations. He noted that in this case death came to those five just at the most fitting moment of their lives, and that this so-called tragedy, as it affected the lives of others, brought alterations in the pattern that spelled in the long run only blessing and peace."

"Yes?" enquired the bewildered Miss Brown.

"I am not at all sure that your tragedy is not going to be a great blessing to me," said Mr. Birley. "That is, if you will be so generous as to make it so."

"Really," said Miss Brown. Her remark again seemed inadequate, but she could think of nothing else to say.

"I think," said Mr. Birley, "that it is now my turn to give you the bare outline of my own history, temperament and needs. To begin with, I live in a Castle. Yes, I know it's surprising. Few people live in castles nowadays. I am one of the few. I keep my allegiance to a dying class and a dying tradition. I have lived there more or less all my life. I was born there, and so were my forbears for many generations. I am a bachelor, as no doubt you have already guessed from my untidy habits. I like to be solitary. I was not the eldest son, you see, otherwise my love of independent living could not have been indulged, for in our family the most important consideration is the production of an heir. But I had an elder brother who produced it, thereby setting me free from any obligation." He paused and smiled at Miss Brown, and she smiled back at him. She realized that he was sacrificing reserve with some effort, just to amuse her and put her at her ease, and she was grateful. "My brother died in the South African War," he went on, "and his son died of wounds received in the Great War, but not before he in his turn had done his duty and produced two sons, my great-nephews, dear to me as my own sons, but probably not such a nuisance to me as my own boys would have been. We three men live in the Castle. I permanently, the boys only during their comings and goings from school and university and the field of war. There is yet another man in residence at the Castle, Boulder, our butler and chauffeur, a man of cantankerous nature and peculiar habits. There is also a gardener, Pratt, with the imperturbability of an owl and the obstinacy of a mule. There is Thomas the stable boy. There is the horse Golden Eagle. There is the dog Argos. There is also a nondescript female who comes up every day from the village to do this and that about the house, but I keep out of her way as much as possible and am unable to describe her in any detail. A resident staff such as one had in the old days is not of course procurable in war time in the country, but there was also, until recently, a Mrs. Weston who was our housekeeper. She had been our housekeeper for twenty years and was the widow of one of our gamekeepers, a kindly body who seemed just part of the landscape. Upon her death a month ago, however, we found to our surprise that she must have been an extremely vital part, for we all, the Castle, myself, the boys, Boulder, Pratt, the dog Argos and the nondescript female, immediately fell into a state of confusion and disorder very distressing to all concerned. I advertised for another housekeeper and had many applications. I chose the most likely, but she drank, and she did not get on with Boulder. I chose another, a stern teetotaller, but so stern was she that she wouldn't let me drink, thinking even one glass of port bad for my rheumatic gout, which no doubt it is, and also she did not get on with Boulder. I chose a third and she just did not get on with Boulder. During these last few days, in the intervals of discussions with my publisher, I have interviewed a few more and disliked them all with an intensity of which I did not know my ageing emotions were still capable. Miss Brown, you in your boarding-house must have had great experience in housekeeping and in the handling of different types of humanity. Do you feel that you could take on the management of the Castle and its menfolk? The Castle is built on a precipice in the woods at the back of beyond, and it is very lonely there. We Birleys are notoriously difficult to manage, though we're nothing to Boulder and the dog Argos. The only thing that I think might attract you, lover of history that you are, is the Castle itself. It may be that you would like to see out the Battle of Britain in a fortress that has already withstood so many centuries of assault and siege. Its stout old walls that have endured so much and still stand, may comfort you as they comfort me."

There was silence in the railway carriage while Miss Brown resolutely and successfully fought down her tears. "Thank you," she said at last. Her remark was inadequate, as usual, but it was the best she could manage at the time.

CHAPTER II

I

AFTER Miss Brown had left him Jo Isaacson put away his violin, poised his battered hat with something of an air upon his bony head, and strode off through the hot streets in the direction of his lodging, walking with the loping dogged stride of those who always walk because they cannot afford to do anything else. And as he walked he looked now and then at the shilling in his hand. He had gone out that morning with the express purpose of earning a shilling, so that he might have the wherewithal to end his life with the assistance of the shilling-in-the-slot gas fire in his room. But he had not expected to earn the shilling so quickly and easily. Shillings were damned hard to come by these days.

It was Jo Isaacson's creed that a man's life is his own and that he has a perfect right to do with it what he will; if he wishes to end it that's his affair and no one else's. There had been many occasions in earlier days when he had been near to ending it, but yet had always been held back by the strange hope that he had always had, the hope of the artist in pursuit of beauty, the hope that there was going to be something incredibly lovely round the next corner. . . . a refuge in the wood . . . something . . . some sort of rest . . . some sort of abiding place.

But that morning he had awakened with hope dead within him and fear gripping him like a vice. The war had taken an apalling turn and his pessimistic mind saw no hope for England. The Jews would be hounded out of this country as they had been hounded out of all the others. He would once more have to make the choice between flight and persecution and it was a choice that he felt he could not make again. He was too tired to make a fresh start, too weak to suffer further.

And this morning he had also faced the knowledge that so far as he could see he was no longer of the slightest use to a single human creature. He had been of some use lately as nursemaid, court jester and fiddler-in-ordinary to his landlady's small daughters Moppet and Poppet, but to-day they were to be evacuated to the country, they would be gone when he got home, and there would be quite literally no one in his life who needed him. His existence would be an empty show. Nature abhorred a vacuum and so did he. If she would not smash the hollow empty thing that was his life, then he would. So he had come out to try to earn a shilling for that gas fire.

Well, here was the shilling lying on the palm of his hand, but with it had come the knowledge that his music still had power to move another human creature. That fact was to him almost incredible. With his worn-out talent and his worn-out violin he had not believed such a thing possible. Yet it had happened. In deadly fear himself he had yet by his playing made fear more bearable for another. The force that in the old days of his fame he had so often felt burning in him as he came forward to the footlights on the concert platform, careless how much it scorched him up if it could only use him as an instrument of strength for others, that fire that for want of a better name he had called life, had used him again. He was still an instrument. The fact was so astounding that he could scarcely take it in. His confused mind groped about it feebly, seeking for its implications, realising that it had somehow changed the current of his life, yet unaware yet what action he must take because this thing had happened.

What were those words of Flecker's that he had half remembered when that woman asked him about the pilgrimage? He had not thought of them for years but he remembered them now.

"But you are nothing but a pack of Jews."

"Sir, even dogs have daylight, and we pay."

"But who are ye in rags and rotten shoes,
    You dirty-bearded, blocking up the way?"

"We are the Pilgrims, Master; we shall go
    Always a little further: it may be
Beyond that last blue mountain barred with snow
    Across that angry or that glimmering sea.

"White on a throne or guarded in a cave
    There lives a prophet who can understand
Why men were born; but surely we are brave
    Who take the Golden Road to Samarkand."

Well, that was almost always the choice of his race; to go on. Brave, yes, but were they not damn fools? Was there anything at the end of the pilgrimage? It was his belief that there was nothing there.

But he hoped he had not let his mockery show too clearly when that little woman made her trite remark about "beyond the veil." What a revolting phrase! But it was a very popular one and he hoped he had not smirched it for her, for women often clung to clichés when they'd nothing else to cling to. She had been a pretty woman, too quiet-looking for most people's taste, but undeniably pretty. He'd always liked pretty women. His love of beauty and his constitutional dread of loneliness had led him to have intimate relations with a good many, only to find to his bitter disillusionment that none of them was what he had thought she was going to be; they all went stale sooner or later. But that woman had had a freshness that was the very antithesis of staleness, and she had seemed to fling her whole soul into the look of compassion she had given him. Quite a charming thing, that look of hers, to be one of one's last memories on earth.

But here his fumbling thoughts came up again against that incredible fact that life had used him, and it did not fit somehow with the fact of suicide.

Yet he told himself that the circumstances of his life were not altered because his playing had that morning pleased one unknown woman. She had been an uncritical creature and the miracle was not likely to occur again. Moppet and Poppet, who had needed him, were still gone from his life. The future was still a thing that he could not face.

God, how he hated the loneliness of perpetual wandering! No satisfactory companionship was possible if you could not strike down roots. It had been partly the fear of loneliness that had made him choose music for his profession, for music is such a companionable thing. But his talent had been insufficient to make a great musician of him. In spite of his Leipzig training and his early successes his talent had been insufficient. You can't manufacture talent. Hard work can lay hold upon many things, but it cannot lay hold upon the gift of genius. Youthful fire and charm and vigour and a passionate devotion to his art had seemed to do as well in the early days; they had made him a capable violinist and later first violin in a famous orchestra; and later still, for a short while, something of a celebrity. Then they had seemed to peter out, and the plodding doggedness, helped on by a good bit of drinking, that took their place had not been nearly such a good substitute. He had played in theatre orchestras, and then in cinema orchestras, and then in the streets. He had fled in turn from Germany, Austria and Italy. He had been moved on until he was sick of being moved on, and now he was fifty-five years old and until this morning's shilling nothing but coppers had come his way for weeks.

How was it possible to go on living under such conditions? God, how his music had lied to him in the old days when it had seemed to promise so much! Side by side with his love of it had come lately a sort of hatred. It was a beautiful but lying jade. It promised what it could not give. The Andante of the Ninth, for instance, what right had that damned lying fool Beethoven to write such a thing! That outpouring of sorrow, that deep grief, interspersed with those strange trumpet calls, then the heavenly melody breaking through the grief and lifting, lifting, triumphantly mounting upon untiring wings—where to? Nowhere. That final hymn in praise of freedom and brotherhood brought him no conviction. The thing ended and the lights went out and you were back in the slime where you'd always been.

He caught his shabby old coat on some barbed wire and cursed angrily. Every reminder of the war made Mr. Isaacson feel sick. Barbed wire entanglements in the streets of London, gun emplacements at street corners, barrage balloons in the sky, men in uniform, women in uniform, all dressed up as smartly as you please simply to kill and be killed in a hopeless struggle. "There'll always be an England," they were singing in the pubs and whistling on the streets, and would soon be hollering in the shelters when the bombs were falling. But Mr. Isaacson doubted it. In his opinion the bleeding Germans had won this bleeding war and soon, if he did not make sensible use of that shilling, he would see in the streets of London what he had already seen in the streets of Vienna. . . . Jews shamefully maltreated. . . . No wonder that woman had flung him that look of pity.

A sudden blind insenate fury seized him. Pity! Pity! If it was not persecution it was pity. Pity was a damned insult. What right had she to pity him? She was perhaps one of those fools who believed in something or other, who was ready like all the other fools to suffer and die for abstract ideas that disappeared into nowhere the moment you came up with them, for hopes that were never fulfilled and lights that went out; but that gave her no right to pity him. Well, let them believe their fairy tales if they wanted to. It did him no harm. Only let them refrain from insulting him with their pity who in his acceptance of negation had now attained to the final wisdom and the final courage.

33

"If in this life only we have hope, we are of all men most miserable."

The clear voice halted him abruptly. Was it that woman speaking? He looked around him a little wildly, but there was no one. He had had no breakfast, the perspiration stood out on his forehead and his hands were shaking. Am I light-headed he wondered? Then he saw the words scrawled in white chalk on a blank wall; and his fury turned to rage that he had been so taken in. It was some fool in the district who went about every night with his bit of chalk ornamenting harmless walls with sentimental clap-trap from his Bible. Such fellows were public nuisances and should be dealt with accordingly. Mr. Isaacson swore and went on.

But his confused thoughts were fumbling now not only with that incredible fact that life had used him, but with the everlasting tormenting question as to the nature of life and the extent of the hope that might be entertained of it. "If . . . if. . . ." It had tormented Hamlet, and rightly, for it was the only question. For if life were the immense thing that that fool with the chalk maintained, then one would not dare to break any instrument that it saw fit to use. One would not dare. One would wait in patience till life itself did the breaking.

He was dizzy from lack of food and the thoughts that whirled round and round in his head, but brought him no nearer to answering the question as to how he was to use that shilling, and he swore again as he tripped over the curb. Why must he go over this hackneyed ground for the thousandth time? Had he not decided long ago that he would believe in nothing of which he had no proof? And there was no proof about the length of life. The travellers to Samarkand never returned from beyond the last blue mountain with any information.

There was the house that he had hitherto called home, even though it was weeks since he had paid anything for the little room he rented in the attic; and inside was the gas fire. But he could think no more. He was too damned tired. He'd just go in and see what happened.

But outside the door he paused and listened in horror. Good God, they were still there! They should have left an hour ago but they were still there. He could hear Moppet sobbing and Poppet bellowing and Mrs. Baxter vainly trying to soothe them. He swore again, for by going out so early to play in the streets he had hoped to avoid the departure of Moppet and Poppet, and the good-byes that he simply had not the nerve for. Well, he hadn't

34

avoided them, and now that he was here he might as well go in and help poor Mrs. Baxter with Poppet's infernal bellowings. He was good with children. He was perhaps nothing but an overgrown child himself, and they claimed him as one of themselves.

He opened the door and stalked in, put down his violin case and demanded, "Now what's all this, Poppet?" in the mocksevere tone that usually made Poppet giggle. But this morning she was too far gone for giggling. She stood in the middle of the Baxter kitchen, ready dressed for the journey, complete with gasmask and teddy-bear, and roared and bellowed with that abandon that nothing will check except the complete collapse of the respiratory organs. Her face was scarlet and her mouth so wide open that Mr. Isaacson could see right down her pink throat. Her eyes were tightly screwed up, lest she should see some amusing sight and be diverted, and with small hands clenched firmly upon the rung of a kitchen chair she held herself braced to give the utmost power and volume to her roars. Moppet, standing beside her between their two little suitcases, clutching a little book called "The Tale of Peter Rabbit," which was to her what his bible is to a saint of God, sobbed hopelessly, and Mrs. Baxter, her face strained and working, was feverishly pinning on her shabby black straw hat at the little glass over the sink.

Mrs. Baxter was a very great woman. Besides Moppet and Poppet, the babies, and three little dead children in the nearest cemetery, she had two sons at the errand-boy stage, mischievous young demons who tormented the life out of her, and a husband in such poor health that he could never keep a job for more than a month at the outside. It was she who managed their meagre income, augmenting it by charing and washing and a lodger, lest they lose their respectability, the one fear of her life. Little beauty was left to her now, and less strength, yet she kept the devotion of her man and her children and she made their clean neat home a place that they did not leave except under violent protest, such as Poppet's at this moment. She was as kind and long-suffering as she was brave, or Mr. Isaacson would have been turned out long ago. She never looked for any sort of reward for all she did and yet she had it in the passionate delight she took in her two little daughters. And now they must be packed off into the void, consigned to the doubtful tenderness of some unknown woman, lest they be blown to pieces by the German bombs. She turned round and looked pitifully over their fair heads at her lodger.

"They should 'ave been at the school an hour ago, Mr. Isaac-

35

son," she called to him above the uproar. "The children were all to collect at the school, but I couldn't get 'em there with Poppet this way. I'm taking 'em to the station meself. If the train's late we'll maybe just catch it."

"But it's your morning for charing at the Bellamy's, surely?" enquired Mr. Isaacson in the sustained roar that was all that could be heard above Poppet.

"Yes, an' I'll get the sack if I don't turn up," shouted Mrs. Baxter, turning desperately to hunt for her purse in the kitchen drawer. "Poppet, ma luvly, for Gawd's sake stop your bellowin'. If you don't I'll smack you. Moppet, where's me purse? I 'ad it last night for the grocer. Where'd I put it?"

But Moppet was not helpful. She merely hiccuped and increased the tempo of her sobs.

"Now don't *you* start, Moppet, duckie," implored her anguished mother. "Try to be a good brave girl. There's a war on an' we must all act accordin'. Where *is* me purse? Be quiet, Poppet!"

"I'd better take these kids to the station," decided Mr. Isaacson abruptly. "So long as they're with you they'll continue to carry on, but with me they'll quieten down. You shouldn't miss your charing, either, you've the future to think of. Come on, Moppet, you carry the suitcases and I'll carry Poppet. Poppet, leggo that chair and come along with your uncle. Leggo that chair, Poppet!" and he bent to unloose the iron grip of her tiny hands.

But Poppet, prised off her chair, merely attached herself to the handle of the violin case on the floor, to which she was much attached because the violin played her so many pretty tunes, and the tumult of her grief all but shook the house. He had to pick her up and carry her out into the street, violin and all, Moppet struggling after with the suitcases.

"But me purse!" cried Mrs. Baxter. "You'll want money for the bus!"

"I've a shilling," called back Mr. Isaacson, and then the sound of hurrying footsteps and the roar of Poppet's anguish died away in the distance.

Mrs. Baxter shut the door and put the kettle on. She would make herself a cup of tea before she went to the Bellamys, for her legs were trembling beneath her. She wished she could have said a proper good-bye to her children, kissed them properly and told them to be good girls, but really she had had no chance with all that hollering. It had been a horrible parting, noisy, turbulent, un-

36

tender, and she had so wanted them to carry away some loving memory of her, for God knew if they'd ever see her again. Well, it was too late now. Their only memory of her now would be of a scolding, shouting woman looking for her purse. She sat with her head in her hands, waiting for the kettle to boil, and hoped she'd done right to send them away. At the beginning of the war, in the autumn, she had refused to let them be evacuated; better for children and their parents to stick together come what might, she had said, and after all it might not be as bad as one thought. But she felt differently now. She had no illusions, now, about this war; how could she when she had seen pictures of dead children lying in the streets of Rotterdam? Churchill had left no room for illusion, either. Blood, sweat and tears, he had promised them. Only that; except, at the far end of this dark tunnel of suffering, the hope of a new world where the children would be safe; she thought he had promised them that too, if they could endure. Yes, she'd done right to send the children away. Blood, sweat and tears were not for little children, only for their mothers. She made her tea, gulped it down and got up, straightening her shoulders. She was not afraid of what was coming. She could take it. She knew all about blood and sweat, and tears too, she who had borne seven children and lost three.

I I

Mr. Isaacson sat in the bus with Moppet and Poppet one on each side of him, and his violin, from which Poppet had now been disentangled, laid across his knees. Moppet was reading "Peter Rabbit" to comfort herself, and Poppet's roars had mercifully subsided. Her respiratory organs had given out and she had no strength left for anything but the depositing of damp kisses upon the nose of her ridiculous teddy-bear. She still sobbed, but not in a way that drew unwelcome attention to the trio, and Mr. Isaacson once more had leisure for his own bewilderment.

Miss Brown's shilling had now dwindled to a few coppers, and a few coppers were not sufficient to purchase death from the gas fire. Others ways of ending his life were open to him, of course, but he found to his surprise that with the breaking up of the shilling the conflict that had been tormenting him all the way home from the Free Library had abruptly ended. Subconsciously he had come to a decision and the longing to end his life had, for the moment at any rate, left him; it had, he supposed, foundered upon the fact of his usefulness; his duties as nursemaid to Moppet and Poppet were still demanded of him.

But they would not be when the kids were in the train, and what then? He didn't know. He now possessed nothing in the world but his violin and fourpence halfpenny. He didn't know and he couldn't think. The bus now seemed to him to be rocking up and down as though it were a ship at sea, and a misty spray was obscuring the windows. For a week now he had been finding excuses for absenting himself from most of the Baxter's meals, because it was not fair to eat their food when he could not pay for it, and starvation can play queer tricks both with one's sense of vision and one's equilibrium. He began to feel anxious. He'd been a fool not to ask Mrs. Baxter for something to eat before he left the house. A poor look-out it would be if he collapsed before he'd got the kids safely on the train. If only the damned bus would cease swaying up and down and behave in a normal way. And now it had stopped with a jolt that nearly sent him pitching forward on to the lap of the opposite passenger. Was this Paddington? He couldn't see.

But mercifully Moppet had more or less come to and taken charge of the party. "We must find Teacher," she croaked hoarsly, poking Mr. Isaacson with "Peter Rabbit." "Get out, Mr. Isaacson. Poppet, gimme your suitcase and take Mr. Isaacson's 'and."

Out in the street he felt physically a little steadied by Poppet, who was clinging to him with the same iron grip with which she had hitherto attached herself to the chair and the violin case. Odd what strength small children have in their hands, thought Mr. Isaacson confusedly. . . . Was this the station entrance? . . . Even a baby will hold on to your finger with the grip of a boa-constrictor. . . . What the devil was the matter with his legs? He could hardly move them. . . . They wanted to feel secure, and they were quite right; life was hell without security. . . . But there would be no security for Moppet and Poppet if he did not get them on this train, and here was he with his legs turning to lumps of lead beneath him so that he could scarcely move them.

" 'Urry! 'Urry!" cried Moppet urgently, pulling at his coat.

But Mr. Isaacson couldn't hurry. Everything seemed conspiring to hold him back; his legs, the swaying of the pavement beneath his feet, and now a huge figure in dark blue who suddenly loomed up before him like the prow of a ship approaching through the mist.

"Platform ticket," said the immense figure placidly. "You can't see the kids off, mate, without a platform ticket." He bent a little, kindlily, hands on knees. "Goin' to the country, kids? Foin, that'll

38

be. Pigs an' all. Me own kids is in the country. Foin toime they're 'avin'."

Moppet smiled wanly; she was an unselfish little girl and always tried to give the right response. Cursing, Mr. Isaacson dumped down his violin and shoved a penny into the machine that also rose up out of the mist and seemed to him to hit him a stunning blow on the forehead. Now he only had threepence halfpenny.

On the platform they were submerged in a surging flood of children. This way and that they swayed, helpless and struggling, until more by good luck than good management they were suddenly washed up at the feet of Teacher.

"Thank heaven!" said Teacher heartily. "Why didn't you turn up at school at the proper time? Poppet wouldn't go? Naughty Poppet! Thank you, Mr. Isaacson, for bringing them. I think it would be best for you not to wait. I'll look after them now." And with a sudden skilful twist she prised Poppet right off Mr. Isaacson and attached her to herself, for if it was not done now, she realised, knowing Poppet, it never would be. But Poppet, in the very act of being transferred from Mr. Isaacson to Teacher, suddenly realised that her teddy-bear was missing. She wrenched her hand away, seized hold of Moppet and burst into roars of sheer fury which for volume and scope easily outdid anything else hitherto achieved. The other three gazed at her, helpless.

"Her teddy's gorn," said Moppet at last. "P'raps it's cos her teddy's gorn."

"Now stand quite still here, you children," said Teacher with bright decision, "and Mr. Isaacson and I will find it. You look that way, Mr. Isaacson, and I'll look this way. Without Teddy she'll yell for the whole journey."

Mr. Isaacson turned blindly in the direction indicated by Teacher; useless for him to tell her he could see nothing at all now through this grey mist that surrounded him. He pushed his way through it, feeling it pressing against him like a solid weight, sapping the very little strength that he had left, until another red machine came at him and hit him another blow on the head. A chocolate machine. A bit of chocolate inserted in her mouth always stopped Poppet's roaring. It was not until he had pushed in a penny and got out the chocolate that he realised that now he only had twopence halfpenny.

He stood there swaying, forgetful of Poppet's teddy-bear. Twopence halfpenny. What could one do with twopence halfpenny? A whistle sounded and something else loomed up out of the mist and knocked against him; a woman this time, who murmured an apology without looking round and ran on to catch her train. It was the same woman whom he had seen outside the Free Library, the woman to whom he had so incredibly been of use. . . . Used. . . . Only by that woman and Moppet and Poppet. By no one else upon the wide earth. And they were all three in that train; the only three creatures in the whole world who seemed to have any use for Jo Isaacson. They might still have use for him. They might come to some harm without him. This problematical fact seemed to him now the only fact left in the world, the only thing left to which he could cling. He saw the moving carriages sliding past him, saw an open door swinging, called upon the last ounce of his strength, staggered through the mist, scrambled in and fell headlong. He lay there on the floor of the guard's van, clutching his violin, a stick of chocolate and twopence halfpenny, and a merciful darkness descended upon him and blotted out his torment.

III

Some while later, white and shaken, he sat with his back against a hamper containing a live puppy and his feet braced against a tin trunk, sipped hot coffee from the top of a Thermos flask and nibbled at his stick of chocolate. Opposite him, hands on knees, sat Mr. Holly the guard, kindly and perturbed.

The situation, for Mr. Holly, was delicate in the extreme, for here was the West Country express bound non-stop for Torhaven, and here was this bloke without a ticket; with nothing, apparently, except a violin, twopence halfpenny and a stick of chocolate; and he hadn't even got that now for with a last swallow he finished the chocolate. It had been some little while before Mr. Holly had found Mr. Isaacson. It had not been until a fondness for animals had caused him to approach the hamper in order to address a few encouraging noises to the puppy, that he had seen Mr. Isaacson lying stretched out behind it. Mr. Holly was a man of fifty, and he had served the Great Western Railway for most of his life. He was therefore perfectly capable of dealing with any emergency, not excluding this one. Having rolled Mr. Isaacson over and ascertained that the life was still in him he had proceeded to apply first aid, and in no time at all had had Mr. Isaacson sitting up and taking nourishment. The bloke's own stick of chocolate being now finished, Mr. Holly dived into the shining oilskin bag in which Mrs. Holly always packed his provisions, produced a ham sandwich, handed it to Mr. Isaacson and embarked upon a little kindly questioning.

"Now where was you thinkin' of goin' to, mate?" he enquired. That, to him, as a railway official, was the first point that needed settling. There was no doing anything with a passenger till it could make up its mind where it was bound for; and quite surprisingly often it had lost its ticket, and its head with it, and had no idea.

Mr. Isaacson seemed to have no idea. Wolfing the sandwich he feebly shook his head.

"Well, now," said Mr. Holly, "the first stop is Torhaven. You could get out there, or you could go further. Do you fancy Torhaven?"

Memory stirred vaguely within Mr. Isaacson. Children he was fond of, children called Moppet and Poppet, had been going to Torhaven.

"That'll do," he said.

"That's right then," said Mr. Holly heartily. "You get out at Torhaven, mate. There's not a finer town in the 'ole of the West Country. Matter of fact, I live there meself. Now about this little bother of you 'avin' no ticket. . . ." He paused, fished out another sandwich for Mr. Isaacson, and scratched his head in some perplexity as he looked at the battered figure before him on the floor, thin and meagre, elderly, obviously potty, swaying feebly to the movement of the train. "Poor bloke," thought Mr. Holly. "Poor old bloke."

Mr. Holly himself was of a substantial build. Years of good nourishment had gone to the making of a fine figure of a man. His face was round and rubicund, his grey moustache bristling with vitality, his blue eyes alive with twinkling light. He had many chins, all of them kindly, for years of security and layers of fat, though they had protected Mr. Holly himself from the slings and arrows of outrageous fortune, and not blunted his perception of the havoc they wrought upon other poor devils. His profession had seen to that. A railway official, one way and another, sees a good deal of suffering.

Hitherto, when trying his kindly best to alleviate distress, Mr. Holly had confined himself to a rather superficial helpfulness; kindly chuckings to the desolate whining puppies in their baskets, a pat on the head for a crying child, the presentation of a ham sandwich to a man obviously hungry, excessive care in lifting an invalid in pain out of a railway carriage. He'd never gone further than that, he'd had neither the time nor the opportunity, and he'd always been stern, as was his duty, about ejecting those desperate travellers who were contriving to escape from something or to somewhere with no ticket and no cash.

But he felt, now, moved to go a little further in his treatment of Mr. Isaacson. He would not, next time the train was halted by a contrary signal, heave him out by the scruff of the neck. He was going to let him go on to Torhaven and, yes, he decided abruptly that he was going to pay for the poor bloke's ticket himself. Such behaviour was going against all precedent, but with the war taking this turn one tended to find oneself more and more winking an eye at precedent. To hell with it, thought Mr. Holly suddenly. With Jerry likely to invade the country at any moment, giving a leg up to a chap down on his luck seemed undoubtedly the right course of action. Prostration, such as Mr. Isaacson's at this moment, was the worst thing possible for the country.

"Well, mate," he said cheerfully, "you're goin' to Torhaven, an' I'm payin' your fare for you so there won't be no defraudin' of the G.W.R., but wot I want to know is, wot was you intendin' to do at Torhaven?"

"I couldn't tell you," said Mr. Isaacson.

Mr. Holly's blue eyes popped slightly, but he showed no other signs of agitation. Best to keep calm when dealing with these poor potty blokes.

"Try to think, mate," he encouraged. "Wot for did you board this 'ere train?"

Mr. Isaacson, his hand to his head, tried to think. He had a vague idea that he had made some sort of choice this morning; life instead of death. He had flung his body into this train much as a man flings a tool to a craftsman who may have use for it. . . . But he could not say that to Mr. Holly.

"Two little kids," he said vaguely. "Two little kids are on this train."

"Two? More like two thousand," ejaculated Mr. Holly. Then he thought that he saw light. "Ah!" he triumphed. "Two kids? Bein' evacuated? Your two kids? You felt you 'ad to keep your eye on 'em? Any father'd feel the same. I should, for one. . . . Mrs. Holly, she lost 'er first an' we never 'ad another. . . ."

He broke off abruptly, again scratching his head in perplexity as he looked at the limp figure in front of him. Mr. Isaacson, propped against the hamper, soothed by the hot coffee and Mr. Holly's kindness, had relapsed into a dreamy sort of state that would soon be sleep if Mr. Holly did not stir him up. He was obviously incapable of future exertion. He was making no effort to deal with himself but was leaving it all to Mr. Holly.

"What's your trade, mate?" asked Mr. Holly loudly, leaning forward. "'Ow did you earn that twopence halfpenny of yours?"

Mr. Isaacson lifted his head, "Playing in the streets," he said.

Mr. Holly clacked his tongue in consternation. A street musician. Not a very paying proposition, by the look of the poor bloke. And he'd have to get a licence before he could play in the streets of Torhaven. How would he exist meanwhile? Mr. Holly made a startling decision. He took a pencil and pad from his pocket, sucked the pencil and began to write, breathing stertorously, for literary composition did not come to him at all easily. Then he put away his pencil, prodded Mr. Isaacson gently, and handed him a folded bit of paper.

"When you get to Torhaven," he said, "you spend that twopence halfpenny of yours on a bus to No. 5 Skinner Street. There you'll find Mrs. Holly. You give 'er that letter from 'er lovin' 'usband, tellin' 'er to give you board an' lodgin' for a week while you get goin' with your fiddle in the streets. No, I don't want no thanks. I ain't never done such a thing as this before, but there ain't never been a war like this before, an' wot I say is, we all need to stand together against these bloody 'Uns."

After this Mr. Holly sat gazing before him in utter astonishment. His own amazing benevolence had knocked him all of a heap.

CHAPTER III

I

MISS BROWN sat in the restaurant car with her host, enjoying such a meal as she had not had for years. Mr. Birley apologized for it. "War-time muck," he called it expressively, if rudely, but Miss Brown thought it a wonderful meal. She worked her way through it all, from soup to coffee, with a quiet methodical enjoyment that touched her host to a condition of amused compassion that he found rather refreshing. He found this nondescript little woman, whom no one in the restaurant car found worthy of a single glance, interesting. She had the simplicity and trustfulness of the nicest kind of child, together with a pride and courage that seemed to him wholly admirable. Her reactions to a totally new environment, her development under the ordeal that awaited them all, would be worth noting, he thought. The development of character, with its inevitable effect upon the course of history, was to him the most interesting thing in the world.

"You know the West Country?" he asked Miss Brown, when her coffee was finished and she had refused a cigarette with a little gesture of rather shocked repudiation that amused him mightily. "If not we might stay here, by this wide window, so that you can welcome the grey stone walls and the friendly hills as they come to meet you."

Miss Brown said she had never been further west than Bournemouth, where once she had visited her Aunt Ada. Her aunt was dead now. Appendicitis, and then complications.

"Really?" said Mr. Birley. "Most unfortunate. I hope you will not find our country life too slow. It is lived to the tempo of the horses who plough the long furrow over the crest of the hill, of cattle homeward bound for the milking through the deep lanes. Personally I hope that tempo will never be lost, for I think it beats time for the only life worth living. But then, you see, I am a West Countryman."

"And patriotic," said Miss Brown.

"Yes," smiled Mr. Birley. "The West is rich in history, a gold mine for a historian. The old and beautiful villages have a very special flavour of friendliness and peace. The hills are round and very green, the lanes and woods bird-haunted, flower-decked. The sea is never far away. The winds blow freshly and the crying of the gulls is as familiar a sound as the song of the lark. There are old castles among the hills and nearly every village has its ancient manor house. Plymouth Hoe still stands, despite all the efforts of the enemy. Drake's drum still rolls in the hour of danger. . . . Forgive me, I am one of those garrulous old men who once the handle is turned run on until checked, and being a writer I have developed a fatal facility."

But Miss Brown enjoyed the unfamiliarity of his pedantic talk. And she enjoyed the quiet hour that followed, leaning back in her seat, relaxed in the dreamy content of a railway journey, peacefully wrapped about by the cessation of normal living. One was for the moment divorced from time and place and the problems of them. One sailed through the air like a bird. Only sun and air and speed existed, only the green fields and the shadows of the clouds that fled across them, the light on the water and the white wings of the gulls against the blue. For the second time that day a most unfamiliar sensation stirred within her. Happiness.

"Isn't it strange," she said to Mr. Birley, "how, sometimes, when everything is unspeakably terrible somehow you suddenly feel happy!"

"Sudden awareness of the things that last," diagnosed Mr. Birley. "Or else sudden awareness of an excellent digestion that has just satisfactorily completed its complicated task. And here we are. There's Boulder. I must get my things. Porter! Porter!"

II

The following hour was painful to Miss Brown. Her happiness fell from her abruptly and she even went so far as to wish that she was back in London with Cousin Emmie. The new and the strange ceased to seem adventurous and lovely and seemed intsead full of menace and embarrassment. Torhaven might be, as Mr. Birley assured her it was, a beautiful town, built upon seven hills like ancient Rome, its white houses thrown like foam over the rocky cliffs, but it was most embarrassing to have to go from shop to shop in Mr. Birley's car, telephoning to Cousin Emmie and buying herself a nightgown and toothbrush and the other immediate necessities of life out of his shabby hogskin purse. And then there was Boulder. He was undoubtedly a menace. He was an erect, thin little man with a face like a tortoise, sad, quenched eyes and the patronising smoothly efficient manners of the perfect gentleman's manservant. He received the explanation of Miss Brown's presence without comment but with a glance of doleful scorn that threw Miss Brown into immediate misery. Mr. Birley might be the soul of kindness, the Castle and its surroundings might be a paradise of beauty, but Miss Brown knew only too well that if Boulder was against her life would be bereft of all comfort and satisfaction. Well, she must put up with that. She hadn't come here to seek comfort or satisfaction. She had come to try to find once more her place in the pattern of things. She had come to play her part in the Battle of Britain within the shadows of a castle wall.

She felt better when her purchases were over and they were speeding out into the country, only Boulder's disapproving back visible as she sat in the back seat of the commodious shabby old car with Mr. Birley. They seemed to slip very abruptly from the bustle of the big town into the leafy stillness of the lanes. Modern villas seemed to change places quite suddenly with white-washed cottages smiling from the depths of gardens that were ablaze with flowers. Gasometers and cinemas were gone and, instead, an ancient grey church towered up above a jumble

45

of old roofs. Hay scented the air, and when the car slowed down the call of a wood pigeon sounded peacefully above the ripple of a stream.

"We are nearly there," said Mr. Birley. They had climbed a steep hill, swept along a road whose track looked as though the finger of a giant had traced a perfect curve along the roof of the world, the great panorama of the moors to one side of them, the sea far away below them on the other, and then slid away to the right down a narrow deep lane towards the woods.

The entrance to them was barred by a gate and beside the gate was another of those ancient cottages with white-washed walls. The front door was protected by a deep porch with wooden seats and behind the lattice windows scarlet geraniums glowed like fire. A little old woman in a snowy apron came out from the cottage to open the gate for them, an old woman whose wrinkled skin and nut-cracker features were irradiated by a toothless smile of such sheer happiness that it caught at the heart. Miss Brown had seen children at the beginning of life like that, but never any one at the end of it; above all not in these days.

Mr. Birley swept off his hat and called a greeting to her as the car slid through the gate. "Mrs. Heather," he said. "Seventy-five years of age and has lived in that cottage ever since she went there as a bride of eighteen. Her husband was one of the Castle woodmen, killed years ago by a falling tree in a big storm. She bore twelve children in that cottage and now lives there quite alone. Nothing will induce her to go and live with one of her married daughters, or go into an almshouse, or do anything whatsoever suitable to her age or infirmities. Visitors who want to see the Castle on Saturday afternoons are shown round by her and buy postcards of it inside her cottage. I cannot imagine why she is always so extraordinarily happy. If you are ever able to find out I shall be most interested."

Miss Brown was scarcely listening to him for the car was sliding down a narrow beckoning track through the woods to she knew not what. Around her the beech trees stood in their ranks, great warriors majestical in silver armour, their branches like lifted arms that held up the shimmering canopy of green leaves. Miss Brown had not known before that trees could grow to such a height, that their trunks could be so mighty or their massed leaves form so impenetrable a green shade, or that their mighty power could impose so great a silence. Nothing moved except the topmost leaves stirred by the breeze from the sea, and they were so far away that their dreamy murmur was unheard; only their stir sent flecked shadows swaying gently over the surface of the road, and the unheard voice of them was crying, "Come this way."

And they went that way, and the car swung out into a small grassy clearing and stopped before the gate of the Castle.

"We get out here," prompted Mr. Birley gently, for Miss Brown sat as though turned to stone. "And then Boulder takes the car away behind those trees, where the garage and the stables and the vegetable garden are. After that he will get our tea. You get out first. It takes me a moment to get the stiffness out of these rheumatic legs of mine."

It was stunning astonishment that had made Miss Brown so incapable of movement. It had been her dream to visit famous castles, but she had never hoped to see one as lovely as this. It was still lived in, still alive, not a relic of the dead past but a vital part of the living present. Its walls, above the vivid green of the grass, glowed in the sun with a warmth that seemed to strike outward from within, as though the heart of the place still burned with valorous fire. Where the glow of the battlements met the shimmering heat of the blue sky one might have imagined that figures moved and that banners stirred a little in the hot wind.

Yet, at a second glance, how old and worn were the glowing walls, pierced with loopholes for the arrows, just the outer shell of a Norman castle, with four towers one at each corner, and a great portcullised archway where a green painted gate stood wide open, so that one could see within an ordered garden full of flowers.

"A Tudor manor house is built within the Norman walls," said Mr. Birley, as he followed her out of the car. "It is a strange and very lovely combination."

Miss Brown walked as in a dream through the shadows of the Norman archway and out into the light and colour of the formal garden, with its paved walks, clipped yew hedges, and brilliant parterres of summer flowers. The archway was in the north wall of the Castle, and the garden stretched from north to south, with the house to the west. The east wall still stood stout and strong but the south wall had fallen into ruin, and here the yew hedges had been discontinued and a low stone parapet took their place. Beyond this was space, for upon the south side the Castle stood upon the rocky summit of a wooded hill that fell precipitously away to a valley far below where a stream was singing. Beyond this valley the ground rose again and rolling wooded hills stretched to the horizon.

The house, facing east, quite filled its half of the space within the Castle walls. It was a small perfect house built of ancient grey stones, with wide, square-headed windows, gabled roof and exquisite tall Tudor chimneys. A flight of steps led up to the terrace that stretched the full length of the house, and the front door stood open within its beautifully arched and carven porch. Although it was as perfectly of its period as were the Castle walls of theirs it did not look out of place within them. The Norman walls, the Tudor house, the brilliant little formal garden, the wide view across acres of glorious woodlands, made a whole so perfect that one was not conscious of the many centuries that had gone to the making of it. Its beauty banished time and teased one out of thought.

"Oh, it is very nice," murmured Miss Brown, standing anchored upon a paved path between beds of nemesia and blue delphiniums, and then, blushing and making a desperate effort to be a little more adequate, "it-it-seems just right, as though it were meant to be here."

"It's been here long enough," said Mr. Birley, smiling. "The first of my ancestors to live here was a Norman, Simon Beaulieu, one of those who fought for the Conqueror. His reward for distinguished devotion to his king was this stretch of woodland to be the possession of his heirs for ever."

He limped to a seat by the south wall, overlooking the valley. "Come and sit down while you look about you, Miss Brown. Simon, no doubt, sitting his horse just about where you are sitting now, must have seen with one flash of his eye how magnificent a site for a castle was this mighty precipice, with stones for the walls all about him and fresh water in the valley down below. The sunshine probably meant nothing to him, nor the view. But he was a good craftsman. He built well and truly, and his heirs enjoyed his handiwork and brought honour to his name. The greatest of them was his grandson, Stephen the Crusader. He, we always think, was the best of us. Twice he left his home to fight for the Holy Places. He endured wounds, famine, imprisonment; but came back at last to die peacefully in the Castle. But after peace comes strife again, by the law of life. The Wars of the Roses sound romantic, but to Richard Beaulieu, who backed the incompetent saint of Lancaster, they brought tragedy. He was besieged here by his enemies, and rather than yield to them he rode his war horse right over the Castle wall, over this precipice, and was dashed to death in the valley below. According to the legend his enemies buried man and horse down there by the

48

stream, no man knows where. Most of the Castle was destroyed and his family driven out into the desolation of the First Exile."

Mr. Birley stopped abruptly. "I'm possibly boring you?" he asked anxiously. "My nephew Richard is continually reminding me that our family history is not of the absorbing interest to others that it is to me. He thinks it hard that guests are not allowed within our doors without a précis of it. I have no doubt he voices the general opinion."

"But don't you remember," smiled Miss Brown, "that I like history so long as I am not living in it?"

"That First Exile lasted for nearly a century," continued Mr. Birley instantly. "It lasted until Tudor days when Harry Birley —you see the name had changed a little by that time—who had waxed fat on the destruction of the monasteries, came back to rebuild the home of his fathers.

"And you see how well he rebuilt it. You see how he retained the outer Norman walls, repairing them most carefully, and how he built his manor house within them of the old stones salvaged from the ruins, so that there is a perfect reconcilement between the one period and the other. He was an artist, that fellow, if a scoundrel. King Henry beheaded him. No doubt deservedly. His family, however, lived on serenely in the Castle, entertaining Queen Elizabeth and rising to great heights of adventurous glory in the days of the Armada and the voyages to the New World. Bad days did not come again until the devotion of Charles Birley to the royalist cause brought ruin in the Civil War of sixteen forty-two. Then there ensued the period of the Second Exile. . . . There is only a little more, Miss Brown, and then you shall have your tea. . . . That lasted until the eighteenth century when Roger Birley went out to India as a clerk in the service of the East India Company. There, by means which it is perhaps better not to enquire into, but also by conspicuous gallantry in the service of his country—civilian service, for even in the thick of the Indian Mutiny it was said of him that he never touched a sword —he amassed an enormous fortune and brought it home to England, together with the rheumatic gout that he has handed on to me and a liver deservedly disorganized by riotous living. He immediately came back to the Castle, where the Manor House, this time, was more or less falling to pieces, built it up again and made this exquisite eighteenth-century garden where formerly there had been only an old paved courtyard. He did not live to enjoy his inheritance. He died of his rheumatism and his liver soon after the garden was finished. But his descendants have lived

49

here ever since, making next to no effort to augment the fortune he left them; it is now diminishing with alarming speed, and serve us right for our lethargy and our parasitic feeding upon the achievements of the past. It is likely that this war will see it dwindle away altogether; it may be that the whole place will be blown to pieces, like your own beloved home. Then will come the period of the Third Exile, from which perhaps, this time, there will be no return. One cannot, you know, always return. For every family, for every nation, for every civilization, there must come, at last, the end."

"Please God not yet," said Miss Brown, for once managing to say what she wanted to say with surprising fluency. "Not yet for England, and not yet for this heavenly place. England, now, is like this place. A castle set on a hill for all the world to watch."

"We shall see," said Mr. Birley grimly. "Now is the time of testing, now is the judgment, no less for nations than for individuals. We shall see. . . . But there was Dunquerque."

CHAPTER IV

I

"MAY we take her in to tea, or are you still only at the period of the Second Exile?"

The voice, mocking, deep, yet silkily soft, broke in startlingly upon Miss Brown, pulling her back abruptly from the past to the present day. She looked up and saw two young men standing there in the sunshine with a huge dog between them, but it was upon the elder of the two, the one who had spoken, that her attention was instantly riveted.

"Miss Brown, Richard, my elder great-nephew," said Mr. Birley. "Richard is, of course, the Castle's owner, the heir of the ages and the head of the family. I just live with him on sufferance."

Richard laughed but a little twitch of irritation drew his black brows together for a moment, and he moved his big shoulders impatiently, as though some burden pressed upon them. Was it irksome to inherit the ages, wondered Miss Brown? His uncle's remark had evidently exasperated him. The observations of the elderly to the young frequently had this unfortunate effect, so Miss Brown had observed from the vantage point of her middle age. Tendentious these remarks so frequently were, and informed with unconscious anxiety that the old trails so painfully blazed out should be faithfully continued by those who came after.

Yet Richard did not look as though it would be irksome to him to follow in the steps of his fathers, for he was his fathers. Miss Brown, in a sudden brief flash of insight, could see them all alive in him. Richard was tall and muscular, a fit descendant of fighting men. He had the dark skin and the almost savagely determined jaw of the man who had followed in the train of a conqueror and conjured a castle out of a wilderness. He had the gay gallantry of the cavaliers who had fought for King Charles, and there was perhaps, in the full lips and the tilt of the eyes, velvety dark yet alight with mockery, a hint of cheerful unscrupulousness that might have come from the scoundrel whom Henry the Eighth had beheaded. But to heredity he added that indefinable something of his own that makes the individual. That twitch of the eyebrows, that movement of the shoulders, told of a hidden conflict, a something in him that was at war with his inheritance, a something that wanted to go free on a new and unblazed trail. He was in his middle twenties and alarmingly attractive, with a very deep, softly caressing voice, and just that overdose of masculinity that would set sparks flying whenever he came in contact with a woman equally vital. Wherever he goes, thought Miss Brown, there's bound to be a good deal of upset and to-do. He'll be difficult about his food and his clothes and his laundry. When he's at home I'll have my work cut out.

"And this is Stephen," said Mr. Birley.

Could they possibly be brothers, wondered Miss Brown? She had Mr. Birley's word for it, so she supposed they were. Stephen was tall but small boned and delicately featured, with beautifully shaped but very tense hands, with the long blunt fingers of the artist. He was quiet-eyed and possessed of a poise that was strangely mature, as though his youthful rebellions against the restrictions of environment and heredity were already over, or had never existed, and he felt himself secure in the place and the life where he would be. Yet if there was no rebellion there was a strained tautness in his bearing that was not in Richard's. There was in his mind just now an agony of conflict that Richard would never know. Before the intensity of the suffering in his smiling face the sensitive Miss Brown dropped her eyes.

"The dog Argos," said Mr. Birley.

Argos was entirely free from conflict of any sort or kind. His was the sublime content of one who feels himself enthroned at the hub of the universe. For him the earth spun and the stars sang upon their courses. For him and for his people God had created the universe and made it good; he could conceive of it in no other guise. He had been named after that hound of Odysseus whose fame has come down through the centuries in one of the most moving of Homeric passages, and as was only fitting he was a dog of Homeric proportions, an Alsatian of unblemished ancestry. He was of a great age and had lived since babyhood in the Castle, outliving all other dogs who had at various times been resident there. Indeed he had himself curtailed the lives of two or three by sitting on them, for he disliked associating with his inferiors. His appearance was more than noble. The ebony and tawny gold of his coat, exquisitely groomed by admiring satellites, rippled to the movement of his muscles like a coat of satin, and his deep chest and long flanks, the great breadth of his shoulders and the superb carriage of his head, told of a breeding unblemished by any turning to the right hand or to the left hand of wayward fancy by the aristocrats who had been his ancestors. Moral virtue had invariably been allied to beauty and courage in the story of his race, and Argos was the fine flower of the alliance. His lustrous eyes were dark and arrogant beneath the fine brows and the erect black silky ears lined with the softest gold. His nose was long and inclined to be supercilious in repose; in action, when snuffing the air or wrinkled to snarl, it could be terrifying. His great jaws were usually benevolently parted, his long pink tongue hanging out and inclining to dribble; when he closed them, lifting his upper lip to show his teeth, it was best to step aside. He had never mauled any one yet, but in the primeval forests from which his race had emerged into the sunlight men had fled in terror from the cry of "wolf." As he stood between Richard and Stephen, regarding Miss Brown with the casual amiability of one whose position in the world is so lofty and assured that one servitor more or less in the retinue can create but little stir, he seemed the reincarnation of all the noble dogs who through the centuries had kept guard over this great fortress. All their dignity was his, their power and confidence and arrogant devotion. When he lifted up his great head and bayed the deep thrilling bell-like note pealed out over the valley beneath the Castle wall like a trumpet call, and Miss Brown's thin body shook as the reverberations of that echo from the past trembled through her nerves and wrenched at her heart strings.

"It's all right," consoled Richard. "That meant he likes you. You are accepted."

"You misunderstood Miss Brown," said his uncle quickly. "She was not afraid. She is a historian and tangible dangers do not alarm her. Yet I think, Miss Brown, even though you are now incorporated into the domestic scene, that you had better leave it to Argos to make the first advances. He is not a bad-tempered dog but he feels it only due to his position that the initiative should come from himself."

"Of course," said Miss Brown. Not for the world would she have touched Argos, or even spoken to him, without his express permission. Before such historic majesty of mien she knew her place.

"Miss Brown has come back with me to be our housekeeper," Mr. Birley explained to his nephews. "I went to London, among other reasons, to search for the perfect housekeeper, and I believe that I have found her. May heaven be praised. Perhaps the dreadful disorder of our domestic circumstances may now be a little abated."

"You'll have a job, Miss Brown," said Richard gaily. "We're in a hell of a mess."

"I hope you'll be happy, Miss Brown," said Stephen. He had not spoken before and his voice, in contrast to Richard's soft deep sleepy tones, had a clear-cut distinctness, like a diamond writing upon glass. Clarity was of the essence of Stephen. His brown eyes were not opaque like his brother's but had the lightness and clearness of certain quickly running mountain streams, and a directness of glance that was hard to meet. His skin was pale and clear, his hair in the sunlight almost silver in its fairness. The smile with which he had originally greeted Miss Brown had left his face and he spoke gravely and wonderingly, as though he very badly wanted her to be happy but thought it most unlikely that she would be. As pain had seized Miss Brown when she saw the children at the station, so it gripped her again. The world was in a poor way, surely, for that age to speak of happiness in that wondering tone, as though it were a star far away in the sky. When she had been his age she had not wondered about happiness; she had just taken hold of it and thoroughly enjoyed it.

"I think," she said, "that if it is possible to be happy anywhere at all now, it will be here."

They were walking towards the house and she and Stephen were ahead of the other two. Unconsciously she had pulled off her gloves and picked a sprig of rosemary from the bushes which grew amongst the lilies and roses that edged the paved path to the terrace steps, and was pressing it between her fingers, just as she used to press her rosemary in the little garden at "Sea View." Its hot sweet scent floated up to her and she was suddenly astonished, as she was for ever being astonished, to find something remaining from the old days that was just as lovely as it used to be.

"It's just the same," she said, opening her fingers and looking wonderingly at the silvery sprig lying in the palm of her hand. "Somehow I had expected it to have lost its scent."

She glanced up shyly at the boy beside her and saw a look of pleasure pass over his face like glancing light, banishing its look of set unhappiness.

"Nothing has lost its scent," he said quickly. "Nothing in the natural world has abated its beauty by one jot. It was the most perfect spring, wasn't it; it is the loveliest summer I ever remember. This place—it's seemed to glow like a jewel all the time——" He stopped abruptly, not with shyness, for with that strange maturity of his shyness seemed a thing long ago left behind, but because Richard was now upon her other side, and it seemed that he did not speak in that way before Richard. What would he have said, she wondered? Would he have said that the whole of the world of nature was crying out to man in his agony, as the beech trees had said to her as she drove through the wood, "Come this way"?

II

They were on the terrace of the house, before the carved porch, and the dog Argos had stalked in first, laying silent majestic stress upon the fact that this place of residence was his. Others might enter under sufferance, but only at his heels. Miss Brown looked up and saw that words were cut over the archway.

> Come in this way, and fear no more,
> Peace in your heart, leave wide the door.
> Turn not the key, nor shut the gate.
> None come too soon, nor return too late.

"This porch, though it is built in the Tudor style, is in reality an eighteenth-century addition," said Mr. Birley. "The nabob of the East India Company built it and carved those words after his return from the Second Exile. Believe it or not, no Birley has locked that door nor shut the gate since those words were carved upon that stone; nor ever will."

"If invasion comes we'll have to," said Richard, smilingly impatient of the whims and fancies that still flaunted themselves in the face of stark reality.

"No," said Stephen.

"Silly old fool," said Richard tolerantly.

"I must tell you, Miss Brown," explained Mr. Birley, easily yet with a trace of strain in his voice that he could not hide, "that Stephen has just come down from Oxford in some confusion of mind. The latest turn taken by the war has imposed a severe strain upon his adherence to the principles of non-violence."

Stephen did not answer. Miss Brown, after a bare twenty minutes spent within these walls, could realize how anguishing a thing it must be to Mr. Birley that one of his breed should not be willing to fight for his country. Yet she thought that he should not have given that piece of information to the stranger that she still was. His bitterness must be uncontrollably great that he had done so. Afraid to look at Stephen she looked at Richard instead.

"Richard," said Mr. Birley, and his strained tones relaxed into relief and pride, "is on leave celebrating the winning of his wings."

Of course, thought Miss Brown. Richard was a Birley from head to foot and through and through. They had won their spurs in the old days, now it was their wings. Yet Richard was obviously in revolt against the romanticism of family history even while he accepted without question the patriotic duty it imposed upon him, while Stephen was at home in the place where he would be yet could not follow without question in the steps of his fathers. Heredity could play queer tricks.

They had passed within the tall fixed wooden screens that protected the front door and were in the hall and main living room that ran almost the length of the house, with a carved staircase leading up to the gallery above. Four of the symmetrical square-headed windows that she had seen from outside, two on each side of the front door, looked east on the glowing garden and the box hedges against the Norman walls, but to the south a big oriel window looked out over the valley and the far lovely wooded distance, and through it the hot sun was streaming. It lay in pools of gold on the dark oak floor, lit the panelled walls to as living a beauty as though the wood of them were still breathing and sighing in the forests, and scattered flower-like points of brightness wherever the carving of the staircase and fireplace and old furniture caught the beams of light on its polished surface. It struck flames of crimson and azure from the fine old rugs on the floor, the curtains, the old brocade cushions in the deep window seats and the many books in the bookcases that lined the recesses beneath the stairs, and sent long dusty beams of light shining from end to end of the long gracious peaceful room whose door was never locked. The windows were wide open and the scent of the flowers in the garden mingled with the scent of tobacco, sun-warmed pine logs in the open grate, and that indescribable smell of antiquity, the mingled scent of very old books, pot-pourri, damp and mice. Miss Brown, her shabby black bag clasped to her bosom, stood speechless and immovable in the middle of the room.

"You aren't saying any of the usual things, Miss Brown," said Richard with approval. "You haven't gushed over the divine staircase, or had a rush of blood to the head over the oriel window or the panelling, and as you haven't even asked what that filthy bit of rag in that hideous glass case is, I'll tell you."

Mr. Birley smiled. Only by sheer good luck, he realised, had the dumbness of astonishment saved Miss Brown from uttering all the admiring platitudes that would have damned her for ever in Richard's eyes. Forewarned, she was silent as he put a hand under her elbow and guided her to the glass case in question, hanging on the wall between two windows. It was an inoffensive glass case, as glass cases go, and within it, stretched out upon black velvet, was a shred of tattered linen still faintly stained with red and blue. A little tingling electric thrill went through Miss Brown at the touch of Richard's hand, so immensely strong was his masculine vitality, yet when she looked up into his dark wild-bird's eyes their glance was easier to meet than Stephen's, that seemed to be searching out all the dark places of one's soul. The mockery in them was a veil that Richard unconsciously let down to hide both from himself and others a knowledge of himself and a knowledge of them that he preferred both parties to be without. What was the use of testing and probing oneself and everyone and everything that came one's way, like old Stephen did, Richard was always asking himself? Better accept the normal standards of conduct without fuss or bother, meanwhile getting rid of the mush of religion and family legend that tended to tie one's legs up with blue ribands, and to get down to the real business of life, action in a world of action, blazing one's own meteor trail of light through the dark spaces of a fighting world.

"The pennon of Simon Beaulieu," said Richard. "At least so we say. He flaunted it, if it's it, while assisting William to advance his territorial claims in Europe and take the barbarians of England under enlightened Norman protection. Later, no doubt, when old Simon settled down to enjoy the fruits of aggression, I mean protection, it floated in triumph from the Castle wall. You can still faintly see the swastika traced upon it in red and blue. Later, with the swastika cleverly converted into a cross, it went on the Crusades with Stephen Beaulieu. Stephen, you know, is revered as the family saint. He is the only ancestor eligible for the position because he is the only one of whom we know just nothing at all; about all the others we know a good deal and the evidence is all against beatification. It's my conviction that Stephen, when at home, took a hand in the English pogroms, but Uncle Charles and Stephen don't take to the idea, and it can't be proved. Later it saw Richard Beaulieu throw himself over the castle wall, and went into exile with his sons, coming home again with old Harry of the Tudor times. Then it went out again with What's-his-name the Royalist and returned home with old Red-Nose the Nabob. . . . At least, Miss Brown, that is the legend. Actually I shouldn't wonder if it wasn't just the old Nabob's night-cap, framed by a doting widow. The frame is certainly Victorian, the only genuine Victorian antique in the whole house."

"Thank God tea's in," said Stephen.

Boulder, now metamorphosed from chauffeur to butler and neatly garbed in threadbare black, had brought in a tray containing exquisite, but oddly-assorted, cups and saucers and a huge Georgian silver teapot. This he placed on a low table covered with a cloth much in need of the attentions of a darning needle, with a plate of bread and butter and an untouched madeira cake that had seen better days. He then stood upright and shot out his cuffs.

"Does the Young Person take tea with you, sir, or in the 'ousekeeper's room?" he enquired of his master in a disagreeable stage whisper that he fully intended to be overheard by Miss Brown.

Mr. Birley adjusted his pince-nez that he might the better direct a chilling glance through them at his erring domestic.

"I have already told you that this lady's name is Miss Brown," he informed Boulder. "And naturally she takes tea with us on her first day."

Boulder shot back his cuffs and departed, closing the door with an exaggerated softness that was somehow grossly insulting.

"Why doesn't he swear when he's put out?" asked Richard. "A good damn relieves the feelings and does no one any harm, but closing the door like that gives one goose-flesh all over."

"Will you pour out, Miss Brown?" asked Mr. Birley, directing a reproving glance at Richard through his pince-nez before casting them aside. "Boulder served in my brother's regiment through the South African war. In the first German war he was batman to these boys' father. He was a very gallant soldier, but now the iron of domestic service seems to have entered into his soul. You must have employed servants in your boarding-house, Miss Brown. Do you know why it is that domestic service has such a corroding effect upon the temper?"

"I never had a servant, at least not the sort that lives in," said Miss Brown quietly, taking both small hands to the huge teapot. "I couldn't afford one. But don't you think it must be dreadfully irritating always to have to do things other people's way, and never your own? I had to work very hard in my boarding-house, but at least I always did the flowers the way I liked, and put the furniture where I wanted it, and that made me happy."

Miss Brown's quiet voice did not falter, but it stopped with an abruptness that was almost like a cry of pain.

"Miss Brown's boarding-house, her furniture, and the vases in which she arranged her flowers, have all been blown to blazes by the enemy," Mr. Birley told his great-nephews. "That is why she has had to come to us."

They were as tongue-tied in the face of misfortune as the young of the English breed invariably are, but after a few stammered phrases that made everyone feel most uncomfortable they began to show Miss Brown how much she was needed in a way that was very comforting.

"Can you make cakes, Miss Brown?" asked Richard. "Whenever I come home on leave—and I come pretty often, for we get a good bit of leave in the R.A.F. to steady our supposedly exhausted nerves—there's never anything but this filthy thing from the grocer's. War-time flying doesn't get me down at all, but mildewed madeira cake does."

"Perhaps there'll be some flowers in the house now Miss Brown's here," said Stephen. "There's been nothing in the vases but spiders since Mrs. Weston died."

It was suddenly perceived that Miss Brown had a very small dimple in her left cheek. Yes, she liked making cakes and doing the flowers.

III

It was Stephen who, after tea, said he would show her the house and help her to settle in. In spite of the blessed fact that poverty did not now stare her quite immediately in the face, and that the to-day of firm foothold had expanded to take in the whole four weeks that must elapse before Boulder could get her ejected like her predecessors, a chill depression had suddenly enveloped Miss Brown, a chill that was all the colder because of the warm enthusiasm for the Castle and its beauty that had filled her before. She felt suddenly very alone in these new surroundings, among these strangers who were neither of her sex nor of her world. Her social standing was not the same as Boulder's, and he disliked her already because she could sit down to tea with his master and he could not, but it was also not the same as the Birleys' and they would always treat her with that particular brand of thoughtful kindness that is an almost impenetrable barrier to real intimacy. They would never tell her their troubles; they would be too considerate to impose their private distresses on one who seemed something of a child to them because she had not grown up so high in the social world as they had. Mr. Birley had told her a great deal about his family history, but of the anxiety which he must feel for his great-nephews he would never speak except involuntarily. Richard's rebellious condition was plain to see, but it would never occur to him to delight Miss Brown by working a little of it off on her. Stephen's misery of mind was already pressing painfully upon her, but it was not very likely that he would think of easing the pressure by telling her about it.

And she was going to love Stephen. Of the two brothers Richard was the most obviously striking, but he had not that mature and sensitive understanding that she was beginning to feel in Stephen. The quick painful love of a woman who has never borne a son, but who if she had would have had him just like this, went out from her to Stephen. She was going to be happy in this place, but she was going to suffer too.

They mounted the great bare staircase together, slowly, as befits those who tread where generations have trod before them. The centre of each wide tread was a little worn, so many were the feet that had passed up and down, yet was polished to a satin smoothness by the caress of the many silk and satin skirts that had slipped from stair to stair through the centuries. The wide balustrade was shining-smooth too; so many hands had touched it as Miss Brown's was touching it now, as she passed up the stairs from one pool of sunlight to another, into the shadows of the gallery.

It was panelled like the hall, and like the hall reached almost the whole length of the house, with doors opening out of it to north and west. But it had only a small curtained window to the south and most of the light came through the east windows looking on the garden, not a bright light at this time of day. And the rugs and curtains were not brilliant in hue like those downstairs. The old brocade curtains swaying at the windows were silver and sea-green, and the rugs on the floor were of a mid-forest green that was almost as dark as the polished oak between them. This gallery seemed as though tunnelled at the bottom of the sea, and through the rhythmic swaying of the shadows shone the white coral faces and the pearly eyes of seamen and men-at-arms who had suffered the sea-change of death more than a hundred years ago.

"They could get so little life into their portraits then," said Stephen. "They all seem dead men, don't they?"

Miss Brown passed from one to another of the Birley portraits; men who wore the pointed beard and white ruff of Elizabethan days above a seaman's cuirass, or whose lovelocks and Vandyke collars of white lace fell over the armour of a fighting cavalier, and men with great curled wigs above the scarlet coats of soldiers who had fought with Marlborough and Wellington. They were most of them, as Stephen had said, rather lifeless portraits, not by the hand of a master, but from under several curled wigs there looked back at her, and followed her about the room as painted eyes will, the keen grey glance of Charles Birley the historian, and above the ruff of an Elizabethan and the lace of a cavalier she saw twice over the vital reckless face of Richard who had won his wings. But Stephen, with his delicate features and disconcerting light brown eyes, she did not see. Nor did she see many women, and the two or three whom she did see were so badly painted that they were completely nondescript.

"There seem so few wives," she complained, up in arms for her sex.

"Well, of course, actually there must have been the usual number," laughed Stephen. "But it seems the Birley men thought it waste of money to paint a woman. Judging by their faces it looks as though they had belonged to two types, the type that women fall for very easily and that does not much value a thing it gets too much of, and the type that goes in for a wife merely as a necessary investment. Rotten husbands they must all have been. Don't you think so?"

Miss Brown, blushing, thought so. She remembered Mr. Birley's aversion to marriage and remembered, too, the electric shock that had gone through her merely at Richard's touch. . . . But she hastened to say that all the Birleys looked very nice.

"Now here *is* a good portrait," said Stephen. "The only one. A Romney."

They had reached the curtained south window and Stephen drew back the curtain that the light might fall on the picture that hung beside it.

"It is Roger Birley of the East India Company," he said. "The man who refounded our fortunes after what Uncle Charles calls the Second Exile. The man who made the garden."

And the man who never touched a sword even in the thick of the Indian Mutiny, remembered Miss Brown, and found herself looking straight into Stephen's eyes.

And very odd they looked in the coarse red face of the man who had died of the effects of riotous living. It was a magnificent portrait, so alive that one felt that at any moment the Nabob must stretch out his hand for his glass, and wink his eye as he described some rather shady business transaction, or else curse volubly as a twinge of the gout went through him. He had a choleric but most humorous face, where a weak mouth contrasted oddly with a jaw whose resolution was not obscured by several double chins. He was beautifully and fastidiously dressed in white powdered wig, plum-coloured satin, and a waistcoat embroidered with forgetmenots and carnations. He belonged to neither of the two types in which Stephen had roughly divided the other men of his family. He was entirely individual and, Miss Brown vaguely felt, the best of them all. "The quick of the tree," was the phrase that occurred to her.

"Human nature is a queer thing," said Stephen. "If he was so fastidious and strong-minded why did he drink so much?"

"Just to follow the fashion of the time?" suggested Miss Brown.

"But he looks such a tough chap, as though he wouldn't care a rap about the fashion of the time," said Stephen. "He's just a mystery. That's all." And he drew the curtain and banished the mystery back into shadowed obscurity.

"He has your eyes," said Miss Brown shyly. "But there is nothing else of you in him, and nothing at all of you in the other portraits."

"I'm supposed to be like my mother," said Stephen. "She died when I was born. I'm not a Birley, yet I'm not at all sure I don't care for this place even more than my uncle and Richard do. Odd, isn't it?"

"Life's very odd," said Miss Brown seriously, and Stephen smiled. The adjective "odd," applied to the life of this summer of 1940, was a miracle of understatement, but like his uncle he felt that Miss Brown's quiet platitudes were going to keep them all upon an even keel in the days that were coming.

"And it's odd," he said, "that with civilization crashing round us we should still be taking an interest in individual personalities. And yet not so odd," he added, "considering that its survival is one of the things we are supposed to be fighting for."

For the next half hour he showed her the way about what he called her "kingdom." The phrase thrilled her, even though the sense of cold lonely depression continued and her heart failed within her at the magnitude of the task that lay ahead.

For a manor house the Castle was small, but it seemed to Miss Brown terribly large. With aching legs she followed Stephen along cobwebbed passages and up and down uncarpeted dark staircases, that twisted round and round their central newels till her head span. The rooms were beautiful with their four-poster beds hung with brocade and their exquisite Sheraton furniture, but they were very dusty and there was no water laid on on the top floor. Her own bedroom, with the housekeeper's room leading out of it, looked westward over the castle wall just below it into the rustling leafy spaces of the woods. It was most lovely but had not been turned out since the last occupant had disagreed with Boulder and departed. Even Stephen, who had seemed happily oblivious of cobwebs everywhere else, paused here and passed a worried hand over his fair hair.

"Should I find a brush and sweep it?" he asked a little distractedly. "It's rotten for you arriving unexpectedly and finding nothing ready."

"Not *you*," said Miss Brown firmly. "I'll see to all this."

"Oh, but I'd like to help," said Stephen. "It's no good asking Boulder to. He won't do anything except his own jobs, the silver and so on, and the cooking when he has to. He's not what I'd call a really domesticated man. Now I am. I'm the girl of the family, I'm always being told. So you stay here while I get the sheets. I know where they're kept."

He was back in a moment, smiling encouragingly at Miss Brown over a pile of distinctly damp linen. She had not the heart to suggest that it should be aired, she just made the bed with his help, hoped for the best and asked gently about the woman who came in by day.

"Oh yes," said Stephen vaguely. "Fanny Treguthwic. I think to-day is her afternoon off, or she'd have been here to help you.

She always seems very slow to me but she's very anxious to please."

"Oh," said Miss Brown in a small voice.

"There's one thing you *won't* have to contend with," said Stephen, anxious to cheer, "and that's evacuated children. Actually I believe another lot of them arrived in Torhaven to-day but the billeting officer is missing out the Castle as she doesn't, thank God, think a household of men capable of dealing with children. She didn't know you were coming, you see. We'll have to keep you dark."

Miss Brown was not so sure that she thanked God, provided the children could have been girls, and without things in their heads. The unrelieved masculinity of her surroundings, with the accompanying cobwebs, pressed upon her spirit.

"There!" said Stephen, thumping her damp pillow with his fist and pushing a collection of fluff out of sight under the bed with his foot, "that looks nice now, doesn't it? Would you like to see my room? It's the best in the house."

Miss Brown said she would, though secretly hoping it would not be at the top of yet another flight of stairs.

But it was, and stone stairs this time. The Norman tower at the south-west corner of the old wall had been repaired and included as part of the Tudor house, and at the top of it was Stephen's room, with Boulder's below it. The staircase, he told her, led right down to the ground-floor, where a door opened out into the woods. It was locked now, and never used.

"Oh," gasped Miss Brown, stumbling from the darkness of the stairs into the brightness and light of this watchtower in the sky. "Aren't you horribly lonely here?"

"I like being lonely," said Stephen briefly, "and look at the view."

The small square room had three windows in the huge thickness of the wall, looking south, west and east. It was the same view as one had from the oriel window of the hall, but infinitely wider because of the height of the tower. The drop of the wooded precipice to the singing stream far below in the valley seemed immense, and from here one could see that at the far end of the valley the stream encircled an old grey stone farmhouse. Climbing woodlands, ridge beyond ridge of them, closed in the view to the south, but to the east one could see the great sweep of the moors, with their strange tors clear-cut against the sky, while to the west, through a break in the woods high up in the sky, was a view of distant gold cornfields and green pasture lands and fields of rose-red earth with a church tower behind them, that was like some far-away glimpse of a country in a fairy tale. The blue limpid scented summer air filled this bowl of loveliness like warm wine, and below it was the rustling of a myriad leaves and the muted bird-song of high summer.

"Perhaps it's loveliest in the spring," said Stephen, "when the foliage is not so dense and you see the bluebells in the woods through a sort of fine mist of new green leaves. Or in the autumn when they are burning brushwood down there in the valley and smoke coils up through the turning leaves. Or in the winter when the whole world is muted by hard frost, with the stream silent and the bare twigs coated with silver. I don't know. I love it always. And nothing can touch it."

Miss Brown hardly knew how to reply. Stephen did not use his uncle's rather stilted phraseology but he had his fluency, and he was too unselfconscious to mind saying what he felt. "It's a nice room," she said lamely, adding with a smile, "and very different from your brother's!"

Richard's room on the first floor, with its four-post bed and thick carpet, had been as luxurious as it was possible for any room to be in this austere house, and all his possessions had been strewn over it like autumn leaves cast adrift by the wind, but Stephen's room was plain to the point of sending a chill through Miss Brown. A camp bed, rush matting on the stone floor, a plain wooden chair and table, bookcases and a gramophone, were its furniture. The only bits of colour were the bright bindings of the books, a few of them verse, most of them books on architecture.

"I hope to be an architect," said Stephen, seeing Miss Brown's eyes upon them. "I had planned to go to Belgium to study architecture when I left Oxford. The war has smashed all that, of course."

He spoke with a bitterness that Miss Brown missed, for she was studying his room with increasing astonishment. Fancy *choosing* to sleep here, she marvelled. Truly the ways of the well-to-do were past comprehension. Had poverty compelled Stephen to sleep on a hard camp-bed in a stone-floored draughty tower-room one would have felt pity for him, but since he did it for choice one supposed one didn't.

"I hate being cluttered up with things," said Stephen. "And I like to think things out alone."

"I shouldn't be surprised," said Miss Brown wisely, "if you thought things out too much."

He laughed. "It's no good, Miss Brown. One either has the kind of mind that asks questions, or the kind of mind that doesn't. One can't change one's kind of mind. As Sancho Panza said, 'Everyone is as God made him, and very often worse'."

"But there's no necessity, surely," argued Miss Brown, "to be worse."

"You mean the questioning mind can say 'stop' to itself before it reaches the peak of torment? No, I don't think it can. You see, though it may shrink from it, it knows that only beyond that place is there any sort of peace. One knows that instinctively, even though one may not have actually experienced it yet. . . . I play my gramophone in the evenings sometimes, Miss Brown. If you hear it, and it bothers you, please tell me and I'll shut up at once."

Miss Brown was a little hurt at the sudden change in the conversation. For a moment they had been very near an intimacy that would have given her joy, and then he had abruptly, though without conscious intention, relegated her again to that place in the social scale that was not quite the same as his. Could not even this war destroy the loneliness of caste? But she accepted the position into which she was thrust with her usual dignity.

"Thank you, Mr. Birley, that's very kind of you," she said as she went down the twisting stone stairs again. "But I shan't mind. I like music."

"For the love of mike, don't call me Mr. Birley," laughed Stephen. Perhaps after all, thought Miss Brown, he would learn one day, and sooner than many, that most of our barriers are better down.

IV

But the rest of the day did little to lessen her depression. When, having done his kindly duty, Stephen abandoned her, Boulder immediately pounced. He had perforce been coping with the commissariat during the interim between housekeepers, but with a woman beneath the roof he had no intention of continuing the practice. "This way, Miss," he said firmly, and shot out his cuffs.

It had not occurred to Stephen to show her the kitchen regions. Possibly he had never been in them. He belonged to the sex and the class that are as the ravens whom the Heavenly Father feedeth. Sustenance always appeared as by magic from somewhere or other and he thought no more about it.

But Miss Brown perceived that she was going to have to think a good deal about it. None of that peaceful raven attitude for her. The lower regions were of Norman architecture, subterranean, dirty, and there seemed nothing in them but a mutton bone. The Tudor manor house had been built upon the old foundations, and doubtless, thought Miss Brown, casting a wild glance about her at the pillars with their carved capitals and the beautifully vaulted kitchen roof, it was all very interesting if you did not have to prepare meals in it. There were, it was true, a few modern conveniences, such as a dilapidated cooking stove and a sink thick with grease, but never in her wildest imaginings had she expected to have to cook for the aristocracy in such a stinking hole. She was horrified to overhear her ladylike mind using such a shocking expression even to itself. But really, she could not say that this kitchen was nice. What would Mother have said? Poor Mother would have died of shock had she known in her lifetime what conditions could exist in the nether regions of the mansions of Real Gentlemen.

"And what," asked Miss Brown of Boulder, indicating the mutton bone, "was it your intention to do with this?"

"A stoo," said Boulder laconically, and inserting his boot beneath the sink he hooked out a basket containing a few mildewed carrots and one tired onion. Miss Brown burst into tears.

But Boulder did not know it. Quick as lightning she snatched the carrots from the basket, turned her back on him, plunged them into the slimy tin basin that stood in the greasy sink, reached for a broken knife on the window ledge and turned the tap on.

As she scraped the carrots she fought down and vanquished her sobs. Fancy crying! She never cried. But then never before, as far as she could remember, except when her parents died, had she been plunged into quite such an abyss of misery and loneliness. Desperately she strove to recover her former pleasure in the kindness of the Birleys and the beauty of the Castle in its perfect setting of summer beauty. But it was no good. This kitchen and Boulder swamped everything. She seemed drowning in a flood of tears and grease.

Then she pulled herself together. She had won as by a mircle what only yesterday she had been longing for with such desperation, usefulness. She was for a while part of the pattern again, she was once more a pawn in the game, she had her place. What did it matter if it was a hard and greasy and lonely one? It did not matter at all. It only mattered that she should do her job.

And, she realised with a sudden thrill of pride, her job was at the moment an exceedingly important one. Four men—not to mention the dog Argos—depended upon her for nourishment, and one of those four was a pilot in the R.A.F. Were she to send him back to the fight with a digestion in good working order great would be the things that he would do for righteousness; but were she to send him back with the headache, the jaundiced vision and the phlegmatic movements of one with a disordered interior, then the cause of God would be put much behindhand. One of her mother's sayings had been, "When great deeds are done by men, my dear, there's always a woman in the background, and generally in the kitchen." With her head up, careless now of the tears on her face, she swung round on Boulder, who in his shirt sleeves, with a green baize apron tied round his thin middle, was polishing silver and gazing balefully at her from the door of a Norman dug-out that was presumably his pantry.

"Look here, Mr. Boulder," she said, "I can't make an appetising meal out of these mildewed objects, and you know it. There's a vegetable garden. Surely there's something eatable in it? What's the time? Half-past six. If we put dinner at eight that gives us an hour and a half. Come here, Mr. Boulder. You've got to help me."

They glared at each other across the gloomy old kitchen and for the first time Miss Brown got a really good look at her adversary. She had already come to the conclusion that Boulder must have a nature warped by something more than domestic service. Now, looking at his lined yellow face, the heavy pouches beneath his sad little eyes and the sweat that stood on the bald head that he tried to disguise with plastered streaks of grey hair, she realised she was looking at a very sick man. Of course. Sick men had absurd fancies, and one of them was that it was the newcomers about the place, and not death, who were inexorably pushing them away out of life. Her father had been like that. How he had hated, during that last year when his powers were failing and he would not admit it, that bright young man who was travelling for his firm so far more successfully than he could do. Yet her father's failing powers had not been the young man's fault. It had been death that was to blame.

Passionate pity surged over her as she looked at Boulder. This man had been a soldier, he had fought in two wars, and now in this third and greatest war he possibly felt himself thrown out on the scrap heap. For almost a lifetime he had served the same family with dog-like devotion; and now he was a very sick man and they had probably not even noticed it. With all their kind-ness she was bitterly sure they had not noticed it. Like all their kind they would regard an old family servant much as they regarded the old family furniture; they would be fond of it, but they would scarcely notice how it was wearing. And it would not be Boulder's place, of course, to mention any indisposition of his own. Well-trained servants were never indisposed. In all proba-bility he was even lonelier than she was herself.

She took a few steps forward and met Boulder's basilisk stare with kindness. "I am sorry I spoke hastily just now, Mr. Boulder. With this horrible war on everyone ought to be friends. And then you and I will never do our job here properly unless we pull together. And it seems to me we have quite a big job to do here. We're not back numbers yet, you and I, by any means. Every English home that keeps going normally and courageously is a slap in the face for Hitler. Don't you think so? But I can't do much good here without you, Mr. Boulder. You will have to help and teach me."

Miss Brown paused, breathless, after what was for her an unusually long oration. Boulder looked her up and down, where she stood in a patch of sunlight looking excessively determined and diminutive, and rather pretty in spite of her tear-stained face, and his bitter mouth twitched a little with amusement. Then he wiped his hands on his baize apron, took his coat from a peg behind the door and motioned her to follow him with a jerk of his tortoise head.

He took her through a small dark tunnel that led from the kitchen regions through the western wall of the Castle to the woods beyond. They followed the path through the trees until they came to the clearing in the woods where were the stable and the garage and the kitchen garden. This was an entirely utilitarian garden but it had been growing here for many years and had a beauty of its own. Cupped in the shelter of the woods, and filled with the golden light of evening, it was fragrant with the incense of sweet herbs and the fresh homely smell of teeming earth. And what earth! Rich and red and moist it glowed almost with the colour of carbuncles, and above it the potato flowers were a mist of mauve and white and the sprays of the runner beans were as leaping flame. Miss Brown noticed espaliered apple trees heavy with fruit, wineberries running riot over a fence, currant bushes and gooseberry bushes and strawberries gleaming among green leaves. There were some homely flowers too, honeysuckle and rosemary and borders of pansies along the moss-grown paths.

The Castle was a self-supporting kingdom, thought Miss Brown, but a kingdom that would run to waste if not taken firmly in hand. She hoped that Pratt, absent at present, would be more amenable to collaboration than Boulder.

Yet Boulder, albeit ungraciously and with no more speed than was absolutely necessary, was setting himself to help her. He fetched baskets from the potting shed and suggested that green peas might go well with the "stoo" and that "some of them strawberries needed eatin'." He helped her to pick them and showed her where the herbs and lettuce and carrots grew, and he carried the heaviest of the baskets as they returned along the woodland path to the house again, and back in the kitchen he threw open the door of a hitherto undiscovered larder and produced milk and butter and eggs.

Miss Brown prepared the meal with all the skill that she possessed, and Boulder cleaned the silver and watched her. Mrs. Weston had been a good plain cook, her successors had been no cooks at all, but Miss Brown, it soon appeared, was an artist. She could make a cream soup worthy of the Ritz out of milk and lettuce leaves and the yolks of eggs, a stew that smelled like heaven out of a masterly blending of herbs and vegetables and the mutton bone, and something that looked like a spring sunset from the strawberries and the whites of the eggs. Boulder was obviously impressed. At seven-thirty he unearthed the best dinner service, a gorgeous affair of scarlet and gold, and polished it up to do justice to her art, and as he came downstairs during dinner with gratifying empty dishes he went so far as to tell her repeatedly, if grudgingly, that "Mr. Birley says you'll do if you go on as you've begun."

Miss Brown suspected that Mr. Birley's commendation had been differently phrased, but she felt happier. If she could feed Boulder well he would not get her turned out yet, anyway.

She refused Mr. Birley's invitation to have coffee upstairs and went early to her room with a supper of hot milk and biscuits, leaving Boulder to the stacking of the plates "till the Young Person what comes in the morning sees to the washing of 'em." She had won him a little, she thought, for when she said good-night he delayed her a full ten minutes telling her about his indigestion, and then he said, with rough kindliness, "You'll 'ear Jerry over'ead tonight. 'E's over most nights, passing over to the ports the other side of the county, but 'e does us no 'arm 'ere. There's no call to worry. Good-night, Miss. I 'opes you'll sleep well."

It was twilight when she got into bed between her damp sheets, hoping for the best, and she did not draw the curtains across her window but lay waiting the coming of the night. It came as it comes in the country in the summer, with the leaves muted to stillness and the dark veils dropping one by one, the stars pricking through and an owl calling a long way away. But it brought her no healing at all. She lay aching in every limb and sobbing with the misery of sheer exhaustion, her body cold but her head hot with a throbbing headache and a procession of nightmare whirling thoughts. The people whose lives had touched hers that day seemed to appear and disappear before her, though her eyes were tightly closed in an effort to stop the passage of those despicable tears. That man outside the Free Library with the panic in his eyes; those two little girls at the station, so afraid for the fate of a teddy-bear, so afraid of the unknown; Mr. Birley, so kind, so learned and controlled, yet bothered about his rheumatism, anxious about his nephews; that sick man Boulder with his fear of being superseded; Richard in rebellion, afraid of being held back from the things that he would do, and Stephen shrinking from the conflict of a mind that longs to conform but cannot deny its faith. Their faces, young and old, lovely and unlovely, the faces of humanity, passed and re-passed before her, etched on the darkness with nightmare intensity, all of them afraid, all of them helplessly lonely by reason of the unlikeness of their fears; yet all of them bound together by their mutual horror at the overmastering anguish of this age, this crashing terror of an era's end. To Miss Brown, between sleeping and waking, with nerves strained to breaking-point by fatigue and strain, fear seemed a presence actually with her in the room, beating all about her, trying to break down her defences, get into her and make her mad. Fighting against it, beating with her hands against the darkness to ward it off, she woke right up and heard the deep warning note of Argos baying in the house below and the throbbing of great engines of destruction overhead.

It was almost with a sense of relief that she rolled over on her back, her nightgown drenched with the sweat of nightmare, and knew the nameless terror for the tangible threat of the German planes. "They does no 'arm 'ere," Boulder had said, but they sounded very ominous in the quiet night. She had been used to hear their throbbing preceded by the wail of the siren and accompanied by the boom of guns; it was more frightening in the stillness. They were right overhead, and she clenched her hands, with a sudden vision of Stephen's young face against the background of the panelled gallery with the sea-green curtains. Then very gradually that hateful throbbing died away, muffled by the night, beaten down by some other sound that rose above it, lamenting yet melodious, sorrowful yet somehow triumphant, full of promise, beckoning, the sound of the wind murmuring through the green shade of a leafy wood. Up in his tower Stephen was playing Delius' "Song of Summer." To its cradle song of wind in the trees Miss Brown fell asleep.

CHAPTER V

I

MR. BIRLEY, though he had scarcely sat down to his after-dinner spell of writing, laid down his pen, cast his pince-nez adrift on their chain, and leaned back in his chair, set before the writing table in his study window that looked out across the terrace to the garden. He found it quite absurdly difficult to write during these days of intense and anxious waiting, those rickety tumbling days when the structure of life as one knew it rocked beneath one. It was only his conviction that those, like himself, who could take little active part in service to their country, must bend their whole strength to keep life running as far as possible in the normal channels, that caused him to keep his unwilling nose resolutely to the familiar grindstone. Orderliness of life and thought must be maintained as far as possible. When these chaotic days were passed what was left of it would form the scaffolding upon which the new order could be built. "Order." A good word. How passionately sane men longed for it, and how incapable they seemed of achieving it with any permanence. How passionately the insane hated it and how easily they could destroy it. Hitler's contemptuous sneer at "the bourgeois virtues of peace and order" was typical of all the anarchists through the ages. Always the perpetual struggle forward of the sane men, the good-hearted, decent, stupid, blundering lovers of God, always the perpetual reeling back as yet another onslaught of the furious men swept in from the sea of darkness. Why so slow and blundering, you children of light? Why so swift and brilliant in dark power, Apollyon? It is easier to be angry than to pity, he thought, to destroy than create, to hate than love. Yet the children of light picked themselves up and went on again, dogged, obstinate, stumbling along after a lost inheritance, blinking stupidly at a half-seen vision of a Holy City far away; and among the ranks of those blundering foot-slogging fools of God there moved here and there the shining figures of the men who led them, the Chivalry, the Knights and Companions of Christ; so few of them, and most of them in such extremity, yet whenever they spurred their white horses forward the ranks of hell gave way.

He looked down at the sheets of manuscript lying on his table. His mind had gone back in these days to the era where as a historian he was happiest and most at home, and he had embarked wildly upon a survey of European history from the Renaissance to the Caroline Age. What a task! He'd be lucky if it was completed to his satisfaction before his death. Yet what a crashing magnificent period, and full of the shining figures of the Knights, Thomas More, John Fisher, John Houghton, Robert Aske, Don Juan of Austria and a hundred more. Their names were like stars in the stormy darkness of their times.

Don Juan of Austria. Lepanto. The names leaped up at him in his own sprawling handwriting. He was back in those days when a distracted and disunited Europe faced the onslaught of the Turk. He saw the evil sweeping across Asia, Africa, half Europe, and still advancing. He heard the shrieks of the massacred, the rattling of chains in the hellish dungeons, the sobbing that broke through the music of the last mass sung in the Christian Church of San Sofia at Constantinople. His mind reeled before the horror of little children stolen from their homes, trained as inhuman robots, and then set to massacre the mothers who had borne them. He sickened as he remembered the stench of the galleys and the whistling of the whips about the shoulders of the straining slaves. To his mind it seemed happening now, to-day, as much of a reality as the torture of Poland, the agony of Rotterdam and the obscene horrors of the concentration camps. He stirred in his chair, restless and sweating in the grip of nightmare. How long, O Lord, how long?

Then, out from the mists of the north a man came riding, a young man with a blood-red banner blazoned with a picture of another young man dying on a cross. And after him rode his companions, laughing, the cold light glinting on their armour, a company too small to be called an army, a chivalry of youth and daring, the crazy knights of God. What madness in the world had ever equalled their madness, who dared to oppose with their mortal bodies and their blood-red banner that great evil multitude whom no man could number?

Yet their madness proved common sense. Europe, amazed, incredulous, looked at that tiny company standing between her and death and rallied. Shamed, inspired, dowered with fresh hope, the stricken nations gathered behind that banner of a young man on a cross, and the fight was joined.

Lepanto. Quite a little battle judged by modern standards, quite a small affair, but tremendous for those days, and momentous by reason of the immense spiritual strength that seemed to emanate from the smaller and the weaker side and swept it along to victory. Mr. Birley could hear the thunder of the guns and see the victorious galleys of the young men sweeping through the blood-stained Mediterranean, with young Don Juan high upon the poop of his flagship and young Cervantes with his shining sword. And, when the thunder of the guns had died away into silence, he could hear the music of Europe's thanksgiving pealing out over the heads of a kneeling multitude through the wide-open doors of St. Mark's at Venice.

And then he came abruptly back to the present, for a door banged somewhere, he heard running feet on the terrace steps and looking up saw Richard crossing the garden, quickly and lightly in spite of his height and breadth, possibly late for some urgent but agreeable appointment. He was in riding clothes and singing and slapping his hunting whip against his boots. He must, his uncle thought, be going out with Prunella Maxwell, the girl of the moment. His vital figure vanished through the castle gateway and the green woods took it.

It is always the same, thought Mr. Birley, it is always the young who do it. When the lethargy of their fathers allows the ramparts to crumble the young men fill the breach. "And ye, dear youth, who lightly in the hour of fury put on England's glory as a common coat." Lightly, always lightly. If their banner was that of a young man dying on a cross it was brightly coloured and it streamed on the wind. It was the old who met these times of crisis with such heaviness. The young were wiser. They sang as they fought.

II

He looked at his watch. He would go for a walk. Dinner had been earlier to-night, for the excellent Miss Brown, though she had only been with them for a bare twenty-four hours, was

73

already getting into her stride. He had time for a walk, and then quite a good spell of work before bed-time.

He put away his manuscript, heaved his long loose body out of his chair and stood grimacing with pain as movement came back to his stiffened limbs. His rheumatism was undoubtedly getting worse. He must fight it harder. His doctor had told him that exercise, though incredibly painful, was the best antidote for the disease. He would set himself to walk a bit further to-day. He utterly refused to become an invalid again. He had been one for a while in his youth and the experience had left him shrinking from illness as he shrank from nothing else in life. He had seen his grandfather and his father each in turn fall a victim to this wretched complaint that was the gift of old Roger Birley to his unfortunate descendants. He'd seen the lives of both of them close in painful helplessness and dependence upon others. Intensely independent as he was, liking to possess the citadel of his own being inviolate, the thought of such an end was a nightmare to him, the only personal disaster that he feared at all. His love of solitude had led to his having neither wife nor child. Now, sometimes, he was sorry. Someone who was part of oneself would not seem such a violator of one's privacy. The thought of a strange nurse possessing intimate knowledge of the functions of his body was so intolerable that it drove him straight away into the hall to look for his hat and stick. He must go out, walk, ward off the danger for as long as he could. "This muddy vesture of decay," as Shakespeare had said of the body with more truth than elegance, "doth grossly close us in." The source of all joy when one was young, it was the source of all fear as one grew older and the independence of the spirit fought against the weakness of the body. Deliverance from the body would mean deliverance both from this conflict and this fear. "Come in this way and fear no more" was written over the door of his home; it might equally well be written over the door of death.

Leaning on his stick, yet walking quickly in spite of his pain, he passed through the garden where at this hour of the evening every leaf and petal was glowing in the golden light streaming from the west. This was the hour that he loved best for a walk. Not only was the hour of sunset more attuned to his naturally solitary temperament than morning or midday, but to his mind the country that he loved was at its loveliest and its most peaceful in this golden light.

He passed under the old archway and into the woods, where the shadows of the tree-trunks lay long and still across the winding road and the song of the birds had taken on that poignant clear note that comes with evening. At the gateway that led out of the woods he paused to wave to Mrs. Heather where she sat behind the magnificent geraniums in her window, knitting an immense shapeless dark-blue garment for her grandson in the navy. She gave him her wide, toothless, happy smile. Why *was* the old dame so happy? Was it because of her astounding success with geraniums? Perhaps her green fingers had made contact with the power that throbs with such terrible force behind the beckoning, whispering, shining veil of nature, and yet to the elect slips through it under the guise of peace. Perhaps. Mrs. Heather had never told him, and he had not liked to ask.

He came out into the short country lane and climbed upwards to the crest of the hill, and here he stopped, for to the north and south, east and west, the country of his birth lay dreaming in the evening light. He could see from horizon to horizon, from the moors to the sea, from the hills to the woods, from the smoke of a distant coastal port whose famous name was almost part of the name of England, to the smoke of his own village of Applegarth that lay on the slope of the hill on the further side from the Castle.

And this his country was in deadly peril. Had he been a woman he might have wept. Had he been a different type of man some slight sound of anguish might have come from between his lips. Being what he was a muscle in his right cheek twitched a little and that was all. The gold of the sunset was deeper than usual to-night. "The splendour of the spirit of God shining out through the big hills, and steep streams falling to the sea." Synge had written those words about Ireland, but Mr. Birley applied them always to this hour of sunset in the West Country.

It was a pastoral country. From where he stood he could see the hills dotted with the peaceful herds of cattle and the folded sheep. He could see the figures of men haymaking, and the chequered fields of corn and barley ripening already to harvest. He could see a team of tired horses plodding homeward in the sunset light, and a flock of mewing seagulls, their wings touched with gold, wheeling up into the sky behind them. Smoke curled up from white-washed farms built in the folds of the hills, and the woods in the valleys were utterly still.

This, to Mr. Birley, was England, the England that was in peril. He knew that a great part of his country was given over to the roar and clank of machinery, to desolate acres of bricks and mortar grimed with the smoke of factory chimneys, to slums where little children lived like rats in the sickening stench of the holes and corners that they called their homes; he knew all that, and the shame of it was a thing that in these days of judgment he took to himself in anguished penitence; but yet to him that was not England. *This* was England, this life of the fields and the farms and the woodlands that had existed long before the first factory had belched its obscenity into the sky, long before the first gun had ploughed a hideous furrow of death through the green earth. This had been from time immemorial, and this would be again when the bitter waters of nemesis had subsided and the men who were left, humbled with their faces to the earth, found out afresh that she was their mother and the one hope left them. "The years like great black oxen tread the world and we are broken by their passing feet." Such were the years of this age, but please God the plough of judgment to which they were yoked would plough up the earth for the green corn.

As he swung down the hill towards the village the great bulk of Beacon Hill to the west seemed to rise up and dominate the whole landscape and he could see the figure of the sentry upon its summit, a motionless figure black against the gold of the sky, gazing out over the sea and the rocky harbours, the fields and the woods and the farmsteads that were England. Once again, as in the Napoleonic wars, there was a sentry on Beacon Hill. A hundred years ago he had stood beside a great pile of brushwood, flint and tinder ready to his hand, and when he sighted the enemy he would have set alight the warning that would flash over England, from hill-top to hill-top in charactery of flame. Now there was no pile of brushwood but down below the boulders at the sentry's feet, in a little hut, there was a telephone. Quite a minor change, thought Mr. Birley. The years between the two times of peril seemed to collapse like a house of cards and the two epochs melted into one. How still and how strangely inspiring was the black figure against the flaming gold. Not a man, surely, but the spirit of England itself on guard.

To come back to reality, who was it up there to-night, he wondered? The sentry was pacing up and down now, and a dog was loping at his heels. All the men of Applegarth, including himself, took their turn on the Beacon. Who was it to-night? He did not remember, and dismissed the unknown sentry from his mind, for he had reached the village and the lych gate of the church, and the fancy came to him to turn in under the great ancient yews, from whose wood had been made the bows that Englishmen had carried at Agincourt. A small wind sighed a little in the branches. How old was this land, old and more than a little weary. Through what dark ages had she not passed. Yet her strength was in her age. Like the great yews the roots from which she had grown reached back into the darkness and sucked forth power.

The church stood among orchards like a great rock in the land. Its grey buttresses were half hidden by the red roses that climbed over them, and by the tall uncut grasses that swayed against them, murmuring with their thousand tiny voices, but the great tower shook itself free and soared up like a banner in the sky. One could see it for miles around. It was almost as much of a landmark as Beacon Hill itself.

Mr. Birley walked through the churchyard and passed into the shadows of the church porch. He lifted the heavy old latch by its iron ring, pushed open the creaking oak door and went into the church. It was like a hundred other old West Country churches, pillared and dim and musty-smelling. Here and there was a stained glass window to throw a pattern of rich colour upon the worn flagstones, but for the most part the windows were filled with dim green glass through which one could see the faint still shapes of the trees. When, as now, the murmur of prayer and praise was stilled in the church one could hear instead the ring of birdsong, echoing, and by some trick of acoustics most strangely intensified. Mr. Birley stood for a moment listening to it, then turned to the chapel in the north aisle that was called the Birley Chapel.

It was a very small place, but Mr. Birley always felt about it as he felt about Westminster Abbey, that here was the shrine of the soul. Were Westminster Abbey to be levelled to the ground he would be alarmed for England. He would feel the same about the Birleys if this Chapel went. He stepped reverently through the old carved screen where the wings of the warrior angels still retained something of their medieval colouring, and stood before the altar with its beautiful Spanish crucifix and candelabra that had been lifted as his perquisites by the Birley of the time from one of the vanquished galleons of the Armada. Above them, a little incongruous but very lovely, was the modern window that had been erected to the memory of the father of Richard and Stephen, and below them the light lit richly upon an altar-frontal of Chinese embroidery that had been looted by another Birley during the Boxer Rising. Not a very virtuous family always, smiled Mr. Birley, but yet sturdy when occasion called.

The memorial tablets that covered the north wall were a long record of heroic deeds.

The south wall of the Chapel was formed by the tomb of Stephen Beaulieu the Crusader, and by a monument to Harry Birley, his wife and his thirteen children. The first was deeply impressive, the second an erection of sheer comedy.

Mr. Birley looked long and reverently at the tomb of the Crusader. Richard might say that Stephen had been lifted to the niche of family saint because they knew nothing about him, but Mr. Birley disagreed with Richard. Though the tale of his deeds, that had once been cut upon the stone of his tomb, had now been smoothed away by time Mr. Birley considered that the carved figure of the man himself, lying above the dust of his bones, was all the record needed. He lay clad in steel, his sheathed sword by his side, his legs crossed to show that he had fought in the crusades. His shield formed a pillow for his head and his feet rested against the figure of a hound, lying asleep with nose on paws. But the Crusader was not asleep. His visor was raised to show his eyes, alert and watchful, and the grim set mouth below the winged and eager nostrils. His hands, lying upon his breast, were not folded in death but set tensely palm to palm in prayer. What more did one want to know about him? thought Mr. Birley. A man of action, a man of prayer, a man who had fought the battle of the Holy Things, one of the Knights and Companions of Christ of whom he had just been thinking; above all, a man still living.

"Would to God," muttered Mr. Birley violently, "that you were here now. Yet pray, wherever you are, pray. For the soil of your country and the altars of your God, for all decency and for all honour, pray, Stephen, and keep your watch until the end."

Was it a fancy that those tense hands bore a likeness to the hands of his own Stephen of to-day? Yes, a mere fancy. His Stephen was no crusader. He was a pacifist who, when the call came to him in a few weeks' time, would refuse to answer it. From the bitterness of this thought he turned aside to the unfailing comic comfort of old Harry's monument.

It was obvious from all the historical records that old Harry, though he might be revered by subsequent generations as the builder of the Tudor manor house, had been a rogue of the first water. Yet here he knelt in his effigy of carved and coloured wood, hands folded on his breast, eyes raised to heaven in an attitude of deep and affecting piety, waiting, according to the Latin inscription over his head, for the Resurrection that would set the seal of immortality upon his innumerable virtues. The inscription described as many of these as there was space for, beginning with Harry's attachment to the family circle and ending with his courage in the face of death. Mr. Birley suspected that the only grains of truth in the whole long list were in the head and tail of it. Courageous on the scaffold old Harry had undoubtedly been, jesting with his executioner and addressing such a rollicking speech to the crowd that they been still roaring and swaying with laughter when the axe came down; to the sound of their merriment old Harry had died and according to the family records there had still been a grin upon his face when his severed head and truncated body had been stowed away in the family vault. As for his attachment to the family circle, that must have been true too, for only a man who was much at home could have found the time to beget so many children. Six stalwart grown-up sons knelt in a diminishing row behind old Harry, and five fine daughters were ranged behind Mrs. Harry, who knelt facing her husband, and two small creatures of the female sex who had died in infancy sat down below in two little baby chairs. These two were the only members of the family who were not praying; perhaps they had died before they had had time to commit any sins for which to ask pardon. They were all very well dressed. Harry wore a fine ruff and a fine scarlet doublet, a hat with plumes set at a very jovial angle and shoes with rosettes. He was a fine figure of a man, stout and rubicund and hearty, with a stylish pointed beard. Mrs. Harry, as was perhaps only to be expected of the wife of so robust a man and the mother of so large a family, was pale and anæmic, and looked as though patient endurance was the only virtue she had been able to keep firm hold of, but she was very elegant in a blue farthingale and a golden coif. The sons and daughters who knelt behind them had not been allowed any differentiation of character or variety of costume. Except for their diminishing size they were all exactly the same, just sons and daughters, just the offspring of old Harry.

But the two little girls who sat in their baby chairs down at the bottom had been most carefully and lovingly portrayed. Mr. Birley, bending down to study them for quite the hundredth time, imagined that the artist who had carved this monument must have known them personally, and been as attached to them as Mr. Birley was himself. They sat in their chairs very sedately, clothed in voluminously bunchy frocks, the elder in blue and the younger in rose-colour, with queer little caps poised on their short fair hair and little feet shod in scarlet shoes with pom-poms on them set neatly side by side upon gold footstools. Their faces had become pale and wan with the passing of the years, but they were not the mere conventional masks worn by their brothers and sisters above, they were full of a childish sweetness and wonder. The smaller infant had a doll in her arms, the elder held a little book open on her lap and was evidently reading aloud to her younger sister. It was still possible, after all these years, to make out the words that had been inscribed in Latin upon the open pages of the book. "The Lord is my Shepherd. Though I walk through the valley of the shadow of death I will fear no evil." What death had they faced, poor little creatures? Then as now "the lean abhorred monster" had lain in wait for little children in many horrible guises. Smallpox? The plague? Down in the family vault below the church their small bones had become dust, and there was no knowing. We do queer things when we are alone, and Mr. Birley was no exception to the rule. Stretching out a finger he gently caressed the wan cheeks. He liked little girls.

III

Twilight was near as he tramped back through the village of grey-roofed, white-washed cottages, deep-set in old gardens, and men home from work were leaning on their gates to smoke their pipes while the women were stepping in and out of neighbours' houses for a gossip before bedtime. They responded to Mr. Birley's greetings with friendliness, for there had always been strong and deep affection between the village and the Castle. Away from Applegarth the men of the village might forget or revile the old ways, but back in this familiar valley their allegiance fled back like a homing bird to the Castle on the hill.

This was especially so in war time. Applegarth men had followed the Birleys to the wars from the days of Stephen the Crusader until now, when all the young men of the village were trying to join the R.A.F. because Richard was in the R.A.F., and the older men took their turn on Beacon Hill because Mr. Birley had led the way. Their war time allegiance was a thing that they neither questioned nor understood. It was as old a thing as their ancient hearth-stones and the walls of the Castle. While the instinct to defend the one still lived in them they would look to the other to show them how.

"So Mr. Richard's 'ome, us 'ear?" called an ancient gaffer to Mr. Birley. "Lookin' rarely brown and well, us be told."

"Yes, Bob, he's home. How's your grandson?" asked Mr. Birley.

"Fine, us be told by 'is mother," said Bob. "Proper masterpiece, 'e be; but 'e don't write much."

"No, they don't write much," agreed Mr. Birley.

"So long as they act right," said Bob, "us be content. Mr. Stephen, e's lookin' well. 'E come to see us Friday. So like 'is mother as two peas 'e be. Good-night, sir. Sweaty weather, but a rare 'ay crop by all accounts."

Mr. Birley climbed up the lane to the main road slashing at the nettles in default of Richard. Now why the dickens couldn't Richard go down to the village and gossip with them a bit as Stephen did? Was it nothing to him that the descendants of the men whom his fathers had led were now following him? Did he not care that the old men and women who had watched him grow up were following his gallant career with eager interest? Was he neither touched, pleased nor proud? Was he just bored? Mr. Birley lunged at a dock leaf in the hedge. He had never yet quite dared to realise how deeply, almost desperately, he loved Richard. To see him soar to perfection he would have endured all the torture that there was. "Go on! Go on!" he was always voicelessly crying to Richard who could mount so high, yet sometimes fail so lamentably. "Go on to the full stature of a man. Round out the full circle to perfection. Do not fail us. Be the final flowering of our breed and race. Go on! Go on! Quickly! While there is time."

For Stephen he suffered less, because he loved him less. Stephen, as old Bod had said, was like his mother, a beautiful, artistic, delicate woman whom Mr. Birley had always considered more ornamental than useful, in spite of her faultless touch as a pianist and her considerable gift for water-colour painting, which had doubtless come out in Stephen as this rather tiresome craze to be an architect, a thing no Birley had ever been. True, she had produced the heir, but only with a great deal of fuss and complaint, and when called upon to make the inheritance doubly safe by the production of a second man-child to fall back on, she had yielded only after much persuasion and then broken her husband's heart by dying of the effort. On purpose, Mr. Birley had always considered, lest she should be asked for a third. Too bad of her. . . . He pulled himself up abruptly, self-accused of most ungentlemanly criticism of a dead woman. . . . Her delicacy had not been her fault, poor soul, and neither was it her fault that

that streak of femininity in Stephen's character had produced the virus of his pacifism.

But here Mr. Birley was right off the rails. Stephen's pacifism had its roots deep in a past that had nothing to do with his mother, and it was the best thing in him.

But Mr. Birley did not think so. To Stephen too he cried, "Go on! Go on! Be strong and of a good courage. Do not fail us. Be a man quickly, for the time is short; as short as this twilight of a summer's day."

For it was almost dark under the trees as he walked through the woods to the Castle. He supposed he had been a long time coming up the lane, wearing himself out with his agonised apostrophisings of Richard and Stephen. Very presuming of him, as well as extremely stupid. The roughing out of character had been performed by heredity and environment and for it the past and not he was responsible; he had done his part when he gave a few fumbling lessons in forms and perspective. The filling in of the picture that would come with the years was the boys' affair and no one else's. He did not now come into it at all. "Hands off!" should be the watchword of the old when the young were fighting for their foothold. He was quite certain that old Harry had never drawn a single agitated breath over any of his thirteen children, not even over those two little girls who had had to face the valley of the shadow at so tender an age. Nice little girls! He went in under the Norman archway, crossed the scented garden, went up the terrace steps and beheld them sitting on the door-step, beneath the inscription that bade whoever came to have no fear.

But they were afraid. Their fear was the first thing Mr. Birley noticed about them, after his startled recognition of the short fair hair, the blue dress and the pink dress, the toy and the open book that he knew so well from the old monument. They sat with their small thin bodies pressed very tightly together for comfort and in the eyes that looked up at him out of their white strained little faces the darkness of fear had quenched all inward light. Startled out of all knowledge of what he was doing, Mr. Birley bent and caressed their wan cheeks with his forefinger. Then he looked at the page of the open book from which the elder child had evidently been reading to the younger. He expected to see the words, "The Lord is my Shepherd. . . . I will fear no evil." Instead he read, "Peter gave himself up for lost and wept big tears; but some friendly sparrows flew to him and implored him to exert himself."

He stood up and began to laugh. Not two little ghosts out of the past but twentieth-century midgets from London. He stepped past them into the house and let out the stentorian cry for help with which from now on the Birley men were to greet all perplexing domestic situations. "Miss Brown!" he shouted. "Miss Brown! Miss Brown!"

Miss Brown came running, her very feminine heart lifting in delight at the urgency of that male appeal. "What is it?" she asked, and her voice held all the maternal solace for a bruised knee, all the maternal assurance that everything would be all right the moment she got there.

"Look at this," ejaculated Mr. Birley between amusement and wrath. "Something must have gone wrong with the billeting arrangements in Torhaven and Mrs. Lovell, the-er-billeting officer, has simply dumped a couple on us without a with-your-leave or a by-your-leave. Must have heard you'd come. There's no such thing as personal privacy in the garrulous West Country and I suppose you'd not been here a couple of hours before the whole village knew it. The infernal cheek! Pleased to do my duty, but not at the pistol's point. Where's Boulder? Presumably she handed them over to Boulder. What did Boulder think he was doing leaving them here alone on the doorstep? Boulder! Boulder!"

So he fulminated, going indoors to give Boulder a piece of his mind, but Miss Brown, with the identical movements of a hen scattering her brood to gather them in, pushed the children apart, sat down between them on the doorstep and flung an arm round each. "It's *you*," she cried. "You little dears! Don't cry, my pets, Miss Brown has got you."

CHAPTER VI

I

RICHARD and Prunella rode along the crest of the hill, towards the east from whence the night was coming. No sign of it as yet; only the glorious reflection of the deep glow in the west.

"You were so late, Richard," said Prunella irritably. "Half an hour late. I waited ages. Now it'll be dark in no time and we'll have to go home."

"Why?" asked Richard. His voice was lazy, as usual, but the

look he gave her, with that glinting whip-lash look in the eyes, was not at all lazy.

Prunella bit her lips in fury because her hands were trembling, and Richard, his eyes travelling slowly over her in that disconcerting way they had, would be sure to have noticed it. She braced her shoulders and lowered her eyes, so that Richard should not see the tears in them. She had not known it was possible to be so deliriously happy, so desperately miserable, so furious and so frightened all at once. It had not been like this when she and Stephen had been in love a couple of years ago. That had been a sort of pastoral idyll, gentle and very sweet. They had lain out on the slope of Beacon Hill that summer when she had promised him that she would marry him, and he had told her how he longed to be an architect and design beautiful buildings, to create, to build up, always to create, never to destroy, and she had passed her hand over the dried heather bells and listened not to what he was saying, because she didn't really care for architecture, though of course in company with all women in love she had not the slightest compunction in declaring that his interests were her interests too, but to their tiny faint chime that was like fairy bells ringing far away in the distance, down in Wild Woods in the valley below them. Of course that had been two years ago, and they had been very young, and so of course it hadn't lasted with Stephen any more that it had with her. It had been just a sort of fairy thing, like the chiming of the heather bells, and she had been very sensible to insist that they keep it secret instead of telling everyone all about it as Stephen had wanted to do, for fairy things are always best kept secret. When she had told Stephen, just last Christmas, that time when Richard had had that long leave, that it had petered out with her, he had just smiled, and hadn't said anything, so obviously it had petered out with him too. She was so glad, for she would have hated to hurt Stephen, even though it had turned out that after all she did not really love him.

Yet she wanted to hurt Richard, whom she loved with a passion that was like a wild beast fastened on her and tearing at her flesh. She wanted to hurt Richard, for whom she would have died. Why was it? Why was she so wicked? She hated herself. She hated and loathed herself. She supposed it was because he all unknowingly tormented her so dreadfully, treating her alternately to tenderness and teasing, passion and aloofness, so that she could never feel certain of him. Perhaps it was this uncertainty that made her want to hurt him. She was so tormented by it that she felt she would not care how much she bruised his wings if she could only have him for her own. Perhaps this uncertain man would not make a very dependable husband; but then, she remembered with a pang, he had not asked her to marry him. Probably he never would, for he hated anything in the nature of settling down. Once you were settled down there was nothing to beckon further, and very little prospect of the excitement that he loved. No, he would not ask her to marry him; at least not for a long time yet, not until life forced him to accept his detested fate as the heir of the ages. He would have to have a son then, and he might ask her to be the mother of it. They would be together at the Castle, but would they be happy? She thought that if she could only possess him she would be utterly at rest and happy. But if he thought of the Castle as a prison, if she held him prisoner there against his will, would she possess him? The essential wild-bird spirit of him would be always beating against the bars, trying to go free, and that terrible paradox would be true again, that to possess is to lose.

"Why?" he persisted. "Don't you like riding under the moon and the stars? Personally, I do. I get quite a kick out of it."

"Actually, I do too," said Prunella breathlessly. "But Grandpa does not like me to be late."

Richard laughed. "Edwardian Pru," he mocked. "Prudent and prudish Pru."

He pushed open a gate with his crop, skilfully holding in Golden Eagle's wild cavortings, and watched her with those lazy whip-lash eyes as she rode her dappled Maria past him through the open gate and set her at a mad canter over the fields towards the lower slope of Beacon Hill. Far above them, against the golden sky, brooded that dark figure of the sentry. Hot with love and excitement they did not notice him. He was nothing to them just then.

"You can ride, Prunella," came Richard's voice caressingly in her ear, as he thundered up behind her. "Gosh, you can ride!"

Yes, I can, she thought wildly. I may be Edwardian, I may be prudent and prudish, but I can ride. He likes me when I'm not afraid. He likes me then. I'll never be afraid. Never of anything. Never! Never! Then he will want me always. I shall have him then.

She rode like a fury through the golden light, madly and recklessly. Her short curly red-gold hair streamed back from her small set face with the wind of her going, and the blue silk blouse that she wore with her jodhpurs was ripped from within its belt and billowed out like a blown flower. Her slim brown hands were easy on the bridle but she gripped poor stout old Maria's heaving sides with her knees as in a vice. . . . Maria was sure she would have bruises there. . . . Her lips met in a thin red line of determination but her beautiful nose quivered with her panting breath. Yet even so she could not achieve anything really impressive. "Easy now!" came Richard's laughing voice, and without looking round she could sense him swinging after her easily and effortlessly, holding in Golden Eagle lest he should hurt her feelings by outstripping her. "Go on, sweetest!" she whispered in the ear of the unfortunate Maria, and Maria, with a wildly rolling eye, a bumping stomach and an agonised tail, went all out in a last mad rush towards the gate of Beacon Hill. Maria's jumping days were over, and she knew it, but to please Prunella she would have leaped through hell itself. She gathered herself together, prayed to Pegasus, jumped desperately, caught a hind hoof on the top bar of the gate and fell headlong, throwing Prunella over her head.

Richard on Golden Eagle had meanwhile soared like a bird over the high hedge, wheeled about, come back and dismounted in a fury of terror. Fear for any one he loved always sent him into a raging temper. "Idiot!" he stormed at Prunella as he picked her up. "Crazy little idiot!" Then he perceived that she was laughing and unhurt, if shaken, and his fury mounted higher as he stood holding her against him. "You're a damn fool, Prunella. What on earth made you put a suet pudding like Maria at a gate like that? Anybody'd think you wanted to break your wretched little neck."

"Sometimes I think I'd rather like to," whispered Prunella, laughing with a touch of hysteria.

"*What?*" demanded Richard, bending his head down to her.

"Nothing," murmured Prunella, and was suddenly quieted, sighing like a tired child. Her head ached after the fall and she shut her eyes and pressed her face against Richard's coat. He was angrily kissing the top of her head and the hands that held her were shaking; one of them passed over her shoulders and gently felt her back and hips, unconsciously exploring for injury. She was so happy that he cared that she might have been killed. She nestled her head against him and slipped her hand inside his coat to feel the beating of his heart. She liked to do that. It made her somehow feel very close to the powerful beating life that was her whole universe. But Richard's heart, that usually felt like an unruffled sledge-hammer against her fingers, now beat

86

unevenly, almost like a wounded struggling bird. It was just because she had given him a fright, of course, yet the uneven movement struck cold terror through her. Richard's life, that seemed to her so powerful a thing, was as frail as a gossamer thread; it was her universe, but women woke up sometimes to find that the sun and stars had fallen out of the sky and nothing was left but a darkness and emptiness to drive one mad. There was nothing so terrible nowadays that it couldn't happen. Just the one thing that you knew you could not bear was often, now, the thing that you had to bear. A fear like stabbing knives went through her. When it had passed she began to sob from the sheer exhaustion of its pain.

"Let's sit down," said Richard. "You mayn't have broken your silly little neck but you're all shaken up."

They sat down in a little hollow of the fragrant thyme-scented, heather-covered hillside, where once Prunella had sat with Stephen. The warm sunset light streamed over them from the west and far away below them, beyond the green of Wild Woods, the sea was a slab of gold. There was no sound except Golden Eagle cropping the short sweet turf, and a soft sigh now and again from Maria, who stood with her head drooping, bruised and shaken and very hurt in her feelings because no one had asked after her at all. There was no human figure to be seen in the whole wide landscape except the sentry far away on the summit of the hill, and his still symbolic figure seemed scarcely human. They felt as alone together as the first man and woman must have done when the sword-gates of Eden closed behind them and the whole lovely curve of the world lay attendant at their feet. Richard held Prunella against his shoulder with the lovely gentleness that blossomed so rarely in him, that seemed to well up with such difficulty from the depths of his nature, yet to express it more accurately than the stormy rebellion that was his common mood.

He looked down with lazy puzzlement at her tired little shut-eyed face lying against his shoulder, and at her relaxed boyish figure stretched out on the grass beside him. He could not imagine why he had come to love her so much, for in her immaturity and childish naïveté she was not at all the sort of girl he usually fell for; he had always liked them with some knowledge of the world, with dash and style and mockery. He had known Prunella for years, of course, for she had lived with her grandfather the old doctor since her childhood, she was fatherless and motherless like Stephen and himself, and he had always liked the downrightness of her simplicity and the courage that lived in her slender little body. But she had always been Stephen's friend, not his. It had not been until last Christmas that he had so suddenly and startlingly wanted her with a longing that compared with previous longings had been like the blaze of the sun to the flicker of candle flames. He remembered the very day it had happened. He had been lounging on the terrace after lunch, in one of the sudden interludes of winter warmth that come in the west, when she had walked in under the old gateway, straight and slim like a boy, gay and unafraid, in a straight green frock like a dryad's, her short curly gold hair an aureole about her eager child's face. And it had suddenly been all up with him. When she had run up the terrace steps he had held out his hand to her and she had come to him as all women came when he wanted them. But she had not come in the same way as the others came, armoured with understanding of him and themselves, aware of their charms and using them with skill, she had come as a trusting child and slipped her hand into his.

And because of her trustfulness he had not been able to have her; at least, not yet. It had made the whole affair most exasperating and difficult, because he wanted her as he had never wanted a girl yet, he was always having to put the brake on, and that made him of a variable temper that tormented her. The only relief to be had was in the excitement of the thing. The ice over which they skated was wearing so very thin.

He looked at her again and wondered for the hundredth time if she was beautiful. No, she wasn't, he decided. She was too vulnerable for beauty. She felt things too much and they showed on her. She was of the type that would age very soon. She was too young for anything to mar the satin smoothness of her skin, like ivory across her forehead and blue-veined temples, where the mop of hair shaded it, faintly golden where the sun had kissed it, but there were disfiguring blue shadows of fatigue under her eyes and however much lipstick she put on her mouth she could not hide the poignant droop that spoiled its beauty. The bones of her face were delicate and lovely but they showed too clearly and when she was unhappy her thin boy's body was tense and angular with it; yet when she was happy it could relax into such grace. She was a funny mixture, he thought, more elfin child than woman, yet sometimes she showed a wisdom and determination that made him feel like a kid in the nursery. Perhaps her startling contradictions were the result of an old man's upbringing. Probably. Anyway, she wasn't beautiful, just almost unbearably dear. Then she opened her green eyes and smiled at him, and suddenly she was the loveliest thing on earth.

"Prunella," he asked her, "why did you say just now that sometimes you think you'd like to break your neck?"

This remark of Prunella's was troubling him. Personally he thought life was a good show on the whole; especially to-day when no one knew what was going to happen next. The richness of its beauty and the grandeur of its courage had a fine light upon them just now, thrown up in bold relief as they were against a background of so much darkness. About this darkness it was, of course, best to think only objectively. It would probably be upsetting to probe into the thing. Regarded simply as a veil that hid the future, or as the source of the thunders that shook the earth and the fiery arrows that were tearing the mundane garment of things to pieces, then it was the source of the excitement and uncertainty he loved and fitted well into his scheme of things. He was exhilarated in this rocking universe and it hurt him that Prunella was not exhilarated too. He would have liked her to have walked gladly with him in his warm rich house of courage, where the arrows were like stars in the darkness and the storm rolled by only outside the walls. "Why, Prunella?" he insisted.

"I don't know," lied Prunella, and she pulled herself away from him and sat up.

"Go on," he insisted, for Prunella was a bad liar. "Go on, tell me."

"It's funny, isn't it," said Prunella in a high strained voice, "that at a time like this, when one would expect to be afraid of bombs and invasions and things like that, one isn't, one's just afraid of one's own private fear like one was before, only it seems to get bigger and bigger the more bombs and invasions and things there are behind it."

"Does it?" said Richard, puzzled. "But what are you afraid of, Prunella? What is it? Couldn't you tell me?"

"Aren't you ever afraid, Richard?" hedged Prunella. "Not of anything? Nothing at all?"

Richard turned sighing to the loathed business of self-investigation. "I hate feeling caged, shut up, tied to things," he said slowly. "That's why I love flying; one feels so free up there. If I were to think about it perhaps I should be afraid of old age and death, and that sort of thing, and of all the fun and games being over. But I don't think I've ever felt really afraid. But I've never really been tested. Not yet."

"It's horrid to think of things being over," said Prunella slowly.

"Is that the trouble, then, Pru?" he teased her gently. "Aren't women unreasonable? Just to escape from the fear of the fun being over you'd like to break your neck on Maria! What's that but the finish? Silly little coon!"

She let him pull her again within the shelter of his arm and she did not say any more. He did not understand and she could not tell him that it was his death she feared, not hers. She shut her eyes and hid her face from him, for she was desperately ashamed; her intolerable fear was so selfish; for it was only half of it for him, the fear of his fun being over, the whole of the other half was for herself, the fear that she would have to endure the agony of his loss before he had ever really belonged to her. She wanted him with a longing so savage that it shocked her, for she never used to have these savage longings, she had only had them since the war had come so close and had pulled every emotion almost to breaking point, as though it were a poor thing on the rack. Perhaps, she thought, when death stalked the world nature increased the longing of men and women for each other just on purpose, so that they should have babies quickly, while there was time. It would be just like nature to do that. Her one care seemed to be just to create, create, create, so that life could go on.

"Don't get frightened, honey," said Richard gently. "You know, I think you are afraid of bombs and things after all. You mustn't be. I'll keep you safe."

She smiled at the way he spoke, as though she were a child. He was so sure that he understood her and all the time it was not her body that was afraid but her spirit. It was funny that he did not understand. But then, of course, he was never interested in people's feelings, as Stephen was, not even in his own. But she loved him as he was. She wanted him as he was. Upon the fact of him only could she build the foundations of her life.

"And," continued Richard, "this is a jolly safe spot, as safe spots in this island go now. . . . Unless of course invasion comes," he added cheerfully, suddenly forgetting all about her supposed fear in pleasurable anticipation. "And then of course everyone on the coast may possibly be wiped out."

Prunella began to laugh and got up, slipping out of Richard's encircling arms and rising to her slender height with one quick graceful movement that was like a flower unfolding suddenly in the light of the sun. How lovely she could be, he thought, when she let her old natural gaiety, that he had first loved in her, melt the unhappiness of these later days.

She stood looking about her at the woods and the fields, at the sheep and cattle folded in the hollows of the hills, at Applegarth Church tower rising from its orchards and at the old grey Castle half hidden in the trees, and suddenly she forgot everything, forgot Richard, forgot her fear, was conscious of nothing but a deep peace reaching back into primeval ages. It was so quiet that one could hear a dog barking miles away, and over it all spread that golden light of evening that seems to come flooding in from another world and another age, clear, cool, magical, the age of the old legend when God had cried out over the darkened earth, "Let there be light!" and nature had been lightened, had known what she had to do and gone on serenely and surely upon her way, godlike, creating, creating, that life might never end.

But man had flung up his arm across his eyes that he might not see the light, had turned his back on the garden of his inheritance, had stumbled out of it and killed his brother. And now he was always fighting. That poor stumbling fool who had covered the eyes and raised his hand against his brother was at war for ever with the man who had talked with God in the garden in the cool of the evening, had called the animals by their names and known his brother as bone of his bone and spirit of his spirit. Only a legend, that story of the lost garden, but something of the truth must lie hidden in it, for one had only to look at oneself to see those two men who are the same man, fighting down the ages, the one a rebel for ever, the other straining back always after the lost inheritance. And the conflict in the individual soul spread out and out, like ripples on the water, to nations and creeds and classes, till one was deafened and sickened by the clamour, mad and afraid. . . . And nature, god-like, went on quietly creating, creating, giving man time.

And Prunella, like all human beings who stand upon a hill top in the cool of the evening when once God talked with man, felt back into the past, longed with a passion that brought her near to tears for the lost union, beat herself in useless sorrow against the mystery of its loss, and cried out to peaceful nature to show her the way back.

Somewhere there must be a place of reconcilement for all conflicts, a path to tread that no one had found yet, a way to live that not all the scholars and saints, stumbling along in the darkness, had been able to do more than guess at. There seemed so many signposts, so many banners of beauty and flames of selfless courage crying, "Come this way!" yet though one heard them calling one was too stupid to follow their directions. "Let there be light!" God had cried, and there had been light, but man had hidden his eyes. "Let there be light!" Cry it again, O God, have mercy, and cry it again.

"What in the world are you thinking about, Pru?" demanded Richard with justifiable irritation. His leave was short and he had not expected Prunella to spend the major part of it standing in a trance on Beacon Hill.

"I was thinking about light," said Prunella.

He came and stood beside her, looking down at the green hills steeped in gold, at the sea and the Castle wall and the church tower among the leaves. The quiet of it laid its hand upon him too and he stood without movement, dark and brooding as he looked out over the lovely land. Prunella slipped her hand into his, leaned against him and waited. She never felt very near to Richard's spirit, only to his so terribly precarious physical existence. She wanted to feel near his spirit. If he would only tell her more of what he felt about things, then she would feel nearer. But he didn't tell her anything.

"Do you fight for this, Richard?" she asked him at last, softly and very afraid, for Richard so hated to be probed and tested and asked questions.

"For what?" asked Richard.

"For this bit of earth. The woods and the fields and the Castle."

"Good God, no," said Richard with some violence. "It wouldn't be worth fighting for. This bit of pastoral life left over from a century ago isn't England, it's just a pretty little museum piece not worth bothering about. Even the Huns don't bother too much about it; they mostly pass over it as though it wasn't there. As for the Castle, that's quite useful on Saturday afternoons, when the proletariat go over it at sixpence a head and get a kick out of gaping at the ancestors, but I don't see what it's good for beyond that, do you?"

"But it's the home of your family," protested Prunella.

"And what use is my family?" flashed Richard. "What use is the class we belong to? Once we were useful, perhaps, once we had creative ideas, but not now."

There was such hurting passion in his voice that Prunella was hurt too. "Go on, tell me," she said, as he had said to her a few moments ago.

"All the self-congratulatory nonsense that people talk about the greatness of England makes me sick," groaned Richard. "It always has. For what was England when this war broke out? A tired old country living on her past, boring everyone to death with tales of the glories of yesterday and letting the wrongs of to-day go by her. A rich country that let her little children live in filthy slums, a country so bankrupt of ideas that she could let her unemployed drift about her streets like grey-faced ghosts in hell and not be able in years to think what to do with them. A leisured country which yet couldn't find the time to lift a finger to save the loveliest countryside in the world from destruction."

"But it wasn't *our* fault, Richard," comforted Prunella. "*We* couldn't help it."

"Couldn't we?" said Richard. "Who's to blame if it's not the men of inheritance? Tired old men like Uncle Charles who sit in comfortable studies in country houses writing about the past and never giving a thought to the future. Rich men like me who have God knows what spent on their education, and then don't know what to do about the distressed areas; don't even want to know what to do with them; don't even go and look at them. Leisured men like Stephen who spend their time running round and round after the ideas in their heads like cats after their tails and don't care what happens so long as they catch the blooming tail." He paused, angrily, glowering at the lovely landscape, and Prunella pressed closer to him. "And then you're surprised that I don't like the Castle. I loathe the Castle. I shouldn't care if it was blown to blazes to-morrow. It's the Castle's fault. If we hadn't had a rich past to feed on we might have bothered about to-day. And now the problems that we wouldn't solve for ourselves, the slum problem and the unemployment problem and all the rest, are to be solved by bombs and pestilence and death, and, by God, we deserve it. The poor will suffer most, of course, they always do, but the rich will suffer too, please God. You asked what I was fighting for, Pru. I'll tell you. Not for my Castle and my traditions. Christ, no! For the grey-faced men in the streets and the dirty children in the slums. For the factories and the built-up areas and the drunks in the pubs. For the millions of tired drab folk who hurtle backwards and forwards in the tubes and sit on the sands on bank holiday spitting orange peel into the sea. For the jerry-built bungalows that ruin the countryside and the whole foul mess that is the England of to-day. That's my country, and I'm fighting in the faint hope that when this hell is over she'll get her face washed and her pants hitched up. It was I, and men like me, who let her down, and I wouldn't mind dying if she could be—what I want her to be."

He stopped, and his body was shaking. Never before had he felt called upon to make such an utter exhibition of himself. He did not quite know what had dragged it all out of him; some longing that was in Prunella or some power in this green-gold still world that liked the truth. Anyway a certain peace descended when one had spoken one's mind.

Prunella rubbed her cheek up and down his sleeve. Now he had really talked to her and pulled her near to the real Richard. Now he was really hers. Now she knew him and loved him as never before. "Keats said that patriotism is the glory of making by any means a country happier," she told him.

"That's the idea," said Richard.

"But you shouldn't despise the past," said Prunella gently. "Isn't there just something in the old Castle that's valuable? *You* came out of the Castle."

Richard laughed. "Only you think anything of me," he teased her.

"And it was looking at the hills all gold and green that made you suddenly start off telling me things like you never have before," whispered Prunella shyly.

But Richard wouldn't own it. He just laughed and kissed her. But he kissed her quite differently from usual, gently and tenderly, with no hot hurting passion, and as they walked back to the patient horses with linked hands childishly swinging she felt suddenly strangely rested. It had been wonderful, just for a moment, to feel so close to Richard. That sort of unity was the sort most worth having for it made one feel at peace.

As they mounted and swung their horses round they could still see the dark still figure of the sentry far up on the hill top, remote and brooding against the after-glow, a figure out of the past.

"Who is it to-night?" asked Prunella.

"I don't know," said Richard. "It's too far away to see. What a tall chap! And he has a dog with him."

"The Crusader and his dog from the church, I expect," said Prunella with comical certainty, and they rode home laughing.

II

It was Stephen and the dog Argos on guard, England spread out at their feet and the sky above them a panoply of gold. When Stephen stood still Argos stood still, when he paced up and down the strip of turf worn bare by the feet of the sentries, Argos padded at his heels, when he sat down to rest on the low rock at the top of the hill Argos sat down beside him, his great body pressed against Stephen's knee. He was fonder of Stephen than he was of Mr. Birley or Richard and was never parted from him if he could help it. Stephen often wondered why. "For you wouldn't be if you knew my sentiments, old chap," he said to him. "You're just the most consistent traditionalist who ever lived, while I'm about as inconsistent as a man can be. What am I doing up here, for instance?"

Certainly the top of Beacon Hill was no place for a pacifist, for in watching for invasion from sky or sea he was materially assisting England's war effort. But consistency for a pacifist was impossible, for there was no way, short of suicide, of avoiding participation in totalitarian war. Nothing to be done except decide just how to participate in it. So far, in the conflict that was raging between his independent mind and his fighting traditions, he had advanced to the position that he would fight for his country with any weapon that came to hand except the sword, but that he would rather be killed than kill his brother. It wasn't consistent, but then neither was the other point of view, a war to end war and all that rot. To his agonized mind it seemed that consistency was impossible for any living creature; there was nothing for each men to do but weigh conflicting creeds in the scales of his own free mind, strike his own balance between them and stick to it. What was important was the freedom of the mind, and the sticking to it. But how hard it was to strike this balance. Oh God, how hard.

All his life, for as long as he could remember, there had been in him this conflict between his independent mind and his proud love of tradition, and it had bred in him a morbid fear of criticism that had poisoned his whole life. For it was always the things that he loved most of all, his home and family and their history, that stood in judgment upon the conclusions to which his intellect led him, and his sensitiveness shrank from their judgment as from a whiplash. This loneliness of being censured, this being driven out into the wilderness was the one thing that he feared.

As he paced up and down, keeping his watch upon earth and sea and air, his mind turned and turned upon itself tormentingly. He wondered if there could be any fight more bitter than this of the individual against the common mind. During these last weeks the weight of the common mind, bent to the task of defending all

95

it held holy from annihilation, had been against him like the whole force of an incoming tide against a lonely outgoing swimmer. While those who had yielded felt it like a great benevolent power lifting them upon wings, he felt it as a cruel thing choking the life out of him with its salt bitterness. There was nothing he longed for more desperately than permission to turn round and go with the tide. . . . Oh God, to turn round and go with the tide!

But he couldn't. Without that striking of the balance and keeping to it that some men called keeping the faith, and others called integrity, one was just an animal. Men had died, and died gladly, not so much for the truth of their faith, which might be proved false by the years, as for the right to think and test and seek and find, and hold what they had found, that made them men. If man had not got that right then there was no hope for him, he would never fight his way back to the ultimate truth that he had lost.

But the last few hideous months had shaken Stephen badly, driven him to fight his battle all over again, for they had revealed that this was no ordinary struggle of rival imperialisms but a fight to save the very things that had been won by man's integrity. It was not this time only a bit of territory that was threatened but the free mind of Greece, the Roman faith to the plighted word, the tolerance of Christ and the honour of medieval chivalry. It was religion and art and thought that might go under. How could one not take arms against a threat so ghastly? He had asked himself again and again through the long days and longer nights of these last tortured months; only to swing back and back to his conviction that victory achieved at the cost of mangled children, shrieking women and men shaking in agony was no victory for righteousness but simply a sin as deadly as the sin attacked. There were no real victories except the victories of the spirit, such a victory as that of Greece over Rome when the mind of the conqueror was in turn conquered by the culture of his slave, or as that of Socrates drinking the hemlock and Christ upon the cross. These were the victories that outlasted the centuries; all the others turned to dust and ashes. In the last war men had fought as they were fighting now, to build a new heaven and a new earth, but when they took their victory and sowed it as seed upon the earth it came up again in the likeness of another war.

In the painful arguments that he sometimes had with Richard and his uncle Richard would at this point sleepily murmur something about Waterloo, and Mr. Birley would rap out, "What about Lepanto? What of the American Civil War? Tyranny and slavery were broken then and no further havoc reared its head," and he would be too weary to suggest that if the Turk had had the whole of Europe he would probably be Christian to-day, or that if Napoleon had conquered Wellington England, minus king and aristocracy, might by this time have swung firmly and happily to that Left where Richard felt so at home. It wasn't any good arguing with them; their convictions were as precious to them as his were to him; they had to keep their faith as he his. Though physical conflict might cease on the earth it would not cease in the mind of man until he had fought his way home and been reconciled.

With what? And where was home? Somewhere beyond time and space but yet permeating time and space like air the lungs? How did one get there? Let there be light, O God, let there be light!

It was no good thinking any more. His exhausted mind simply went round in circles. He stood still looking at the sea, so far and lovely, lit with so fair a gold, and at the little rocky bays set about with peaceful harbours and small towns climbing the cliffs. Was the gold sea to spurt flame in the months that were coming, and were those harbours and beloved little towns to crumble into ruin before the enemy's guns? God, how hideous was destruction! Must he waste years, he who had planned to spend his life in building and creating, in helping this insane age to smash its most precious possessions to pieces? It was hell to be an artist at this time, sheer hell. The creative urge, frustrated, turned to iron in one's soul. He turned savagely on his heel, with Argos following, and paced back to the other end of the track. He wished he were Richard with his unquestioning, uncreative mind. They said that at the bottom of one's heart one never really wanted to change with another, but from the bottom of his heart he wished he were Richard now.

And there, riding through the gate from the road far down below him, were Richard and Prunella, and the unhappiness that he had felt before was as nothing to the breathless misery that gripped him at the sight of them. He stood watching, while the whole friendly landscape receded from him, leaving him alone with the fact of those two distant moving figures. He saw Prunella break into that mad canter, attempt the gate, fail and fall, while he stood in the leaden paralysis of nightmare. He saw Richard pick her up, caress and comfort her, and he saw them

97

sit down with Prunella within the shelter of Richard's arm, in the hollow of the hillside where once he and Prunella had sat together. Then he remembered that one must not look on at another man's love-making and somehow turned his back on them and dragged himself back to the other end of the track and stood where he had stood before, looking out to sea. Argos went with him and kept pushing against his thigh, but he did not notice it.

The sea and the small friendly harbours and the climbing towns still held themselves withdrawn. He tried stupidly to get them into focus, tried again and again with a half-angry doggedness, as though the getting of those rocks and harbours back into the circle of his life again were the most important thing that he had to do. Why in the sheer depth of misery did everything leave one alone? One must not let oneself be left alone, or one would go mad. One must run after the receding world and catch hold of it, like a child clinging to the skirts of a mother who is going away, and hold there with the whole of one's strength. There was a gold-crested cloud floating over the sea and he looked at that, set his rocking mind to cling to it with all the strength that he had. "Let me not be mad, sweet heavens! Keep me in temper: I would not be mad."

The cloud trailed a lovely shadow over the sea, and he looked at that, and out of the shadow came a little boat speeding for the shore, and he clung to it and sailed into a harbour beneath the cliff. Now all the details of the scene were in focus again and he was aware of Argos pushing against him. He sat down on the rock and Argos flopped across his feet.

He pulled Argos's ears and cursed himself for a fool. Why suffer like this? He was not the first man to be in the grip of this pacifist question, that nowadays seemed to have taken the place of what one's forefathers had called "religious doubt," nor was he the first to have a longed-for career interrupted by war, or to see the woman he loved turn away from him to another man. They were all common misfortunes; probably it was quite common to suffer the three together. One was a fool to suffer so. A selfish fool. He shut his eyes and thought of the suffering of other men; dazed and hopeless peasants driven from their homes, frenzied men in concentration camps, men who had lately endured the thunder and torment of modern war and would carry the scars of it in mind and soul and body until they died. One needed to take one's own microscopic pain and fling it into the flood of human anguish. There it would be lost, and freed of the weight of it one could get on with the business of living. One had to live. Life had got hold of one for its own purposes, and until it had torn from one what it wanted it would not let one go.

He opened his eyes. "I'm a rotten sentry," he remarked with truth, and got up. Argos got up too, and though heartily sick of the whole business fell into line behind him as he paced up and down. They must have been quiescent for a long time, for Richard and Prunella had disappeared and the sun had gone down. The twilight of a summer night fell about them, veil upon veil, and the great stars blazed in the sky. It was too early yet for the bat-like horrible passing of the great planes overhead. Peace reigned, and the man and the dog, pacing up and down, were the guardians of it.

CHAPTER VII

I

MOPPET woke up first, wakened by a long-drawn snuffle beneath the door. It was That Dog again. Neither she nor Poppet could get hold of the name Argos. It was a name that struck no chord of memory, and so it just would not stick. Argos was That Dog to them, and would be till the end.

"Poppet," said Moppet, poking her younger sister awake, "it's That Dog."

Poppet sat up. "So 'tis," she said. "Come in, dog."

Argos leaned his great shoulder against the massive old oak door with its inadequate modern latch, pushed it open, entered, pushed it shut, approached the right-hand side of the four-poster from which a small hand was held out to him, licked it, went round to the other side, licked the even smaller hand held out there, and then jumped up, stretched his great length across the foot of the bed, sneezed, and fell asleep.

The two little girls sat and looked at him. They had been at the Castle for three weeks now and every morning, just when the birds were singing their loveliest chorus in the woods and arrows of sunshine were trying to force their way through the chinks of the drawn curtains, he had come to them like this. At first they had been terrified, as indeed they had been terrified of everything and everybody in this huge great horrible place where they could not find Mother, but when morning after morning he did nothing worse than lick them, sneeze and fall asleep, they realised that his intentions were good, and by the end of the second week it was borne in upon them that he loved them, and liked to have them there, just as the birds did when they sang to them so loudly in the woods every morning, imploring them, as the sparrows had implored Peter Rabbit, to exert themselves and be good children.

The Lady loved them too, so she had told them over and over again as she bathed them or brushed their hair; they were glad that she loved them, though they wished she would show it in some other way than this perpetual bathing and hair-brushing and putting them in and out of hundreds of clean new frocks which she seemed to sit up half the night to make for them. They did not dislike cleanliness, for Mother had always washed them when they were dirty, but they disliked unnecessary cleanliness, and surely it was quite unnecessary to wash a body that had no dirt on it and brush hair that had not had time to get matted since it had been brushed a couple of hours ago. But they bore it all with exemplary patience, Moppet with no outcry at all and Poppet with only occasional roars, because they liked The Lady, who was kind and sweet-voiced and never smacked them, and because the birds said that they must be good.

There were other people in this new strange world besides The Lady and That Dog. There was the Old Gentleman, tall and thin and so loose-limbed that he seemed always about to fall to pieces, but apparently well-intentioned and amiable, for whenever he saw them he poked them in the stomach with his finger and said, "Well, young ladies?" in quite a kind sort of way. They never spoke when they were with him, partly because they were so afraid he might fall to pieces and they not know what to do about it, but also because his pokes in the stomach hurt. This hurting was unintentional, they knew. Possibly the Old Gentleman did not quite know where their stomachs were; no doubt he, being so grand, kept his in a different place.

Then there had been the Dark Young Gentleman who had said "Gosh!" in a frightened sort of way when introduced to them, fled, and been seen no more. They were glad of that for he had been taller and a great deal stronger than the Old Gentleman, and if he had started poking too perhaps they would have died of it.

The Fair Young Gentleman never poked, and they liked him better than any of the indoor people expect The Lady and That

Dog. At first he had seemed as frightened of them as his brother had been, but he had got over that, and now he played them tunes on his gramophone that comforted them a little for the loss of Mr. Isaacson and his violin, and took them to the stable to gaze at a safe distance at that alarming snorting creature Golden Eagle, and drew them the most glorious pictures of rabbits on the backs of envelopes.

As for Mr. Boulder, they fled at the sight of him. "If you kids keep out from underfoot there won't be no trouble," he had told them the first day, "but if you keep worritin' around my pantry I won't be answerable for the consequences." And there had been a gleam in his eye that had caused them to believe him. Wherever else they might be found it was never beneath Mr. Boulder's feet.

They liked Fanny, who was of their world although she talked so funnily, and they liked good-natured Mr. Pratt the gardener and Bill the stable boy, and Teacher and the other children at School. Those latter, of course, were not so very different from London, except that School was much smaller and nice smells came in through the window. And they adored old Mrs. Heather.

They still hated the Castle. The size of it terrified them, and so did the whispers and shadows in the great dim rooms, and the dark twisting passages that seemed always full of people whom you could not see, people who were there by night as well as day, as though they had no watches and paid no attention to time. Also the Castle was built in such a way that however hard you sniffed you could never know beforehand, or afterwards, what there was, or had been, for dinner. This robbed dinner of the pleasures both of anticipation and reminiscence and was a very great misfortune indeed.

As for the great world outside the Castle, the world of the whispering woods and the sunflecked meadows and the round green hills reaching to the sky, they had not yet made up their minds what they thought about that. To get to school they had to go along the road through the woods to Mrs. Heather's cottage, and then down the lane to the village between high fern-covered banks, and they walked always very quickly, hand in hand, and sometimes they ran; they had never yet stood still to listen in the woods, or climbed the banks to see what was beyond them. They knew there was a great deal to hear, and a great deal to see, but they were afraid. It was so very still in the woods, frighteningly still to ears accustomed to the roar of traffic, and they knew that beyond the high hedges the fields went on and on and then seemed to come to an end in a line against the whiteness of the sky, and they were terrified of falling over the edge into that terrible thing called space. Perhaps one day they would be able to make friends with the unseen people in the passages who did not bother about time, perhaps they would stand still to listen to the voices in the woods, and climb the banks to find out what space really was; but not yet; it was all they could do just now to adjust themselves to The Lady's perpetual washings and the Old Gentleman's pokes.

I I

That Dog was a great help. They did not know why; he just was. Argos, of course, if dowered with the gift of speech, could have enlightened them, for he was well aware of the affinity existing between children and dogs. He knew, and so did they, how to round each day into a perfect circle, leaving no gaps through which could blow the cold winds of remorse or anxiety from past or future, enjoying what was to be enjoyed without fear of its loss, taking the weight of what must be borne minute by minute, without any torment of why? or how much longer? Living, in short, with sense. Argos found it unspeakably good to be with children again. When he had first known Richard and Stephen they had had a little sense, but it had not lasted very long, Stephen relapsing into idiocy at an earlier age than Richard, and he still missed their youth intolerably. There were, of course, a great many children about in the passages, all the children who had ever lived in the Castle, but it was difficult to make any satisfactory contact with the creatures because the vital spark of them and fled on beyond the darkness of this world long ago and what was left was only memory; living, of course, but exasperatingly elusive.

But these children were solid enough. He half woke up and shifted himself to lie with his great head thrust between their bodies that he might feel the companionable solidness of their flesh and bone. And they had nice little sparks burning in them, not very strong as yet, but quite bright and promising. He was getting old now, and his own light burned low, folding it upon itself like the petals of a flower that close at evening, that it might shield the garnered treasure of a lifetime, and he liked to warm himself at the light of others. That was why he was so fond of Stephen, for though Stephen had lost the sense of his childhood's days at an early age his light was unusually bright and strong. Argos pushed the children a little further apart that he might not feel too cramped, sneezed and fell asleep again.

Moppet stretched out a hand to the window beside their bed and lifted the curtain a little. It was full day outside now, so she pulled the curtain back as far as she could and the arrows of sunshine that had been trying to force their way in for so long flew into the room in a great shower of brightness. It seemed as though the bird-song came with them, cascading against walls and ceiling and then surging out of the window again, taking one's heart with it back to the great green woods. The children's room was next to Miss Brown's and looked straight out into the woods. The trees pressed quite close to the window, whispering, calling to one to go and find one's heart again where the birds had hidden it, in the green shade. One day, when one was not afraid any more, one would go.

Moppet and Poppet looked an attractive couple sitting up side by side in the old four-poster. Their fair hair had been so improved by Miss Brown's brushings that it shone like spun gold and was as soft as satin to the touch. It curled a little at the ends now, softening the little pinched faces that were beginning to show a golden tan and a more childish roundness. Miss Brown, disapproving strenuously of pyjamas for the female sex, had made them some little new nightgowns with old-fashioned toby frills round the necks, like ruffs, which gave them an Elizabethan appearance in keeping with the bed, the old furniture and the dim blue curtains.

"Read 'bout Peter," said Poppet, and taking Teddy from beneath the bedclothes she kissed his nose and sat him up on Argos's back. Argos, however, objected even in the depths of his slumber with a low rumbling growl which shook the bed, and Poppet withdrew Teddy and laid him to repose against her toby frill. Argos disliked Teddy and invariably frustrated Poppet's persevering efforts to get them acquainted. He had always disliked associating with his inferiors in the animal kingdom and Teddy was about the shabbiest, most down-at-heel animal he had ever seen.

Moppet drew "The Tale of Peter Rabbit" from beneath her pillow and turned to the first page. She knew the story by heart, of course, and so did Poppet, but the test of a classic is whether or not it will bear re-reading, and God alone knew how many times "Peter Rabbit" had been re-read by Moppet and Poppet.

"Once upon a time," recited Moppet, "there were four little rabbits, and their names were—Flopsy, Mopsy, Cotton-tail and

Peter. They lived with their mother in a sandbank, underneath the root of a very big fir tree."

Poppet suddenly began to roar. Her eyes closed up, her face became scarlet, her mouth opened wide and the tears cascaded down her face with such speed that her toby frill was sopped through in a moment of time. With one hand she flung Teddy on the floor and with the other, flung out in the abandon of despair, she knocked poor Moppet prostrate against her pillow. Her legs thrashed up and down beneath the bedclothes, waking up Argos and sending him leaping for the floor with snorts of indignation. Her grief was so terrible that the whole bright day was darkened, and so loud that it brought Mr. Birley hurrying along the passage in his dressing-gown, one side of his face lathered and the other not, and Stephen tearing down from his tower in shirt and trousers. Miss Brown entered last upon the scene because though her room was next door she had to wait to get the folds of her shirt blouse properly adjusted within her waistband. Not though the heavens were falling would Miss Brown have appeared before Mr. Birley or Stephen with a single hair out of place or a single garment missing.

"Is she hurt?" demanded Stephen anxiously, pulling up his slipping trousers. "It's Argos! Argos, you brute, you frightened her."

Argos stalked silently and majestically from the room. He was always being misunderstood but it was beneath his dignity to answer back. If any one was hurt upon this occasion it was himself; his head was drenched with moisture. He sneezed and went downstairs.

"Something has disagreed with her interiorly, no doubt," said Mr. Birley. "I am thankful to find it no worse. I had feared some serious fatality," and he too withdrew. Since the arrival of Miss Brown he had been continually withdrawing before the onslaught of domestic disturbance, for he found Miss Brown entirely adequate to the labours she had undertaken. It was a highly satisfactory state of affairs.

Stephen, however, having adjusted his trousers, remained. It was typical of him, Miss Brown was discovering, that when anything went wrong he always remained. They stood one on each side of the bed and endeavoured to soothe Poppet; but their blandishments were without effect; Poppet roared on.

"What's upset her, Moppet?" enquired Stephen. They were always asking Moppet what was the matter with Poppet, for it was felt that as a member of the family she ought to have an understanding of Poppet's startling moods that was denied to them. Moppet, however, was never much help. Poppet had the artistic temperament and she had not, and between the have-nots and the haves in this connection there is for ever fixed a great gulf of non-understanding. Your artist is always searching behind the appearance of a thing for its hidden meaning, or is reminded by something of something else, and raised up to the seventh heaven of delight, or cast down into the deepest pit of desolation, not by the thing itself but by the thing behind. Your non-artist sees nothing but the thing itself, and if the thing is distressing is distressed by it, and if it isn't, isn't.

"I don't know," said Moppet, and looked uncomprehendingly at the bare statement of fact that she had just read aloud to Poppet; but Stephen took the book from her and understood.

"Of course," he said, showing it to Miss Brown. "Four little rabbits, and they lived with their mother in a sandbank, underneath the roots of a very big fir tree. It's concisely put, but I don't think I've ever read a more perfect description of cosy domestic life in a restricted space. No wonder Poppet's homesick. Four children, too. Poppet's one of four."

"Four *living*," corrected Moppet. Her mother had always been insistent that she had borne seven children; only three were partially in heaven and partially in the cemetery, so couldn't be seen.

"Four *living*," Stephen obediently corrected himself. "Now listen to this, Poppet, 'Now my dears,' said old Mrs. Rabbit one morning, 'you may go into the fields and down the lane, but don't go into Mr. McGregor's garden. Your father had an accident there; he was put into a pie by Mrs. McGregor.'"

At this tragic statement a tear trickled down the cheek of the hitherto dry-eyed Moppet, and even Miss Brown looked sad, but upon Poppet it had the opposite effect. Her roars of grief turned to roars of laughter. She rocked from side to side in an apparent ecstasy of enjoyment. She rolled an eye over Teddy's drenched head, caught Stephen's amused understanding glance and exploded afresh. "Your father had an accident there." The comedy of under-statement had hold of them both, they were taking refuge in it, as do all the sensitive, from the hard pressure of brutal fact. The other two, of course, thought them quite heartless, though Miss Brown was much relieved to have the storm tempered.

"Thank you," she said to Stephen. "Now get up, my pets, breakfast time." And she attempted to lift Poppet out of bed.

Poppet, however, giggling and wrinkling her nose rabbit-fashion, eluded her and plunged beneath the bedclothes. She had suddenly thought it would be nice to make a burrow down there. Patiently Miss Brown pulled away the blankets, but she swarmed over the foot of the bed and disappeared into the wardrobe. Miss Brown sighed. Stephen, pausing at the door, thought she looked very tired.

"They'll be off to school soon," he said sympathetically.

"It's Saturday," said Miss Brown resignedly, and opened the wardrobe door with care, but not with sufficient care to prevent Poppet slithering between her legs and disappearing behind the dressing-table. "They don't go to school on Saturdays." And she reached behind the dressing-table and grabbed the tail of Poppet's white nightgown.

Moppet meanwhile was laboriously washing her ears. She had never been used to washing her ears and thought it sheer waste of time, for sheltered beneath her hair as they were they never got dirty, but Miss Brown liked her to wash her ears, and she was trying her best to make up for Poppet't deplorable behaviour. Poppet was roaring again now, grief-stricken because Miss Brown did not seem to understand that she was cast for the part of Mr. McGregor, who pursued Peter Rabbit throughout a summer's day but never, never caught him. Miss Brown should know that. Hadn't she read the tale to Poppet at least fifty times? Hadn't she any memory? Frantically Poppet hurled herself from side to side, trying to jerk her tail free of Miss Brown's grasp, but Miss Brown held on.

"I'll look after them this morning," shouted Stephen above the now really terrible uproar.

"But you're going to the dentist," protested Miss Brown.

"I'll take them along," he said as he escaped. He liked spirited women, imaginative women, fine artists and actresses, but not all rolled into one before breakfast. If at the end of this war the Victoria Cross were not presented to all foster-mothers the country would stand convicted of shocking ingratitude. Nothing could relieve a foster-mother of her duties, neither wounds nor leave nor change of quarters. She had to keep at it until the end.

III

Up in his tower after breakfast, changing his coat and searching for cigarettes before they started for Torhaven, he put Tchaikovsky's *Andante Cantabile* for strings on his gramophone, and almost at once he heard through the music high sweet voices, and the pat-pat of small shoes upon stone that meant that the children were creeping cautiously on all fours up his tower steps. They nearly always came when he was playing his gramophone, and unfailingly if he played the *Andante Cantabile*. He often wondered why. Even the *Snow-white* records were not the unfailing magnet that was the other. It touched him that music seemed to draw the two little things as the moon the tides, and he often put on record on purpose to hear that pat-pat on the stairs, and then the fumbling of small hands on the outside of the door. At first when he had opened to them they had just come in, but now, instructed by Miss Brown, they took a deep breath and said in breathless unpunctuated chorus, "If you please Mr. Stephen may we come in and listen to the music"—pause for another deep breath—"that is if we will not be in your way but if we would be in your way be pleased to mention it and we will go away again." At which point they immediately entered without waiting for reply and sat side by side upon his bed to listen.

They looked very enchanting this morning, having been arrayed by Miss Brown in new blue linen frocks that she had made for them, smocked in scarlet, with their hair brushed to admiration and their noses shining with soap. Poppet carried the inevitable Teddy and Moppet carried a small scarlet reticule recently purchased by herself at Woolworth's. Mr. Birley gave them sixpence each every time they went to Torhaven, just for the amusement of seeing what they got with it. The unselfish and domesticated Moppet nearly always purchased something useful for her mother or Miss Brown, a handkerchief or a duster or a little hour-glass for timing the boiled eggs; the little scarlet reticule was the only thing she had ever purchased for herself, and that was not so much for her own enjoyment as to have somewhere safe in which to keep the Old Gentleman's sixpences. Poppet always let herself go completely with her sixpences. She bought balloons and pistols, or anything at all that looked bright and went bang.

She looked so good as she sat there listening to the lovely lilt of the *Andante Cantabile*. Moppet wriggled now and then, and looked about her, but Poppet never moved. With her lips a little parted and her great blue eyes gazing unseeingly out of the window she seemed to be drawing every note into herself, like a small round bumble bee sucking honey from a flower. When the music had died away into silence she sighed, came back to herself, and smacked Teddy hard. Thus did she express the dissatisfaction of us all when the beauty that has raised us up out of mundane affairs, like a mother lifting her child out of the mud, puts us down again and goes away. "Gorn," she said, and flung Teddy on the floor.

Stephen went down the narrow spiral stairs with Teddy under one arm and Poppet under the other, lest she should fall and bump herself. Moppet followed with her reticule, peeping fearfully down the last dark bit of the stairs, that led down past Mr. Boulder's room to the door to the woods that was never used, before they turned aside to the passage leading to the gallery. That door to the woods both fascinated and frightened her. She had seen it from the outside and it had ivy growing over it.

They descended the great staircase from the gallery to the hall with caution, Poppet walking now but holding tightly to Stephen's hand so not to slip on the old worn treads. The sun lay in a great pool of light on the floor below, and when they reached it the two little girls stood still for a moment, stretching out their hands half unconsciously to feel its warmth, a bright sweet picture of blue and gold. For the hundredth time Stephen wondered what would happen in the future to these children of the Great Dispersion. These two were as much in a foreign land as would be those other children who were even now setting sail for Canada and the United States. Would they gather to themselves strength and riches from the strangeness of new experiences that in the age that was coming would help them in the rebuilding of a shattered world? In the short while that he still had at home he would show Moppet and Poppet all the beautiful things that he possibly could, just in the hope that they might remember.

From his study window Mr. Birley watched the trio cross the garden to Richard's and Stephen's old battered two-seater car, waiting for them beyond the archway. Only Stephen drove it now, for Richard's mad driving had led to a dramatic collision with the laundry van, and the suspension of his licence for several months. He watched with pen suspended while Stephen sat the two children upon the seat beside his, and wound up the old car, whose self-starter did not function. He did not go back to his work until they had roared away through the woods and silence reigned again. How different were his two nephews. Richard, if forced to appear in Torhaven with two small children attached, would have endured agonies and looked ridiculous, while the socially unselfconscious Stephen never gave a thought to appearances yet always took his place in the picture of things with sureness and charm. Yet in thought Stephen was self-conscious and self-tortured while Richard was simple, sure and unhesitating, and because simplicity of thought is a happier thing than simplicity of behaviour he was the more fortunate of the two, though he might not travel so far. No, not so far, thought Mr. Birley. Conflict is creative and the harder it is the finer the soul it makes. Then his heart smote him that he was belittling the more deeply-loved Richard. The simple in thought have the pent-up strength of their simplicity. When events strike down to bedrock it leaps out in the swift clean certainty of action that can win eternity with a little hour.

I V

As they drove up and down and around the green hills, yet always dropping imperceptibly from the heights to the sea, Stephen showed the children many pretty things; a shepherd going leisurely along with a flock of sheep, a child upon his shoulder, a bunch of white butterflies tossing in the blue air, wild roses starring the hedges, and sudden glimpses of the sea or of the moors seen between the folds of the hills. They listened and nodded their fair heads but he did not know if they really thought that these things were pretty; they would not, he noticed, look to the far distance, though they would consider things that were close at hand. Once he stopped the car and picked them a handful of wild strawberries; they ate them with enjoyment but asked between mouthfuls why they never had faggots for dinner at the Castle? Stephen said humbly that he did not think they knew about faggots at the Castle, they were an ignorant lot there, but if possible they would buy some of it—or them—to-day in Torhaven.

They were very happy when they reached the town and saw the buses and the cars, and they snuffed up the scent of the petrol with ecstatic quivering noses. But they liked the seagulls, too, sitting one behind the other on the sea wall, and all the little ships gathered within the shelter of the lovely harbour beneath the great cliffs where the white Victorian houses sat on their rocky ledges, looking down at the sea at their feet with incomparable dignity, yet half afraid, surely, of over-balancing and falling in.

Near one of these Stephen parked the car, lifted the children out and pressed the bell.

"'Ow many are you 'aving took out, Mr. Stephen?" asked Moppet with eager interest.

"None," said Stephen.

"What 'ave you come for then?" asked Poppet.

"Stoppings," said Stephen.

They blinked at him. Mother and Dad never had stoppings, whatever they might be. They waited until they could endure no more and then they had them out. Mr. Stephen, as far as one could see, was enduring nothing, and yet was visiting the dentist. It was very odd.

In the waiting-room Stephen sat the two little girls side by side upon the seat of a plush armchair, gathered up all the copies of *Picture Post* with their ghastly photographs of the agonies of war, hid them behind the aspidistra, presented Moppet and Poppet with an innocuous copy of *Good Housekeeping* and told them to be good girls until he came back. They regarded him with wide reproachful eyes as he left them. They had thought they were going to watch him have his teeth out and they were very disappointed.

But Stephen's sufferings from his teeth, though not apparent to Moppet and Poppet, were none the less real, and a grim forty minutes awaited him. So much did he suffer that his mental agonies slipped into the background. Dimly, as the machine whirred, he remembered that England stood in great danger, and that he could not finally make up his mind whether it was his duty to defend her or whether it wasn't. Vaguely he remembered that he loved Prunella, had loved her always with all the force and personality that he had, and that she had left him for Richard. Then he forgot about England's danger, and about Prunella not loving him. Then he forgot there was either an England or a Prunella. Then he was conscious of nothing but the whirring machine and his pain, and a patch of blue sky with seagulls floating across it that was all he could see through the only unfrosted pane of the surgery window, and upon which he tried to concentrate his whole attention, lest he yell. Though it is unflattering to human nature, which if really noble should surely suffer more from mental pain than from physical, the fact remains that at a certain pitch the ignominious suffering of the body can be the only suffering there is.

"Very near the nerve here," remarked the dentist unnecessarily, and it was just at that moment that the tunes began. Someone was playing the violin, and Stephen, dragged from the depths more surely by music than by other forms of art, felt as though he were mounting step by step out of the darkness of the mental misery of so many weeks, and the physical pain of as many minutes, into the light again. Each tune was a step upwards, each pause an acute fear that there might not be another, each fresh beginning a gasp of relief. Gosh, but the man could play! He had a magician's fingers, a fine fiddle, and the timing and phrasing of a perfect technique. If his playing lacked the depth of genius it had a freshness and spontaneity that were somehow childlike and infinitely touching. And he played the things that were good music and yet tuneful enough for a child to love. He played the *Serenade* from Mozart's *Night Music* and the air of the *Intermezzo* from *Cavalleria Rusticana*, a little of the *Rosamunde* music and the *Dance of the Hours*, the *Invitation to the Waltz* and one of Elgar's Bavarian dances; and finally he played the *Andante Cantabile* and Stephen was liberated.

"Who on earth?" he demanded, when the dentist had removed the impedimenta from his mouth and straightened an aching back.

"Rinse, please," said the dentist.

Stephen rinsed and repeated the question.

"Just some down-at-heel fellow who plays in the streets," said the dentist a little shortly, for he was incredibly tired and the international situation weighed upon him. "Now I've merely the filling to put in." And he busied himself over his mixing palette while Stephen relaxed in his chair, glad that the worst was over, and glad that a stricken world was still so full of tunes. "A little wider, please," said the dentist, and the unseen violinist, after a longish pause, plunged abruptly and gloriously into the first violin part of the *Andante of the 9th*. He played with a touch of genius now and Stephen's imagination supplied the missing background of the second fiddles, the 'cellos, the double bass and the wind, saw the rhythmical movement of the bows like the bare branches of trees in a storm and heard the great lamenting music with its trumpet calls, felt the melody lifting, lifting—where, for what purpose, to what end?

"*Rinse*, please," said the dentist grimly, for the third time. "That'll be all for to-day, but I've by no means finished with you," and he bent over the engagement book on his desk.

Stephen rinsed, got up, and stood waiting, looking out of the window at the gulls mounting against the blue sky. The music had stopped and the lifting wings of it were receding from him. Where to? They did not come back so they must go somewhere.

"Next Wednesday at eleven-thirty?" suggested the dentist, and swung round, his observant professional eye running swiftly over the figure of the tall young man standing erect and still with eyes fixed upon the gulls beyond the window. A strange boy, he thought, maturely poised yet with a childish trick of abstraction, and with that pale skin, fair hair and very clear eyes, giving a rather striking impression of lightness and clarity. A nervous temperament, obviously, but well controlled. He had probably suffered more than most people would have done during the last forty minutes, yet showed less sign of it.

"Wednesday. Eleven-thirty. Thank you," said Stephen, and was gone with a swiftness that would have seemed arrogant had not his voice and movements held an inherent disarming courtesy. The dentist washed his hands and meditated a little bitterly upon the advantages of breeding. Only the aristocrats can be rude with grace.

But Stephen was reproaching himself for his abruptness as he opened the waiting-room door. . . . But he had to get the kids quickly and find that violinist.

But the kids were gone. The war pictures that he had so carefully hidden from them behind the aspidistra had been unearthed, enjoyed to the full and scattered about the room, but the children themselves had disappeared.

He went out into the narrow street before the house, where only a rail intervened between the steep drop of the cliff to the harbour below, and looked anxiously over. There were no small lifeless bodies to be seen; only the small ships lying at anchor and the white gulls circling; but from some spot out of sight below him there floated the strains of Chopin's *Nocturne in E Flat*. That was it, of course. Music had pulled them down to the harbour wall just as it pulled them up the steps of his tower.

He went to the end of the street and followed the narrow winding lane that led down to the harbour, and here, at the end of a small jetty that ran out into the sunlit water, were assembled a little group of loafers and children and dogs gathered round Moppet and Poppet and a tall battered musician in a shabby overcoat, his derelict hat set beside him on the cobbles, playing as one inspired.

Stephen sat down on the harbour wall to listen. Moppet and Poppet had not seen him. Hand in hand, entranced, they stood before the musician gazing up into his face. No wonder, thought Stephen, for the fellow was compelling. A Jew by the look of him, lean and gaunt, with strong fierce bones jutting through a yellow skin, the reddened nose of a hard drinker, brooding dark eyes and a bitter mouth that were only partially softened by the music he was playing. There was a certain style about him; some lingering grace in his battered figure, as though once he had learned how to hold himself as the central figure on a concert platform, a look almost of breeding in the lines of his face and a something about the derelict hat that suggested it had been well chosen in its day.

The violinist looked up and saw the young man sitting on the wall.

A king in Israel. The phrase came into Stephen's mind as though a voice had spoken it, visiting him as phrases often visited him, with a queer insistence that was never without effect upon his actions. A king in Israel. One of that great race who drift like autumn leaves over the face of the earth, clinging desperately now and again to some cranny that offers shelter, only to be driven on by the unceasing wind of persecution that can torture but never destroy, scatter but not quench. Blown by its bitter breath the flame of vitality and genius leaps only higher and higher to the just heavens whose vengeance tarries. Kings of the earth, kings unvindicated. It is to them that their persecutors turn in need; their wisdom, gold, science and art that bring salvation again and again. And yet they are nailed unceasingly to the cross, despised and rejected of men, the superscription over them always the same. . . . King. . . . How long, oh Lord, how long? Surely the flame is bright enough now for the coming of the kingdom and the ending of the pain.

Stephen realised suddenly that the hot angry thoughts that were racing through his mind were not his own but had come to him from the mad fierce music that the violinist was playing. What was it? Nothing he knew. The man was extemporising. There was no beauty in his music now, only hatred and despair and a quite appalling fear. Its power was immense. Stephen felt himself cast by it into some dark stream that was flowing down a narrow street between tall overhanging houses; they were twisted and dark and evil belched from them like tainted breath. And the stream that flowed between them was a stream of human refugees. They wore dark stained caftans and their beards were matted with the sweat of their terror. . . . Stephen Beaulieu had fought in the Crusades. What hand had his brothers or his sons taken in the pogroms that had been their ghastly corollary in England? . . . Hot panting breath fanned Stephen's face and the stench of blood and sweat and garlic that clung to the garments of the men about him was nauseating, horrible. And they were so silent in their fear. They neither shrieked nor cried, just stumbled on and on to get away. And then they stopped, surged back upon themselves, reeled and staggered, and cried out at last in a terrible voice upon the God of Israel. For the street was blocked at both ends. There was no more hope. My God, my God, why hast Thou forsaken me? They were trapped. . . . Who had trapped them? . . . The bitterness of death swept the narrow street, cleansed it and was gone.

Stephen was once more conscious that he was sitting on the harbour wall. The music was silent and only Moppet and Poppet were left of the little crowd who had listened to it. Over their fair heads Stephen and the musician looked at each other, a long look that left them both oddly confused and shaken. Where had they been together? Who had blocked the street at the other end?

Stephen got up, and all the loose change that he had in his pocket was dropped into the hat upon the cobbles. But even as he dropped it he was hot with shame, for there was no possible restitution to be made for that act of treachery. Yet for it I shall suffer, he thought, I and my race, if there is justice upon this earth.

The violinist bowed with something of a royal air, as though he were taking the applause at the end of a concert, king of the occasion. He could behave normally again, and so could Stephen, but they were both badly disturbed by the queer emotion that had lately gripped them. Then they thrust it away into the surrounding mystery of things from which it had come. Stephen did not ask the violinist about the music he had just been playing, and that had apparently been wrested from him by Stephen's presence, and he seemed not to want to be asked, for he immediately broke into explanation upon the subject of Moppet and Poppet.

"Nice little kids, sir," he said. "I knew 'em in London."

"It's our Mr. Isaacson!" cried Moppet and Poppet, jigging up and down. "Our Mr. Isaacson!"

"Mother's lodger," explained Moppet.

"He played tunes," said Poppet, "and we went."

"Shall we all have some coffee together?" suggested Stephen. "That is," he added, putting a hand in his empty pocket, remembering his beggared state and smiling at Mr. Isaacson, "if you will be our host?"

Mr. Isaacson's lean unhappy features were suddenly irradiated by a smile whose charm almost took Stephen aback, for he could not know what a fine and courteous host this vagabond fiddler had been in the days of his prosperity, how he had delighted in hospitality and how many bitter years had passed since he had been able to practise it.

"Will you come this way, sir?" he said. "Just along here there's a quiet place where they both serve hot coffee and don't mind my rags and tatters at a table."

He led the way with confidence, as a host should, and Stephen fell into step beside him, but silently, for Moppet and Poppet, clinging to Mr. Isaacson's coat, were pouring forth such a torrent of information that no adult word could be slipped in edgeways. By the time they reached the quiet little sailors' restaurant at the end of the quay, however, Stephen had been fully if confusedly informed about Mr. Isaacson's relations with the Baxter family, and Mr. Isaacson had groped his way through a welter of boulders and castles and woods and young gentlemen and old gentlemen and a lady to some knowledge of the Birleys and their home.

"Two cups of coffee, please, Miss," he said to the waitress, when the strange quartette had seated itself at a little table in the window. "Two glasses of milk and two large buns."

His eyes met Stephen's and they smiled. Buns, one hoped, would momentarily check the conversation of Moppet and Poppet, but meanwhile it flowed on quite unintelligibly upon the subject of rabbits and the two men could only smoke Stephen's cigarettes and appraise each other in silence.

An unusual boy, thought Mr. Isaacson, confusedly. Odd how as soon as he saw him sitting on the harbour wall and looking at him with those clear light eyes he had suddenly started improvising on his fiddle, a thing he had not done for years, and improvising such crazy perilous stuff, too, stuff that had seared him even while he played it. Odd how the boy had chucked all that money into his hat, almost as though he owed it to him. Graceful friendly manners he had, setting a fellow at his ease. Strange how quickly he had found the kids. He'd been playing the *Andante Cantabile* and the other stuff they liked up and down every street in Torhaven, just in the mad hope that the kids were living in the place, would hear him and come out. . . . But it had been a mad hope that he'd never thought to have fulfilled. . . . Odd how his ruddy luck had turned since that day he'd fallen fainting into the train at Paddington. That last corner that he'd turned, the one that he'd thought would be the last, the most despairing and desperate of all his corners, had turned out to be the one to have something round it. . . . Hope. . . . The smile that he turned on Stephen, who had made him a host again for a short half-hour, had a luminous grateful tenderness that smote Stephen. . . . For who had blocked the other end of the street?

The buns came and a merciful silence fell.

Stephen leaned forward. "Thank you for the *Andante of the 9th*," he said. "I heard it from the street above. You seemed to summon up the full orchestra."

"God knows how many times I've played it with the full orchestra," said Mr. Isaacson. "The last time was in Vienna. Then not again till now."

He too was leaning forward, his coffee cup between his thin nervous brown fingers, his tragic eyes on Stephen's. They spoke both of them quickly, eagerly, as though there was much to say and much to understand while this queer bond forged by mad music still held them together. Presently it would break, for it was not normal. Soon they would be themselves again and might not understand each other.

"A black time in between?" asked Stephen.

"Black?" said Mr. Isaacson, and laughed, with no charm this time. "Hell. Bloody hell. One does not play the *Andante of the 9th* in hell."

"No," said Stephen gently. "If one could play it, or even manage to listen to it, hell would be over." He paused, side-tracked into the old controversy. "I think the last movement's a failure, don't you? The *Andante* lifts you to something that not even music can describe, and then Beethoven tries to describe it with a hymn to brotherhood inspired by the French Revolution. The French Revolution! Surely the ghastliest human parody there's ever been of the sort of union he had in mind."

"All these human attempts are ghastly parodies," said Mr. Isaacson, his voice heavy and flat. "And there's nothing there to parody except a dream."

Stephen was humbled. Several times lately he had thought himself in hell. But he was wrong, for he had been able to listen to the *Andante*. He knew nothing as yet about suffering. Nothing. He had touched only the edge of it. "The pulp so bitter, how shall taste the rind?"

"A fugitive Jew in Europe," said Mr. Isaacson. "That's what I've been this last decade. Well, I don't need to speak of it. You know a little of what that means, if you've read your papers, but not much, for the truth don't make pretty reading for respectable folk. I got to England a couple of years ago—I was born in England—but I've not done much good. Too many other Jews about. You tolerate us—that's your policy for the moment—but when we starve among you you don't seem to notice it. You don't notice anything you don't want to, you English. It takes bombs down the chimney and invasion on the doorstep to make you open more than half an eye. Well, it wasn't all your fault. I was no genius, you see, only a man with talent, and talent is not enough, and when I got sick and tired of music the talent went too."

"Not permanently," smiled Stephen. "What gave it back?"

"A bloke in the train," said Mr. Isaacson. "He took me in and gave me free board and lodging for a week. His doing that seemed to freshen me up, if you know what I mean. Things seemed worth while again. I'm still lodging there, but paying my way now, for I make quite a bit in the streets; down here they've more time than they had in London, and they seem to like to listen."

"I don't blame them," said Stephen, smiling. "You've a grand assortment of tunes."

"And they're a friendly lot down here," said Mr. Isaacson. "That bloke in the train, now—God knows what made him give me a leg up that way. I doubt if he has much idea, either. Seemed as astonished as I was."

"The war, perhaps," said Stephen. "Both eyes open for once and you in the line of vision."

"Maybe," said Mr. Isaacson. "Another cup of coffee, sir?"

Stephen had one, though it was bad coffee, for Mr. Isaacson looked eager to be host for a little longer. While he drank it he tried to say a little about himself, for Mr. Isaacson looked as though he wanted that too. He had just come down from Oxford, he said. He had hoped to be an architect, but all that must wait now. He had always been a pacifist and now he did not know what he ought to do.

"Fight, sir," said Mr. Isaacson. "I'd no use for the war a short while back, but now I'm not so sure. This town, now, it's a good town, with the gulls and the sea and the white houses on the cliffs. It's given me my health again, and the, mind you, a short while back, what with the drink and one thing and another, I was as near to a madman as makes no difference. I'd take my oath that in spite of the war there's more happiness here, with all these kids about, than in most other towns in Europe to-day. I'd not like, I've thought lately, to see the things going on here that I've seen going on in other cities. Better fight to keep 'em out, I've thought; better fight to the last penny and the last drop of blood to keep this country sane. You English don't do as much to help the fugitives as we think you might, perhaps, but at least in the past you've let us in and let us be."

"Did you ever read Queen Elizabeth's prayer before the

Armada?" asked Stephen. "She prayed that England might be a help to the oppressed and a defence to the persecuted."

"I always say there's no harm in prayer," said Mr. Isaacson kindly. "No sense in it, but no harm, and often a bit of good. What a man jabbers to is himself, of course, the conscious to the subconscious. 'Give me courage, give me light,' he says, and up it comes from somewhere below."

"Or from outside," said Stephen. "From the woods in autumn or the spring wind. Or from a voice speaking words that slip into your mind and underline themselves there. Haven't you experienced that?"

Both men were silent and in the silence the sentences that just now were underlined in their two minds spoke themselves aloud.

"If in this life only we have hope. . . ."

"A king in Israel."

"That voice speaking is no more than the subconscious thrusting up something one has read or heard somewhere," said Mr. Isaacson, firmly on the defensive.

"Yes, but why is that particular phrase thrust up at that particular moment?" asked Stephen. "And from where does the subconscious draw its courage and its light? It's no good, you said there was nothing to parody, but nothing makes sense unless we're in touch with another country. What you said just now about the preservation of England's sanity proves it; for why do we keep on trying to build Jerusalem? We've been at it for several thousand years, and it seems a hopeless business, yet we're for ever shovelling away the ruins of the old attempts and starting again. There's no explanation except that there's a model somewhere, and we've seen it vaguely through the debris. Man will go on till he's got the thing right at last."

The children had finished their buns and their milk and sat panting with the effort, white moustaches upon their upper lips and eyes alight with a lively sense of favours to come. Smiling tolerantly, Mr. Isaacson wiped their mouths with a practised hand, lifted them down and paid the bill. He put sixpence under the plate for the waitress, and led the way out with an air. There was a lot of the child in him, queer old fish that he was, Stephen thought, watching him so delightedly playing the part of a man of means; and Mr. Isaacson thought the same of Stephen with his young, green ideas and his childish willingness to speak of them. Queer young fish. He'd never been up against it. They always talked this bloody rot when they'd never been up against it.

Out in the street again a change gradually came over them both. Though unselfconscious as ever Stephen seemed to withdraw a little into himself and Mr. Isaacson, looking at him, realised suddenly, as he had not realised before, that this young toff lived a life so far removed from his own that it might have been upon another planet. And Stephen, looking at Mr. Isaacson, was more conscious now of the shabby street musician than of the king in Israel. That strange union was over, perhaps never to come back, though surely never to be forgotten. They strolled along with friendliness no whit abated but intimacy gone, and talked of music very superficially indeed.

"Faggots!" cried Moppet, running along at their heels.

"Faggots!" shouted Poppet, bustling after.

"What *are* faggots?" Stephen enquired of Mr. Isaacson. "They want some and I promised they should have what they want."

"A mix-up of animals' innards," said Mr. Isaacson. "Very tasty, but I doubt if you'd care for it yourself. This way, sir, there's a shop up here that sells it."

The four mounted serenely through the crowd of shoppers on the pavements of the steep busy street that climbed a ravine between two of Torhaven's seven hills. Clean water from the distant moors had perhaps once flowed down this valley, and the surge of traffic reminded one of it. There was something about this town that kept the natural loveliness it had superseded perpetually in one's mind; it was continually breaking through in the graceful contour of roads taking the curve of the hillside, in the brightness of blue sea seen at a street's end, in a rustle of green leaves about a roof tree and a breath of flowers over a garden wall. Its air was clear and sun-warmed, and in spite of camouflaged guns and barbed wire entanglements an atmosphere of holiday-making still pervaded it from its riotous and happy past.

But like every other lovely town it was befouled by butchers' shops. His childish horror of them still remained with Stephen, and as they stood waiting, breathing in the sickly slimy scent of death, he repeated to the children one of the rhymes he had remembered since his childhood because of his passionate agreement with the sentiments of Walter de la Mare therein expressed.

> "I can't abide a butcher,
>   I can't abear his meat.
>   I always think a butcher's shop
>   The ugliest in the street."

Moppet and Poppet did not agree with him. They snuffed up the familiar scent with joy and pointed out a revolting-looking mass as "Faggots!" with cries of ecstasy. Stephen borrowed more money off Mr. Isaacson and purchased some from a kindly, smiling butcher, watched it wrapped up in the outside sheet of a picture paper decorated with pictures of dead bodies being lifted from a bombed building, and carried it out into the street fighting an attack of nausea that all but brought him to open humiliation in the main street of Torhaven at the busiest time of the day. What a world! Yet children and butchers moved through it for the most part with such smiling joy. Were they right or was he?

On the way from the butcher's to Woolworth's, Poppet in one hand and the faggots in the other, Mr. Isaacson beside him with Moppet attached, Stephen met a number of acquaintances. He bowed with his usual ease; it was the acquaintances who were disconcerted. At Woolworth's Moppet and Poppet bought a kettle that went off like an air-raid siren when the water boiled, and a rubber bird of a billious yellow hue that blew up, and then died slowly with shrieks. After a demonstration of these articles Stephen found that as well as feeling sick he had a headache. Then they went back to the car park and Stephen and the children climbed in, while Mr. Isaacson stood watching them rather forlornly.

Stephen strove to recover his fast scattering wits, so as to know what to do about Mr. Isaacson. Full reparation had not been made, either by the Birleys to those men with the blood-stained caftans and matted beards who had died in agony in the narrow street, or by a man who had much to a man who had little. But he could not think of anything to do except write out the times of the buses on the back of his card, so that Mr. Isaacson could come out to the Castle and see the children when he felt so inclined. Mr. Isaacson took the piece of pasteboard with a bow, but in a rather sardonic silence, and when Stephen held out his hand he took it with an exaggerated politeness that hurt after that hour of strange and perfect intimacy. The gulf of their social difference was yawning between them again like an ugly leer. Curse it, thought Stephen, as the car sped homeward, where did I go wrong? Did I show how I loathed the faggots? Was it obvious that I was shaking hands on purpose so that he should not be hurt by my not shaking hands? Somehow I was a blundering fool, and he'll not want to come to the Castle now. Oh, hang!

The children sat beside him chattering joyfully, and alternately blowing up the bilious bird and peeping inside the newspaper at the faggots. They had had a lovely morning.

When they got home Miss Brown met them at the front door, received the faggots with no shadow of shrinking, promised to prepare them for human consumption, admired the bilious bird and said she loved kettles that went off like air-raid sirens. She's a damn fine woman, thought Stephen. I'm glad she's come.

CHAPTER VIII

I

LUNCH was over and Boulder and Fanny Treguthwic stood in the kitchen sorting out its aftermath. Miss Brown, coming downstairs to help Fanny with the washing up, marvelled for the hundredth time at the horrid appearance of things that have been emptied of their virtue. The children's banana skins, with bananas inside them, were a pleasing sight, but emptied of banana their look of limp yellow emptiness was positively dissolute. Tomato skin without tomato is a revolting sight, while as for a whiting's head and backbone minus the whiting—Miss Brown shuddered and looked the other way. Though she had been washing up for other people all her life, and supposed she would continue to wash up for them till she rested from it in the grave, she could never get used to the grease of it, the smell of it, the exhaustion of it and its heartbreaking monotony. Lucky children, playing in the kitchen garden, lucky Mr. Birley and Stephen, sitting upstairs with *The Times* while the remnants of their whitings were dealt with down below. But she did not allow the slight discouragement of these thoughts to become visible; that would have been against her principles.

"Isn't it a nice day, Mr. Boulder?" she said brightly, as she buttoned a chintz overall over her green linen dress. Boulder gazed at her in gloomy irritation, for nothing exasperated him more than being cheered up when he didn't want to be cheered up. But he was obliged to own that she looked neat and fresh, and so kind, as she stood there smiling at him with her one dimple faintly showing and her smooth dark hair gleaming in the sun. Inoffensive sort of little woman, thought Boulder. A pretty voice, she had, and never gave one a back answer. She was a good worker, too, and unlike most women she was content to do her duty in silence, as a matter of course, without perpetually drawing attention to the excellence of her technique. Boulder had decided quite a while back that she should stay. She showed no sign of wanting to oust him, quite the contrary, and one way and another she took quite a lot off him and he thought highly of her. He did not let her know this, of course, that would have been contrary to the guiding principle of his existence, which laid it down as law that as soon as a woman was praised for her virtue she lost it. Virtue was not inherent in a woman, Boulder thought; she merely put it on like a hat to attract the males and once she had attained her object she chucked it away. . . . Look at that tart who'd been married long ago to the young fool crazed with love that he'd been then. She'd even gone to church with him in their courting days and it hadn't been until a month after their marriage that he'd found he was expected to father another man's child. He'd done it: he was not the man to expose his own wife to shame. He'd forgiven her, and then after the birth of the child she'd gone after yet another man, and he'd been so crazed with furious pain that he'd tried to murder the fellow and been had up for assault. She'd died when he was in South Africa, poor girl, but he'd always done his best for her child. He'd not been sorry when she died, for he'd come to hate her; though even now in his feverish dreams he sometimes saw her round blue eyes and her doll's face mocking at him because he had believed it possible that she could love a stick like him. Even now at nights he felt again the agony of his love and humiliation; not by day; by day he had enough to do to keep his pain and weakness sufficiently battened under him to get his work done, so that no one but himself should have knowledge of that cancer in his chest.

"Nice day?" he said repressively to Miss Brown. "Nice, is it, with the garden goin' to rack an' ruin an' the wells runnin' dry, an' so 'ot a fellow can't get 'is breath at night? You'll be tellin' me it's a nice war in a minute, Miss. A nice war! An' 'ere we are with invasion expected hourly an' the income tax bringin' the 'ole lot of us to ruin!" And he picked up his tray of glass and silver, carried it into his pantry and banged and locked the door.

"Us don't know how to please him, Miss, do us?" said Fanny, aggrieved. "If us is cheerful he don't like that, and if us is gloomy, see, he don't like that neither. I'll wash, Miss, if you'll dry."

"He's anxious about Mr. Richard," explained Miss Brown. "He should have come home on leave yesterday and he never came, and sent no message. Mr. Boulder naturally feels anxious."

"No call for him to," said Fanny. "Mr. Richard never does anything he says he will. He don't like being tied down to things, Mr. Richard don't."

"And then Mr. Boulder's not well," Miss Brown further excused him. "When one is not well everything that everyone else says seems to be the wrong thing, somehow."

"Mr. Boulder's not the only one to have the indigestion," said Fanny, splashing indignantly in the soapsuds. "Mr. Pratt has it something cruel and never a sharp word do us get from him."

"Pratt has not got so much to do as Boulder," said Miss Brown, and smiled a little as there rose before her mind's eye the slow perambulations of Pratt about the garden.

Fanny pushed the soapsuds off her fingers and indignantly straightened an aching back. "And if Mr. Boulder's overworked, Miss, what about you and me?"

"It can't be helped, Fanny," said Miss Brown quickly. "I asked Mr. Birley the other day if we could have a little more help in the house and he said he was very sorry but it was impossible. You heard Mr. Boulder mention the income tax just now. It is very high, owing to the war, and I believe it is pressing most cruelly upon gentlemen in Mr. Birley's position."

Fanny looked meditatively out of the window. "Mrs. Heather told me there used to be a staff of ten at the Castle," she said. "Five indoor and five out. Mrs. Heather used to help hull the strawberries for the dinner parties, and hang little coloured lights all over the garden when they had a dance in the big hall. Fine, it must have been."

Both women were silent, and Miss Brown had a sudden odd little vision of Stephen in trim black and white standing at the top of the terrace steps to welcome his guests, dancing in the great hall to the music of the violins and standing in the shadows of the scented garden with a girl in his arms. But the tunes that the violins played were not the tunes that Stephen knew, and the girl in his arms, with her billowing white muslin dress and her great coronet of golden hair, was not a woman of to-day. Stephen had got into the wrong age, somehow. It was a pity. Before the queer little vision faded she saw that if he had lived in that other time he would have had a happiness he would never know in this one. Oh, the pity of it. Recurrently, as man struggled on, a whole generation was broken at the wheel. Somehow, somewhere, was there reparation made?

"Well-there," said Fanny cheerfully, bending again to her

labours, "times change, and if we're all dead by this time next week we shan't be worrying."

Miss Brown laughed. Fanny with her utter lack of imagination was comfortable company these days. She was comfortable to look at, too, with her rosy country face beneath the absurdly sophisticated "perm" of fair sausage curls that covered her round head. She was slow of speech and slow of thought, and typically West Country in the way she combined slowness of movement with a capacity for getting things done notwithstanding. She lived for the moment as the children did. Though she knew that death and destruction might descend upon her at any moment, she would not visualise it until it happened. Watching her slow unthinking routine with the dishes Miss Brown felt steadied and comforted. Supposing that by this time next week the worst *had* happened, and supposing that they had not died, what would she and Fanny be doing? Washing up, of course. Possibly for the enemy, but still, washing up. It was one of the eternal verities. One could cling to it and feel secure.

I I

With his door safely locked upon those chattering women Boulder sat down on his pantry chair, his head in his hands, groaning softly, and in spite of his pain a great wave of relief swept over him that he was alone. These moments behind locked doors were the best moments that he had. They were to him what a cup of tea was to Miss Brown and his gramophone to Stephen. It was not only the thing done that brought relief, the drinking of the tea, the listening to the music, the luxury of letting the groans come through, it was even more the cessation of the fight, the momentary suspension of living to which these trivial things admitted one. "Oh Gawd, oh Gawd," groaned Boulder through his pain; but yet he was at peace; in these moments of quiet he somehow reached out to the eternal quiet and was no longer afraid.

But these good moments never lasted long. The pain increased and with it the tempo of his mood quickened from acquiescence into a goading fear that drove him straight away into the battle line. He got up, his hands shaking and the sweat standing out upon his upper lip and forehead, and began mechanically to wash up his silver and glass. Washing up. He was for ever at it. He did not doubt that Jerry would catch him at it, dishcloth in hand, when he landed; Jerry who last time had had to encounter Herbert Boulder with a bayonet instead of a dishcloth, and some nice little Mills bombs handy. He was not afraid of Jerry, indeed he was distinctly sorry for the poor blighter, for years ago he had proved himself a better fellow, man for man, than that poor bullet-headed driven conscript, nor was he afraid of death, that he had seen too often to regard as anything but a mere commonplace, but he was deadly afraid that Mr. Birley would discover his illness and send for Dr. Maxwell, and that would mean hospital, and he'd never get out again. That was what goaded him forward in his tremendous, heroic fight. That fear was the mainspring of his whole existence.

For he knew what was the matter with him all right. His father had died of it. He had had his suspicions of what his end might be since that day in nineteen fifteen when that great Boche prisoner had suddenly gone berserk and gone for Captain Birley, Richard's and Stephen's father, before they'd had the time to tie his hands; Boulder had just had time to step in between and take the terrific blow instead; a blow often started it, one had heard. And he knew he was pretty bad. If it was found out it would mean the hospital, and he'd never get out.

He did not analyse his fear of the hospital; he just had it. In reality the whole thing went back to a night nearly half a century ago when he and the Major, Captain Birley's father, had sat out under the blazing South African stars and he had told him about that tart who had let him down. Stephen had said he was no Birley, but then he had never known his grandfather; his quick intuitive sympathy had come to him from that great man. Major Birley had known there was some bitter shame hidden behind the mask-like face of his ugly insignificant little Cockney servant; he had sensed the blazing passion of the man, the pride, the infinite capacity for dog-like love. Bit by bit he had got the whole story out of him, and bit by bit, as the days went on, by a deliberate reliance upon Boulder, by deliberate trust in him, by a purposeful taking of the little man into his life as an integral part of it, he had drawn out the shame and cleansed the wound and given back to Boulder his self-respect.

But the Major had not quite realised how fierce would be the devotion of the re-orientated Boulder. It clamped down upon him like a vice, to his great inconvenience at times. But it was the result of his own action and he accepted it humorously, together with Boulder as a life-long incubus; and when Boulder's devotion later widened to enclose all the Birleys in a hoop of most uncomfortable steel they did the same. Feudal friendliness was still strong in them. The nasty-tempered little man was theirs, and they would stand by him till the end.

As he would by them. Deep in his subconscious was the conviction that if he were separated from them he would be damned. He would be back again in that place of madness from which they had saved him. And once he went to hospital his union with them would be snapped. He would never get out.

And he had to be doubly careful now, for Dr. Maxwell was on the alert. Whenever he met him the old man's eyes went through him like a couple of gimlets, almost as though they saw right through his clothes to the Thing that he had. "Come and see me, Boulder," the old man had said one day, but he had headed him off with, "No thanks, sir. Never felt better." His set face suddenly relaxed into a smile as he worked. He could fool 'em all. Yes, he could fool 'em all up to the end.

His pain had lessened as he washed up. It often did. "Work it off, work it off," he would say to himself sometimes through set teeth, and the knowledge that he was keeping his end up, keeping the hospital at arm's length, acted on him like a stimulating drug. So it did now. His mind, hitherto stunned by the pain, began to work again, and he returned to his perennial worrying over the decline of the Birley fortunes.

This soaring to fresh heights of the income tax, for instance. Mr. Birley and Mr. Stephen had talked of it at lunch. Things would be worse than ever. Damn Hitler! For years now he had had to watch the slow waning of the family glory, and it hurt him far more than it hurt the Birleys. Mr. Birley and Stephen were facing probable ruin calmly, if with pain, content that it should be their gift to their country in this epic hour of her danger and glory, and Richard thought it would be a jolly good thing if they were ruined, but Boulder faced the probability of a Third Exile with rebellion and despair. If only he could last out a bit longer, with his saving of a penny here and a penny there, his careful turning off of lights that the young gentlemen left burning, his careful pressing of Mr. Birley's clothes so that they should last as long as possible, his perpetual harrying of Fanny lest she eat too much, then ruin might be staved off, but if things were found out and he was taken to the hospital. . . . Well, he'd left all his savings to Mr. Richard. There must be quite a tidy little sum by this time. For years he had scarcely spent anything out of the generous wages that Mr. Birley refused to cut down. They were piling up for Mr. Richard; or for Mr. Stephen if Mr. Richard died; and his will was safely lodged at the bank.

But here his thoughts turned abruptly from a possibility they would not face. All the world seemed to him to revolve about Richard. All the past glory of the Birleys rested upon him and the future looked to him for the hope of its birth. He seldom spoke to Richard. His passionate love for him was so great that the very power of it kept him inarticulate; a great flood of feeling pressed inwardly against the doors of speech and kept them closed. It would have been a relief to him if he could have occasionally answered Richard's careless kindness with even a look of affection. But he did not know how. He could only go away and reckon up how much his savings amounted to now; leaving Richard with the distinct impression that the queer old cove simply hated him. Boulder spent hours unnecessarily brushing Richard's clothes and polishing boots that already shone like glass; and when he was away he would waste whole days pottering about his room, rubbing up the furniture and rearranging the treasures on the mantelpiece. If Miss Brown or Fanny, who were responsible for doing the other bedrooms, came near Richard's room he snarled at them like a wild beast. . . . And Mr. Richard should have come home yesterday, and he hadn't come.

III

Someone tried the pantry door and then knocked at it.

"Oo's there?" demanded Boulder savagely.

"Me, Mr. Boulder," came Fanny's plaintive voice. "It's Saturday, Mr. Boulder, and Mrs. Heather is here."

He had finished his washing-up now and his blessed moment of peace behind a locked door was over. He must open and admit the world. And it was Saturday, that cursed Saturday when the Castle was open to visitors from three to six, and Mrs. Heather took them round at sixpence a head. Though the sixpences were useful for the upkeep of the Castle, Boulder hated the business. He loathed seeing trippers from Torhaven exclaiming at that tattered flag in the glass case, fingering the furniture, mounting the great staircase and gaping at the family portraits. The whole thing seemed to him a desecration, and he hated those harmless trippers to the very depth of his passionate soul.

But it appeared that Mrs. Heather took the contrary view. When Boulder came trampling angrily out of his pantry, like a lion from his den, she was sitting serenely on one of the kitchen chairs, smiling her lovely childlike smile, her wrinkled hands folded quietly on her spotless white apron and her old black bonnet like a crown upon her snowy hair. Miss Brown and Fanny, though they had finished their work, had lingered to smile back at her. They adored Mrs. Heather because she was always so happy; though they did not know why she was so happy, or why she was so especially happy on a Saturday. One would have thought so old a woman would have found the perpetual showing of visitors round the Castle both fatiguing and monotonous; but Mrs. Heather adored Saturdays. When Mr. Birley had suggested relieving her of the duty she had shown the first signs of distress that he had seen in her for twenty years, and only his hasty assurance that never, while she lived, should any one else take on her work, had brought back her smile again. "But why, Mrs. Heather?" he had asked. "Why do you enjoy it so much?"

"I like to be the one to show 'em what the Castle means, sir," she had said. "What does it mean?" Mr. Birley had asked. But she had not explained herself further than that. She laboured under the delusion that Mr. Birley knew more than she did and would have considered it presumptuous to try to explain anything to him.

"Saturday, Mr. Boulder," she said now in her sweet quavering old voice, surprisingly clear to-day because she had got her teeth in. She did not hold with false teeth as a rule, thinking them contrary to nature, but she always wore them on a Saturday, so that the visitors should not miss a single word of her narration of family history. This narrative had been written out for her years ago by Mr. Birley himself, and she had learnt it by heart and never forgot a word of it. "Saturday, a quarter to three, an' the gentlemen have forgotten as usual and are in the rooms."

"I'll shift 'em," growled Boulder, and went upstairs. He had so hoped the war would have put an end to this degrading perambulation of trippers round the Castle. But it hadn't. With the characteristic determination of the British not to be heaved up out of their customary rut if by any means in their power they could contrive to continue in it, those who were accustomed to take a little holiday at this time took it if they could, trippers stonily determined to trip, war or no war, invasion or no invasion. "Mayn't be 'ere much longer," was a remark that Boulder frequently overheard now on a Saturday afternoon. He did not know whether they referred to themselves or the Castle, but judging by the extreme cheerfulness with which they spoke he supposed it was the Castle. Individual human beings, he had noticed, seemed always to expect still to be here, the one per-

manency in a tumbling universe. Though in theory they must
know that they had to die yet in practice they seemed to look out
from their personalities as from some impregnable island.
Boulder had felt like that himself once; until that day when he
had known that death was living with him upon his island. Even
now, on occasions, he felt like that still; though with a difference;
it was not his life that seemed to him now inviolable but a something within him that his life had made.

He entered the great hall where Mr. Birley and the dog Argos
sat submerged in newspapers and an after-luncheon somnolence.

"Saturday, sir," he said apologetically.

Mr. Birley and Argos woke up.

"Not again?" complained Mr. Birley. "It's always Saturday."
And poising his glasses upon his nose he gazed wildly around,
wondering which of the personal possessions strewn about him
he must take with him into the fastness of his study. Only the
garden, hall and gallery were opened to visitors, and he and
Stephen could inhabit their own rooms and the study and use
the back stairs, but they always seemed to leave the very book
they wanted behind in the hall or gallery. Always. Argos was
more fortunate because for purposes of instruction, amusement
and admiration he found himself perfectly adequate. He arose
slowly, stalked down the length of the hall, leaned his shoulder
against the study door, entered and lay down upon the hearth.
Here he would lie, lost in contemplation of his merits, from three
till six.

"*The Times*," fussed Mr. Birley. "Where's *The Times*? And
what the deuce have I done with my pipe? And Trevelyan. His
history. I had him not two minutes ago. Find Trevelyan. . . .
And Boulder, I should like you to ring up the aerodrome presently and see if they have any notion of Mr. Richard's plans for
his leave. Odd that he's not written."

"Very good, sir," said Boulder imperturbably, and gathering
up an armful of papers and books he shepherded his agitated
master towards the study door, shut him in and came back to
plump up the cushions. Then he went up to the shadowed gallery,
where the dim dead faces peered through the green light and
Stephen sat in the grateful coolness reading the poetry of Mr.
Stephen Spender.

". . . and it is death stalks through life
Grinning white through all faces
Clean and equal like the shine from snow.

129

In this time when grief pours freezing over us,
When the hard light of pain gleams at every street-corner
. . . our strength is now the strength of our bones
Clean and equal like the shine from snow. . . .
And it is the strength of our love for each other."

The dim white faces of the dead seemed to gather about him
in the green light. . . . Give up, they said. There is no ecstasy like
the ecstasy of loss. Give up all that you have, everything, even
the right to hold a faith of your own. Fight in the white light of
death with a million others, one with them, loving them, one
bone and sinew with them, one cause, one faith, at peace. Give
up and be happy. Give up. Give up. . . . So they crowded about
him, whispering, and he felt himself slipping. It would be so
sweet to give in, so happy. Might one not be happy for a little
before one died? Yes, surely. Give in. Give in.

"Saturday, sir," said Boulder.

"Oh, damn!" cried Stephen, and jumped up, his book crashing to the floor. A draught from an opening door below sent the
curtain over the south window blowing out into the room and
the light fell upon the gross full-blooded fighting face of Roger
the Nabob. . . . Give up? Not this way. Not just to be happy,
with the fight not fought to a finish and the faith not kept. There
is a joy of oneness that is only a joy of this world, just a shadow
on the wall, a prophesying. Will you sell your birthright for a
mess of pottage? Coward! Fool! Hold on. Hold on.

"Oh, damn," groaned Stephen again, stooping to pick up his
book. In another moment, but for Boulder and Roger, he would
have given in. In another moment, he would have been happy.

"Sorry for the interruption, sir," said Boulder severely, for he
considered that Stephen was making an inordinate fuss about
nothing. "But these Saturdays, they do come round. Anythin'
else you're requirin', sir, from this room or the 'all?"

He shepherded Stephen firmly from the room, rearranged the
folds of the curtains and descended once more to the kitchen
regions. "Shifted 'em, Mrs. 'Eather," he said.

IV

Mrs. Heather rose with alacrity and made her way upstairs
and across the garden to the great gateway, where a charabanc
was already waiting. Only a dozen or so inside to-day, where
before the war there would have been fifty. Mrs. Heather felt a
little pang of disappointment. This lot could be taken round in

130

just one party and she like to have a succession of parties, all the parties she could get, perhaps a couple of hours of story-telling, two hours of "being the one to show 'em." Well, one party was better than none and she nodded and smiled encouragingly as five women, three men, three little girls and one small boy descended from the charabanc. "That's right, then," she said. "Come along, my dears. Best to make the most of one's chances, these days. . . . The Norman gateway of the original Castle, built by Simon Beaulieu in 1069."

She was off, repeating the first sentence of the little history taught her by Mr. Birley as though it were an incantation, or the first phrase of a piece of music, and the trippers followed her with as much eagerness as though she were Simon himself.

And so she was. As she led them through the garden and hall and showed them the treasures there, telling them of Simon and the first Richard, Roger and Stephen the Crusader, as she showed them the portraits in the gallery and told them the tales that matched each painted face, she was each of these men in turn. It was a very odd experience to go round the Castle in her company. Though she did nothing except narrate the bare facts of family history in her sweet old sing-song voice yet she invariably held every one of her audience, even the most unimaginative, gripped by her story. So utterly was she at one with the life of this place that they were at one with it too. The immense strength of her personality pulled them with her into her own selflessness. They lost themselves. They saw the sun rise upon the Castle wall and listened for the music of the trumpets, they heard the ripple of a flag in the wind, the sound of bells in the evening air, the tramp of armed feet upon stone and a woman singing. Courage was suddenly theirs, and strength and beauty. They swung to a marching song over the green hills and felt the hot blood drumming in their veins. They charged to a battle cry and felt the ripple of horseflesh between their knees. They sailed the seven seas and saw the wonder of new lands beneath new stars. They were saints and they were heroes, they were priests and scholars and plain coarse men of the earth. They loved and fought and hated, suffered and died. But they were not dead. The white flame of life that surged through their agonised bodies tore something out of them, despite their screams and curses, and carried it on. They lived.

But the multitude of stupefied, tired, frightened human beings whom Mrs. Heather shepherded round the Castle at various times were scarcely aware of their own experience. They knew they had escaped somewhere, but they did not know what into. They knew they had possessed something but they didn't know what. And when it was all over they were aware of nothing except that for a little while they had been happy. They drove away still thinking that they were lonely, though the rustling of a multitude had been about them, inheritors of a kingdom who did not feel the pressure of the crown upon their brow. . . . Yet they remembered that they had been happy, and some of them forgot Mrs. Heather.

To-day there was one man who would not forget Mrs. Heather, a tall gaunt red-nosed man of Jewish appearance who strolled along a little apart from the others, his hands clasped behind him, his battered hat poised at an angle. So absorbed was he in Mrs. Heather herself, so aloof did he hold himself that he might observe her, that he failed to lose himself as completely as did the others. He stood on the bank, as it were, the stream rushing by him, and observed Mrs. Heather.

He had seen that particular look of happiness upon a face before, but not very often. Once seen, it was unforgettable. He had seen it upon the face of a monk in France, carrying the Host through a crowded street to the dying, of a great pianist surging through a concerto to that last resolving chord when the longing and striving of the dominant seventh and the rest and fulfilment of the tonic are forever reconciled, of a child absorbed in a game and a scientist risking death in his laboratory to fight disease. All of them, except the child, had had faces ravaged by conflict of some sort or another, but conflict past. To all of them something had happened, perhaps gradually, perhaps in one flashing moment, that had been as a dividing line between the conflict and the joy. It was as though they had been reconciled and had come home. Conversion, some called it. Others spoke of purgation, the dark night of the soul, illumination and the apprehension of reality, but they had never made themselves very comprehensible to Mr. Isaacson. There was no explaining the thing, of course. Even those to whom it happened could not explain it, for though they were convinced that they had seen something they had not seen clearly enough for clear words. They spoke the language of dreams that brought no conviction. If he were to ask the old woman what had happened to her she would tell him some simple childish sort of tale that would simply make him laugh. Immensely important to her, it would just sound silly to him. Whatever it was, before it happened self-enjoyment was at rock-bottom the guiding principle of life, afterwards, self-loss.

Wretched creatures that we are, thought Mr. Isaacson, fighting to enjoy ourselves in a world like this one, with all the time that new principle of life struggling for birth like a child in the womb; afterwards, it seems not to matter much what happens. He looked at Mrs. Heather again. To-day, at this hour, there seemed something almost callous about her peaceful happiness. We don't understand, we ordinary folk, thought Mr. Isaacson. It's as though the others were already citizens of another country whose language the rest of us do not speak.

Another country. He remembered that the tall young chap had mentioned it during that utterly crazy hour that they had spent in each other's company. "If in this life only we have hope—." Damn, thought Mr. Isaacson, suddenly disgusted with the thoughts that would keep pushing up nowadays through the habitual despair to which he was much attached because he was so accustomed to it. Damn those perpetually recurring words that he had seen chalked upon that dirty wall. They haunted him like a cheap catchy tune, underlining everything he saw and did. Nothing in it. Citizens of another country, these queer cards? No. Just mad. He looked again at Mrs. Heather, pulling back the curtain at the south window in the gallery that the trippers might gaze upon the face of Roger the Nabob while she told them how he had made the garden. Her sing-song voice, combined with that strange serenity, quite clearly proved the old dame more or less potty.

"And it was said of him that he never lifted his hand in hate against any man," chanted Mrs. Heather, her small wrinkled hand laid caressingly and with reverence upon Roger's gilt frame. "Not even in the Indian Mutiny. No, he never lifted his hand."

"I should say not," boomed Mr. Isaacson suddenly from the background. "Too busy lifting his elbow."

Mrs. Heather stopped in her story, halted by a phrase she did not know, her puzzlement a tiny shadow on her happiness.

"The old gent liked his bottle," explained someone near her, and someone else guffawed, for Mr. Isaacson's interruption had momentarily broken the spell in which Mrs. Heather had hitherto held them.

But with comprehension Mrs. Heather was herself again. "Maybe he did, sir," she called to Mr. Isaacson defensively, her head up. "Loneliness is a hard thing to bear and there's many a one takes a drop too much because of it." And her bright keen old eyes came to rest innocently upon Mr. Isaacson's nose.

He turned and went out. No, the old dame was certainly not

potty. A sharp old dame. Too sharp by half. So she thought that old chap in the picture had been lonely, did she? Quite possibly. It must have been an uncommonly lonely thing to be a pacifist in the heat of the Indian Mutiny. Nothing harder than fighting the common mind. Arresting eyes the old fellow in the picture had had; now he came to think of it that young fellow for whom he had come searching, a pacifist too, had had the same eyes.

He had come to-day because he wanted to see Stephen and Moppet and Poppet again, and he had lacked the courage to accept Stephen's invitation and come by himself on the bus and ask for them. But now, going softly down the great staircase, he did not know what to do next, for how in the world was he to find the children, or the young fellow? He had hoped just to run into them casually, but they were nowhere to be seen. He had not realised that with the proletariat trampling over their ancestral halls it was only to be expected that the family should clear out.

In the hall below him a quite extraordinarily disagreeable-looking butler was answering the telephone, and he stopped. He would wait till the fellow had finished and then ask him where he could find the children. But his heart beat uncomfortably as he stood waiting, for nowadays he was terrified of butlers, and he had to detain his evaporating courage with the pleasing thought that he was as good a fellow as the other. Better, in fact. He had been a gentleman once and that butler quite obviously had not. I tipped butlers in the old days, he thought, to keep up his courage. I handed them my hat and coat and tipped 'em. In old days I'd have tipped that little worm. But it was no good, his courage would not stay with him, and he would have fled back to the gallery and abandoned the search for the children had he not been arrested by what the butler was saying.

"Not back yet, sir?" said Boulder in a precise Cockney voice. "A reconnaissance flight. Failed to return. Thank-you, sir. No cause to worry yet. Thank-you, sir." He kept repeating the words in a dry heartless sort of way, over and over again, rather as though he were wound up and could not stop. Unfeeling brute, thought Mr. Isaacson, and rubbed his hands, suddenly grown moist in the palms, on his handkerchief. "Failed to return. Thank-you, sir," went on Boulder, and then with a great effort checked himself. "I think sir," he said in a different tone, high and forced, "that I'd better fetch Mr. Birley. Hold on, sir, if you please."

He put the receiver down and turned round, his face colourless and rigid almost with the rigidity of death, as though carved out of grey stone. Then he saw Mr. Isaacson and the furious blood suffused it, bringing life back again. He came to the foot of the stairs and glared up at this stranger.

"'Ere, you! What do you think you're doin'? Eavesdroppin' in a private 'ouse? Get out!" He paused, struggling with an anger that seemed tearing him to pieces. "Get out afore I wring your bloody neck!" he concluded.

"Steady on, old cock," said Mr. Isaacson. "Getting out is what I'm after, but with you blocking up the stairs it's none too easy." He spoke gently, aware that the man's anger was directed not against him but against a scheme of things in which it could fall out that planes failed to return. That anger had been his so often, that hideous futile anger at the whole damn mess that was the scheme of things; and upon which one's rage made about as much impression as though one had spat into the sea.

"It's no good swearing, mate," he said compassionately. "It's just no blinking use. . . . And that bloke on the 'phone's still holding on."

Boulder turned blindly from the foot of the stairs to the study door, paused, straightened himself, shot out his cuffs, opened the door and went in with the cat-like softness of the well-trained servant. Mr. Isaacson went with long strides across the hall and the terrace, down the steps, across the garden, under the archway and out into the woods. No use looking for the kids now, and in his present mood he had no taste for the company in the charabanc. He'd walk home.

v

But in the woods he paused. Passing quickly through them in the closed charabanc he had been only aware of a compassionate coolness, a lovely shimmer of healing green, but now the spirit of the great woods laid a hand upon him and whispered "Come this way." He obeyed, and turned off along a narrow path that led west, deeper and deeper into unfathomable peace. The soaring tree trunks were all about him, the pillars of a city beneath the sea whose green waves swayed so far above his head that he could hear no sound, only see the dim shadows of their rhythmic movement stirring about his feet. The small woodland sounds, the echoing song of a bird, the rustle of a little animal moving in the undergrowth, the crack of a twig beneath his feet, came to him so muted by the immensity of these green-vaulted aisles in

135

which they had their being that they were scarcely sounds at all; they were more like the pulse-beats of this living silence.

Liberation came suddenly to Mr. Isaacson as he passed through the woods, with the thought of their green peace the only conscious thought in his tormented mind, their beauty folded about his persecuted drink-sodden body. He stepped right out of the sordid years and was as he had been in the morning of his life. Young and strong, he strode on and on. And then, suddenly, he was ridiculously tired. He sat down on a fallen beech tree, his back against the trunk of another, and by chance he saw his own hands, knotted and veined and quite incredibly ugly with those broken nails of ill-health. He looked at them and smiled sardonically, his illusions slipping from him as his body enclosed him again and the years rolled back. Yet peace remained, and would while he stayed in this place. It struck him that these woods, with the whole of nature, were like those people he had been thinking of, those mad and happy people who had lost themselves, not momentarily, as he had just done, but with the permanent losing that is an eternal finding. Or not quite like, for these woods had never had themselves, with them there had been no sharp dividing line between self-seeking and self-loss, from the very beginning they had been utterly yielded to the purpose of their being; they had lost themselves in it as individual shapes and colours were lost in the depths of their green shade. Lost in it himself Mr. Isaacson smiled at the foolishness of man, who thought he had conquered nature yet in spiritual knowledge was outstripped by her utterly.

But Mr. Isaacson's thoughts did not swing back at this point, as they had done in the gallery, to their habitual bitterness, for within the compassion of the woods there was no place for it. Their green was so kind to the eyes, their coolness so gentle to a fevered body, that instead he fell asleep.

He woke up not with the usual start of fear, the usual shock of realisation that life and its anguish were with him again, but quietly and happily, as a child wakes, and found himself looking at the pitiful eyes and poignant mouth, the sweet wondering sorrowful face of compassion itself. And the face was completely familiar. He had seen it before. He had even run after it, he remembered, and through devious ways it had led him to this green peace. Then full consciousness returned to him and he saw a slim small woman in a green dress standing quite still in a patch of sunlight, gazing at him, the woman who had spoken to him outside the London library and knocked against him on the station platform. She was a pretty woman, prettier now in that summer frock, in this perfect setting, than she had been before. He jumped up and held out his hand to her, not so much in a gesture of politeness as a gesture of pleading. "Please," he said stupidly. "Please." He was asking her for something that he knew only she could give him. Some sort of rest. Some sort of abiding place. Something. He was not quite himself at the moment.

Miss Brown remembered him. She smiled and put her hand into his, and he held it so hard that she flinched, his hungry eyes devouring her face. She tried not to draw away, but she did not like it very much. She was so dreadfully sorry for him, but the smell of his old clothes nauseated her a little and she noticed, what she had not noticed before, that this was a man who drank. She was also a little frightened of the hunger in his eyes; for it was lonely in the woods. She could not quite check a slight recoil.

But he saw it and dropped her hand, stepping back, a queer shadow passing over his face as though he had dropped a blind in a pitiful effort at self-effacement. It was gone in a moment but in that moment she wondered how many times in his life he had looked like that, and knew it was many times. He was not indifferent yet to the things that were done to him; neither to the bad nor to the good. There must be greatness in him, a kingliness of feeling that would not at whatever cost let itself be blunted. A lesser man would have been utterly hardened years ago.

Quickly careless alike of her safety and her fastidiousness, conscious now only of this man's need of friendliness, she sat down on the tree trunk, smiling at him. He sat down too, but not too near this time, taking up as little space as possible, his knees tightly together and shrinking in upon himself. So since the days of adversity he had been accustomed to sit in buses and tubes all over Europe; for a down-and-out who was also a Jew had always been looked upon with repulsion in those conveyances. Unconsciously, because of Miss Brown's recoil, he adopted this attitude even in the compassionate spaciousness of the woods. Looking down at his hands laid on his knees, angered by their deformity that seemed to him like a dirty smudge upon the beauty of this place, he waited for her to speak.

"Only the utterly unexpected happens nowadays," said Miss Brown. "In little things as well as in big. I remember thinking to myself, that day when we met outside the Free Library, that I should never see you again."

"Did you want to see me again?" demanded Mr. Isaacson with a childlike eagerness that caused Miss Brown to tell a really staggering lie with an ease astonishing in one so unpractised.

"Yes," she said. "I felt that we might be friends."

Mr. Isaacson turned and looked at her curiously. No, she was neither coquettish nor bold, she was simply self-oblivious, like these woods. Her recoil, he decided happily, had not been from repulsion but from modesty. Modest! What a funny old forgotten word! But that was what she was, this prim pretty little spinster. He did not move any nearer to her, for he realised he must go carefully, but his whole attitude relaxed from the tight painful shrinking into a blessed ease. Miss Brown saw it and was glad. She remembered suddenly how she longed for Mr. Birley and Stephen to tell her personal things about themselves, so that she should not feel so lonely, and how they didn't do it. Vigorously repressing a desire not to do it either she began to tell Mr. Isaacson how it was that in this time of storm and chaos she came to be sitting here with him in the silence of the woods. She told her story very badly, because it was somehow difficult to tell it to him, though it had been so easy to tell it to Mr. Birley. Everything that she gave to Mr. Birley, knowledge of herself, service, admiration and gratitude, she gave with ease and eagerness; increasing eagerness as the days went by. She was astonished, and even a little frightened, by that ease, there was something inevitable and menacing about it, as though it were the first tentative movement of a landslide that might be rather terrible for her.

But Mr. Isaacson was unaware of her difficulty and inexpressibly touched by her confidence. In return he gave her a diluted version of his own history, with all that was hideous in it most carefully omitted. There were things that had been done to him, things that he had seen, obscene things worse than the worst horror of pain, of which he would never tell her, however intimate their relationship might one day become. It was to keep the likes of Miss Brown even from the knowledge of those things that men were dying to-day with gladness.

Yet Miss Brown was aware of the gaps in his little narration, abysmal gaps full of darkness. Her own ignorance was so equally abysmal that she could only say simply, "I am sorry," and then, "Isn't it odd how strangers talk to each other nowadays? English people used to live each in his own box with the lid on, and now we talk to strangers in railway carriages as though we'd known them all our lives."

"To our great advantage, surely," said Mr. Isaacson.

"Oh yes," said Miss Brown eagerly, thinking of Mr. Birley. "Oh yes. Oh yes."

Mr. Isaacson thought she was thinking of him, and drew a little nearer.

"It's because we're all shut up in England now like beleagured people in a castle on a hill," said Miss Brown. "Outside is that great evil army battering to get in; and it does not do to think of it too much. It does not do to think of to-morrow either. It is right that we should all be friendly, for we have only to-day, each other and our pride."

"And to-day," said Mr. Isaacson with sudden astonishment, "to-day, sitting here with you in the woods, is good."

They were silent, and the shadows swayed about their feet, and far over their heads the waves of that inland sea were as the waters of forgetfulness.

But nowadays one did not forget for long. Suddenly Mr. Isaacson remembered something, and the woods darkened. "I'm sorry about that young chap, whoever he is, being missing," he said.

"Missing?" asked Miss Brown sharply.

He told her about the telephone call, and without a word she jumped up and ran away from him through the woods. He got up too and strode after her, crying to her to stop. He strode on and on, but she had simply disappeared, down some path to the Castle that he did not know of, disappeared as completely as though she had not been a human woman at all but just some green wraith conjured up by the magic of the woods. Useless to look for her; her heart was in the Castle where he could not follow her, not with him. He strode on without a pause, trampling down the undergrowth like a wild beast in his angry pain. She had not said goodbye. She had not told him how or where they could meet again. After their conversation she'd had no right to treat him in that way. Had she been simply playing with him? No, not that, but she had pitied him, as she had pitied him outside the Free Library, and pity was a damned insult. He'd not come near the place again, no, not even to see Moppet and Poppet. What was the good of it? Down and out. There were few phrases more accurately descriptive. Down in the ditch, outside the wall, where the defeated are. And this wall was a castle wall too high to be scaled, and the ditch had slimy sides that gave a man no foothold. When they had nothing better to do they could be kind, those people who were not yet defeated, but one could have no real companionship with them. Once you were out of their world you could not get back. She had held out a hand to him, that woman, and then in the act of helping him up had pushed him back. It had not been liking, only pity.

He tramped out of the woods and up the lane to the main road, then on and on, mile after mile, back to Torhaven. It struck him that his race was always walking, always going on somewhere else and never wanted when it got there.

VI

Miss Brown, Mr. Isaacson utterly forgotten, ran back to the Castle. Richard, whom she scarcely knew, meant little to her, but the anxiety of Stephen and Mr. Birley meant her whole world. Miss Brown was not a woman who gave much attention to her own emotional and mental states, or it might have struck her as odd that after such a very short time they *should* be her whole world. Nothing struck her at present except the necessity of getting to them as soon as possible.

In the garden she found Stephen furiously struggling with a patch of docks under the Castle wall. He seldom gardened, for though he loved gardens he was one of those who prefer other people to do the work. He hated dirty hands, and bending his slim height double made him ache in the middle. When he heard Miss Brown's quick footsteps he straightened himself and smiled at her.

"Docks are like besetting sins," he said. "You can never really get them out."

For a moment she wondered if he knew; then she realised that the exhaustion of his look was not entirely due to the docks. Her heart ached for him, as for her son. "Oh Stephen, I am so sorry," she cried. "I am so terrible sorry."

His face hardened. "Thank you very much," he said stiffly. "But it's only missing, you know. Just overdue on a recon-naissance flight. They turn up again. Did you have a nice walk, Miss Brown?"

"Very nice, thank-you," she said, repressed, and went swiftly across the garden and up the steps to the house, but before she had time to turn the handle of Mr. Birley's study door Stephen had followed her.

"Miss Brown, please don't."

She dropped her hand instantly.

"Let him alone, Miss Brown. He's that sort."

"Certainly," said Miss Brown. "Of course. It was very presumptuous of me." And she smiled at him and went quietly away up the stairs. But her smile had not hidden her hurt and she moved as though her limbs were intolerably heavy.

"Oh God, how we have to hurt each other," groaned Stephen, as he went back to the docks. "We're jostled so close together these days, we're so sharpened and so vulnerable, and we hurt each other." Then his anxiety for Richard swept over him again and he forgot Miss Brown as completely as she had forgotten Mr. Isaacson.

As she went along the passage to her room she passed Richard's. The door was open and Boulder was inside, polishing the furniture with the same fury with which Stephen had been attacking the docks. Poor Boulder, she thought. Can there be anything more hideous than to be old and have the young die for you?

She gained her room with a gasp of relief, locked the door and made for the bed. Women are said to be inordinately fussy about their beds; they are laughed at because they are perpetually rearranging them, embroidering fresh counterpanes and curtains for them, studying bed fashions just as they study dress fashions. Yet heaven knows her bed is as important to a woman as her body. It holds her in its arms through all her troubles, and of the weeping of a proud woman it is the only witness. No wonder that in the strictest of convents the nuns move to a fresh cell every day lest they grow too fond of their bed.

But Miss Brown was not of those who fling themselves upon their beds like a child into its mother's arms, and bellow into the pillow, for even when she was quite alone self-restraint was a thing that she never let go of; she knelt down rather primly beside it, leaned her arms upon it, as though upon her mother's lap, her face hidden, and gulped down her bitter draught. Until she had done that she could not turn to action like Stephen and Boulder.

It is a bitter draught that you love more than you are loved and there are few whose pride lets them face it. But it was Miss Brown's habit to face everything, to get things clear, as she called it. She got everything clear before she'd done. I'm not a self-sufficient woman, she said to herself. I can't get along unless I can be indispensable to someone. That's not unselfish, really it's selfish. It's a love of being important. Mother and Father found me indispensable, and I loved them and was happy. And then I made "Sea View" into a person, and was indispensable to it and was happy. And then no one wanted me, I fell out of the scheme of things, I was quite unimportant, and so I was miserable and terrified. Then Mr. Birley picked me up and put me back and made me important, and so now I love him with my whole heart. And I love Stephen too. They have come into my life like husband and son. But naturally they don't love me. I'm only their housekeeper. And so I'm suffering. I'm suffering the pains of hell, and I deserve to, because of my abominable selfishness. We're all selfish. Bone selfish. We all revolve round and round ourselves. . . . Except just a very few who have learned how to break free of that dreadful circle and go free, and they are the ones who are happy.

Then, as she realised and for the first time faced the nature of her love for Mr. Birley, shame seized her and a maidenly blush swept in a crimson flood from her forehead to her neck and right down under her neat green linen frock. For really, it was simply disgraceful. She did not just love him, she was in love with him, at her age, with a man in an entirely different stratum of society, her employer, and quite an old man. It's not decent, whispered Miss Brown, it's simply not decent. And why should I do it now? I've never been in love before, not even with Mr. Jobson of the gents' underwear department who looked like the Duke of Wellington and was so in love with me. Why now? You'd have thought I'd have been safe at my age. I suppose a woman is never safe, least of all in war-time when one's emotions are on fire. And then those two and this place stand to me now for what I've always loved, the great men in the history books, all that is gallant and beautiful. Those things used to seem at a distance from me, now they have come right into my life, and so of course I have to love them. What shall I do about it? Had I better give notice? Oh God, please be so kind as to tell me what I ought to do.

But there was no direct reply, nothing but a recrudescence of that awful creeping fear of being cast out of the pattern of things again. Perhaps it's a right fear, thought Miss Brown. It's right to want to be in the pattern, even though most of us want to be in it for the wrong reason. So I'll stay. Unless they turn me out. I'll see things out with them here until the end. I love them, but it would embarrass them horribly to know it, so they shan't know it. It will be good discipline to hide my love. Nothing is better discipline than letting no one know what you are feeling. And why should I be ashamed of love? I won't be ashamed of it. Requited love gets as much as it gives, but unrequited love gets nothing for itself and so it must be the best sort of love that there is. Perhaps it will teach me how to break away from that circle of myself.

Miss Brown got up, tidied her hair, and sat down to the darning.

CHAPTER IX

I

PRUNELLA, that night, had her usual nightmare, in which Richard was in danger and she was running to warn him of it against a great wind that advanced against her like a wall of darkness, and finally brought her to a standstill, beating against it and crying out, spent and agonised. But to-night the dream did not end in the usual way. Usually the thing that was up against her suddenly gave way before her furious onslaught, and she fell down and down into some horrible dark abyss whose bottom she never reached because just as she was getting there she woke up, drenched with sweat, sobbing and frightened. But to-night, after the dark wind had solidified against her, it seemed to become a sort of door. She did not beat against it to-night, for she knew that she could not pass through. She leaned against it, arms outstretched like one crucified, and listened intently and with desperation, as though her life depended upon overhearing something from the other side. And she did hear something. Very distantly she heard the sound of trumpets.

And then, quietly and gently, she woke up, and the first light of dawn filled her little room and very faint and far away she could still hear the trumpets. She jumped out of bed, flung on her dressing-gown, ran to the window and leaned out. Dr. Maxwell's old grey stone house stood on the hill just above the village of Applegarth, looking out over the roofs of the village, over the woods and pasture-lands to the sea. She caught her breath at what she saw. She had been born and brought up in this land of beauty, yet its perpetual changing loveliness would go on surprising her until she died. There had been a drenching thunderstorm the evening before and as a result of it the valleys below her were filled with mist lying flat and level like a milk-white inland sea. Roofs rose out of it, conical hilltops and the tufted tops of trees, as in some Japanese picture. Just below her it melted into nothingness against the hillside and far away on the horizon ended in silver spray against the line of gleaming gold that was the real sea.

And rising above it was a gorgeous mass of cloud, purple and crimson and rose-pink, with towers and battlements of pure gold, like a great city in the sky. It was still very early, the air cold and rarefied after the storm, and one great planet was burning above the cloud city like a lamp upon the tallest tower . . . Civitas Dei. The City of Peace. . . . Far down in the depths of that strange milky mist the cocks were crowing, and further away the trumpets answered, as though from the battlements of that strange city in the sky. What was it? In this exquisite unearthly dawn it was difficult to think in terms of this world. She could not think. She could only kneel at her open window, her arms laid along the sill, her curly head resting on them, and look and be glad. Did not people sometimes think of the natural world as the garment of God? Once, she remembered, there had been a woman who had touched that garment and been healed. She felt healed at this moment, healed of all her fears. . . . If only she had had a little boat, and she and Richard could have stepped into it and sailed away over that milky sea to the city of peace where there'd be no more war.

And then, most strangely, the bells began to ring. There was a glorious peal of bells at Applegarth Church, very old bells that years ago had been baptized by the bishop with holy water and annointed with oil and salt and cream in the name of the Trinity, and that for centuries had rung out over these hills and valleys to the glory of God. They were silent now, for the first time in all their long life, and so were the other bells of England in the churches and the great cathedrals, resting with bent heads and silent silver tongues. When they lifted their heads and spoke again it would not be to call men to the worship of God but to ring out the tocsin of danger over all the land.

But the Applegarth bells were ringing now, and other bells from other little villages hidden in the folds of the hills were answering. Belfry after belfry was taking up the tale and flinging it inland, and towards the sea, where a big military camp was hidden beneath the mist, the trumpets were calling sleeping men to arms.

Prunella jumped to her feet just as her grandfather's knock came at the door. "Get up, Pru," he called. "Get up and dress."

She ran and opened the door. Grandpa, tall and robust and hearty, looking bulkier than usual in his voluminous dressing-gown, his hands in his pockets, was swaying from foot to foot, as he always did when he was interested or excited. His bright blue eyes sparkled under his bushy grey eyebrows and his grey beard jutted truculently. He was enjoying himself.

"It appears there's some idea of invasion, Pru," he announced.

"Really and truly or just a scare?" gasped Prunella.

"It strikes me as being a lot too picturesque to be true," said Grandpa. "A great deal too picturesque. But there's always hope." And crossing to Prunella's window he looked out over the milk-white mist, straining his eyes to see the Rider on the Red Horse, riding up out of the tranquil sea. But there was nothing. Only the steadfast blazing planet still hung like a lamp over the city in the sky.

"Do you *want* to be invaded, Grandpa?" marvelled Prunella.

"I want to beat 'em back," growled the old man.

"And what do we do now?" asked Prunella. She liked to behave properly, and invasions were as yet outside her experience.

"We behave exactly as usual," Grandpa instructed her. "You go to early church—if you were going to early church—and I slaughter slugs in the garden till you come back. Then we devour eggs and toast and tea. Then we shall see what we shall see. Either we shall say, 'Now, God be thanked who has matched me with His hour,' or else we shall say, 'All my eye and Betty Martin.' In any case I think we should get dressed now."

When they had got dressed it was still much too early for church, and they sat together on the seat outside the front-door, facing east to the glory of the sun that had now drunk up the mist and restored the world to the normal loveliness of high summer.

Prunella looked about her with a queer wondering intensity, telling herself that she might be looking at all this for the last time, yet somehow quite unable to believe it. Her intensity was echoed in the world about her. The sky was now a dazzling blue, the flowers in the little old garden a riot of colour and perfume, tossed and luxuriant and burning-bright. The bees were humming and the birds were singing and the pulse of the world seemed beating high with passion and pride. Whether they were invaded or not this day that had begun with trumpets in the dawn was going to be great day, Prunella knew. Richard had written that there was a chance that he might come home this week-end. Perhaps he had come yesterday and she would see him to-day. Her eyes were bright with anticipation. This would surely be a great day. When its burning hours had passed away she would not be quite the same Prunella.

She was not the same Prunella now that she had been some months ago, thought her grandfather, observing her very acutely, though apparently immersed in meditation and his pipe. She was living too intensely, the lovely thread of her being stretched too tightly on the trembling framework of this chaotic age. Yet the heightened living gave to her variable beauty a great loveliness at times: as now, sitting beside him with the soft silk folds of her buttercup-yellow Sunday frock lending grace to her tense, slim, boyish figure, her curly gold head almost aflame in the sun, her sweet sensitive lips parted in excitement, her green eyes bright and her cheeks flushed with expectation. The hollows at her temples and the shadows beneath her eyes were not so noticeable when she was ablaze like this. What was she expecting to-day, beyond the possibility of death? All the other things that live so certainly within its shadow? Love, ecstasy, illumination? He wished he knew. He wished it was her habit to confide in him.

It never had been, even though they loved each other deeply and generously. Since the death of her parents eight years ago little Prunella had burned in the centre of his life like a flame upon the hearth, and with a selflessness that amazed him. She knew that she was all he had and with a quiet matter-of-factness she had set to work to make that all worth having. When she had left school she had insisted upon coming home to live with him, "for keeps" as she said, though surely she must have wanted a career of her own like other girls. But if she had she had never shown it. She had seemed utterly contented with keeping his house in applepie order, mending his clothes, looking after her pack of Brownies in the village, riding her fat old Maria through the lanes and over the green hills. Even in these war days she would not leave him to do anything spectacular. She wound bandages, minded dirty children, knitted socks, collected the village war-savings and waste paper, and did all the other dull deeds that are not performed to the sound of trumpets, just so as not to leave him.

Maria was practically the only pleasure that she had, for they were not well off. Dr. Maxwell had always been too truthful a man to be a successful doctor. Only a really astonishing ability could have counteracted the effect upon his practice of his habit of telling people they were fools when they were fools, that they ate too much when they did eat too much, that there wasn't a thing the matter with them when there wasn't, and though his ability was adequate it was not outstanding. His practice had dwindled now to the Castle, that had a feudal feeling for him and so would never desert him, and to those poor of the neighbourhood who couldn't afford to call him in unless they were really very ill, and who experienced then nothing but his skill and a bluff hearty sympathy that was the kind they understood.

And so Prunella had had to plan and contrive to buy the materials from which she made her frocks, and had worked hard and played little, and had not grumbled. When at the age of twelve she had solemnly taken on Grandpa as her life's work she had made up her mind that she would not grumble. But this non-grumbling had bred in her a habit of reticence that he deplored most grievously now. For she never told him anything. With his quick, trained doctor's observation he had observed her recent unfolding and awakening with accurate ease and great anxiety, but because she did not confide in him he felt himself powerless to help her. He had always been afraid to force the locked door of her delicate reticence, blundering male that he was, lest he do more harm than good by his violence. But he knew that she was too ignorant, too generous, too vulnerable. She lacked the worldly wisdom that he might have given her, the self-restraint and the touch of hardness that might have kept her from too much bruising in the tempestuous world she had inherited. He had been too cowardly, too lazily indifferent to the passing of time that had made her a woman before he realised it. He was to blame, and he knew it. He wished he could be the only one to suffer.

He remembered vividly the wave of relief that had swept over him when he had first realised that Stephen loved Prunella. His cowardice and laziness were not going to be visited on his or Prunella's heads after all. They were going to be let off. She had got the right man. She was safe. Stephen's sensitive gentleness would be unerring in the ways of love, and she would suffer no bruising at his hands. And in worldly ways she would be safe too, he had thought, for he was one of the few who were aware of the toughness of fibre in Stephen. For Stephen, the old doctor realised, was like one of those slender trees that are bent but never broken by the storm. And he was not the dilettante that he sometimes seemed. Whatever he did he would do well, and neither in thought nor in action would he ever turn back. He might change his opinions, as those who are sufficiently courageous to face ridicule frequently do, but not until the final bitter end of having them proved false by experience, never for reasons of expediency or ease. His integrity would give him the best sort of success in life, the success of trustworthiness and dependability. Prunella's life, linked to his, would be grounded on a rock.

But the old doctor had reckoned without Prunella herself. He had kept Prunella a child too long, and Stephen's gentleness had not been able to break through her immaturity to the woman in her. It had taken Richard's force and vitality to set her so dangerously ablaze as she was now, and the tempestuous variable Richard was not the man he wanted for Prunella. It is one of the tragedies of a woman's experience, thought the old doctor, that the best men are sometimes unexciting lovers, and often the exponents of unpopular creeds.

"Stephen still a pacifist?" he asked suddenly.

"I think so," said Prunella. "How *can* he be, Grandpa? How *can* he?"

"We need them," pronounced Grandpa. "We need their witness to the fact that war is bestial, wicked, degrading, futile. It may seem to most of us that when there is no way left of confronting evil except with the sword, then it is better to draw the sword than to allow free passage to the evil. But it is necessary to remember that our way is the lesser of two evils, not good. The pacifists help us there. They are men in advance of their time, men prophesying of a state of affairs that has not come to pass yet, crusaders, the voice crying in the wilderness."

"What a lecture, Grandpa," laughed Prunella. "And I thought you were asleep."

Asleep, thought the old man? And here have I been worrying over the child till every fibre in me is awake to the point of agony.

"Time you started for church," he said a little irritably. "And for the love of heaven wear a hat, and wipe that red stuff off your lips."

"But I always wear a hat for church, Grandpa," said Prunella patiently, fishing out a little blob of something yellow from the fuchsia bush beside her, and poising it upon the side of her head. "And I haven't done my lips this morning. I never do when I'm going to early service." And she bent over and kissed him, darted through the garden like a yellow butterfly and was gone.

What a child, groaned her grandfather. In spite of everything, what a hopeless child still.

11

Now, why *don't* I do my lips when I'm going to early service? wondered Prunella as she walked down the lane. I get them as bright as I can when going to matins. How very odd of me.

Her own oddness was constantly in Prunella's mind these days. She was for ever questioning her own conduct in a way that she had never done before. She supposed it was because humanity itself was, to put it mildly, behaving so very oddly just at present, and feeling oneself a part of it one scrutinised one's own behaviour in a way that one had not done before, saying where am I wrong, where are *we* wrong, that we've come to this?

Wrestling with the present problem she decided that she went to matins just because she always had, and because she liked to look at people's hats, and gossip with them in the churchyard afterwards, and for these social affairs one always did one's lips. But she went to early service for quite a different reason. She could not explain very well for what reason, for the doctor was no churchman and her religious upbringing had been very sketchy, but she expressed it to herself by saying that she went because it was so quiet; quiet with the sort of quiet that came to one in one's mother's arms; if one had a mother. There was a sort of oneness there. For such an occasion one did not dress up. . . . Was that what was the matter with oneself and everybody else, a lack of oneness?

And what funny trivial things one does think of, thought Prunella. Fancy thinking of one's lips when there's an invasion perhaps on the way, and when Richard may be coming home. In great moments one should have sublime thoughts. It is a pity that one doesn't.

But it was hard to believe in invasion in this small, deep lane running downhill to the church. There was a riot of summer flowers in it, brilliant with the sun shining on their wet petals, marjoram and valerian, irises, wild yellow snapdragons and meadowsweet, and the butterflies were flitting joyously over them. These deep sheltered west-country lanes were always a treasure-house of flowers. In winter, after the November gales, it was strange and beautiful to see the trees leafless, but the sheltered lanes below them still bright with periwinkles and pink campion. To many people now war meant a sort of imprisonment. They could not go about and see their friends as they used to do. But our prison here, thought Prunella, where it's so old and beautiful, is like the prison King Lear dreamed of but never had; we can laugh at gilded butterflies and tell old tales.

She was very nearly late, as usual, and ran like a child down the last of the lane and through the churchyard, and made a terrible noise, also as usual, in opening the heavy old door. The handful of old ladies and the two old men who were kneeling in their pews looked round in annoyance, as they always did, at the row she made. Their hearts were unsoftened by the radiant vision with the gold curls, in the yellow dress, burning like a flame in the dim old church. For they disapproved of Prunella. She would have been astonished, perpetually teased by Richard as she was for being so prudent a village maiden, to know that they thought her a Minx. It did not surprise them that now, instead of sitting decorously in some obscure seat suited to her tender years and complete unimportance, she went straight to the Castle pew, where Stephen was kneeling, and knelt down beside him. Nodding their heads with a sort of gloomy satisfaction, because she was running true to form, they bent again to their devotions.

Prunella never enjoyed sitting in the Castle pew because it looked straight into the Birley Chapel and it depressed her quite dreadfully to look at all those tablets to the dead men round the walls; and many of them men who had died young. But none of the tablets was quite so depressing as an empty space on the north wall that was shaped just right for a tablet but had not got one yet. Nowadays that empty space not only depressed but frightened her. Whenever she looked at it she said firmly to herself, "That's where Mr. Birley's tablet will go when he is dead. Poor, dear old Mr. Birley. It will be nice for him to get rid of his rheumatism."

But she had to go to the Castle pew to-day because she thought Stephen looked lonely all by himself in it. She was very fond of Stephen, even though she had been quite mistaken once in thinking that she was in love with him, and she did not like him to be lonely. She knelt down as close to him as she could get, a fact not unnoted by the old ladies, who left a certain amount of space between the gloved fingers that covered their faces as they prayed, and tilted her adorable little face to smile at him.

But when Stephen lifted his face from his hands to smile back at her, her own smile faded. For he looked so odd. As though he had not slept all night. As though something had happened. And he immediately went back again behind that impenetrable barrier of his hands, as though he did not want her to look at him.

She tugged at his coat. "Stephen! Stephen! What is it?" she whispered.

Stephen dropped his hands again. "What is what?" he asked with deliberate stupidity. He was not going to tell her that Richard was still missing. If he could spare her even a couple of hours of misery, before some busybody told her what had happened, that would be something. Even a couple of hours salvaged from sorrow, a couple more hours to see the brilliance of the flowers and the dancing butterflies before grief closed down on you and the world went dark, was a great thing upon the credit side of life. Two hours was quite a long time. But his vagueness did not deceive Prunella.

"Did Richard come home yesterday?" she whispered.

"No," said Stephen.

"But he's all right?"

"Of course he's all right. Don't be a goose, Prunella."

"Then why are you looking like that?"

"Didn't you hear the planes in the night? And the bells?"

Prunella, reassured, smiled at him tolerantly. Silly old Stephen always crossed all his bridges long before he got there. "Duffer," she said. "It hasn't happened yet."

But by this time Miss Black, who sat only a couple of pews behind them, could stand their outrageous behaviour no longer. She leaned right over and prodded Prunella with the handle of her parasol. "Prunella, my *dear*," she said in pain, "the Vicar has come in."

The Vicar of Applegarth stood before the altar of his church in his clean Sunday surplice, just as he had stood for the last thirty years, and as his predecessors had stood for centuries before him, and his fine old voice echoed through the quietness just as it always did. "Almighty God, with whom all hearts be open, all desires known, and from whom no secrets are hid; cleanse the thoughts of our hearts. . . ."

Prunella's curly head dropped on her arms and she was quieted. Now she was feeling as she always did, as she imagined one felt when one lay in the arms of a mother who knew everything.

The Vicar made no change in the service, except that he used the prayer of Queen Elizabeth before the Armada, omitting only a word here and there to bring it completely up-to-date.

"We do earnestly beseech Thee of Thy gracious goodness to be merciful to us, at this time compassed about with most strong and subtle adversaries. Let Thine enemies know that Thou hast received England into Thine own protection. Set a wall about it, O Lord, and evermore mightily defend it. Let it be a comfort to the afflicted, a help to the oppressed, and a defence to Thy Church and people persecuted abroad. And, forasmuch as this cause is now in hand, direct and go before our armies both by sea and land. Bless them and prosper them, and grant unto them honourable success and victory. Thou art our help and shield. Give good and prosperous success to all those that fight this battle against the enemies of Thy Gospel. Amen."

In spite of his anxiety for Richard, a thrill of pride went through Stephen. That old man before the altar, the old ladies behind him and little Prunella, had come to church exactly as usual, and the old ladies had disapproved of Prunella just as usual, as though they had not heard those bells and trumpets in the dawn. If they felt any fear they gave no sign of it. A good breed, after all.

III

The service ended and they filed out into the churchyard and stood listening, the Vicar with them, but there was no sound except the familiar country sounds of cows lowing and dogs barking and birds singing in the trees.

"A false alarm?" asked Stephen. "If so somebody will get into trouble for starting those bells off."

"Perhaps they started and were turned back," said the old Vicar. "The R.A.F. is nowadays that wall for which Queen Elizabeth prayed."

This was an unfortunate remark, for it caused Miss Black, an old lady as renowned for her lack of tact as for her ability to know all the things about everybody that they would prefer her not to know, to say to Stephen, "Oh, Stephen, I am so sorry to hear that Richard is missing. Fanny Treguthwic told me. So dreadful for you. Such an anxiety for your poor uncle. I *am* so sorry."

"Thank you very much," said Stephen stiffly but courteously, as he had said to Miss Brown, and he gripped Prunella's hand.

"Miss Black, I want your opinion about my dahlias," said the old Vicar suddenly, and Stephen and Prunella escaped through the churchyard and into the lane so quickly that he hoped no one saw her face. Well, he had only saved one hour of happiness for her, not two, and now she did not see the brilliant flowers and the dancing butterflies. He looked at her and saw how small and pinched her face had become beneath the riot of golden curls. A face like that was not in keeping beneath curls like that, he thought with a sort of savage irrelevance.

"One does not get the wind up just because a pilot is a few hours late," he said matter-of-factly. "Especially when the pilot is Richard. He's like a cat, that always comes down on its feet. He's always been like that."

"I'm not getting the wind up," said Prunella flatly, and pulled her hand away. She wished he would go on ahead and leave her. She didn't want him. The immediate problem was to find some way of getting through the hours until she knew if Richard were alive or dead, and it would surely be easier to find out by oneself. She stumbled on the stony path, for it was difficult now to do any of the ordinary things, like walking or breathing, that were part of living. For Richard was her life, and how could one live without one's life? But this sort of anxiety would be recurring, it would be going on all through the war, and one must find out how to deal with it. One must turn into a sort of machine, she supposed. One must concentrate on the wheels going round. So she was careful where she put her feet, and at the garden gate she said politely and childishly to Stephen, "Thank you very much for seeing me home."

"I may not see you again, Prunella," said Stephen. "I'm going up to London to-morrow. There'll be lots of work there presently, digging people out of ruined buildings and so on after raids. That's not fighting. And seeing war at first hand will help me to make up my mind about things before the time comes to face my tribunal. Good-bye, Prunella."

"Good-bye," said Prunella, but he doubted if she had heard what he said. He smiled at her and went away, even his body seeming to ache with the dual pain of Richard's danger and Prunella's indifference. It would be good to be in London. In London, presently, there would be no time to think, scarcely time even to feel.

Prunella went indoors and put the kettle on. The machine idea was a great help. As she got breakfast in the loneliness that she had craved, she found that it was the solution, and she bent her whole will to the task of not thinking of Richard, for machines don't think. She concentrated instead on how long the eggs had been boiling, and if the toast was done yet. At breakfast she said to her grandfather, "Richard is missing, Grandpa, but Stephen says it would be very silly to get the wind up just yet," and took the top off her egg.

Her grandfather, while agreeing most heartily with Stephen and telling her tales of all the reappearances of lost pilots of which they were perpetually hearing, watched her anxiously as she worked her way doggedly through her egg and two pieces of toast and two cups of tea. She was far too young to have to face up to this sort of thing, far too young. Yet it pleased him that she was going the right way about it, sticking to her job instead of shutting herself up in her bedroom.

"After you've made the beds we'll weed the garden, Pru," he told her. "It's a disgraceful sight."

The rain in the night had loosened the weeds and they came up easily. Hope flamed stronger in Prunella as she worked, with the raindrops falling on her hands, the sun on her back and the happy living things growing all about her. She always felt the weight of things lightened when she gardened, for life was all about one then, not death, and one was comforted like the Ancient Mariner when he saw the beautiful little fishes.

> O happy living things! no tongue
>   Their beauty might declare:
> A spring of love gushed from my heart,
>   And I blessed them unaware.
> The self-same moment I could pray;
>   And from my neck so free
> The Albatross fell off, and sank
>   Like lead into the sea.

After lunch their daily maid came to wash up and Prunella looked at Grandpa with despair, for what in the world could she do now?

"The surgery is in a great mess," said Grandpa. "I should like a little help in dealing with it."

He meant well, but tidying the impedimenta that was necessary for dealing with human pain always depressed Prunella at the best of times, and to-day it was like a nightmare. Instruments, bandages, anæsthetics, sterilisers; they reminded her all the time of all the appalling things that can happen to a human body in an accident. Her imagination began to slip out of her control and run riot. She fought desperately to keep a hold of it, for if she didn't she was very much afraid that she might begin to scream.

And then the telephone bell rang in the hall. "I'll answer it," said Grandpa. "It'll be Mrs. Anstruther's sixth."

He went out of the room and shut the door. Prunella went on polishing instruments, very slowly, while the sweat trickled down the back of her neck and her body turned ice-cold all over. At first she could not hear what Grandpa was saying, though she strained till it seemed her body must break with her straining, then suddenly he raised his voice very loudly indeed, as though he wanted her to hear. "Splendid!" he ejaculated. "Grand! Hold on a minute."

Prunella laid down the things she was holding and gripped her thin hands between her knees. Of course it might just mean that Mrs. Anstruther was now fully embarked upon her sixth, for Grandpa liked people to have babies.

But when he came in it was with a broader smile than was usually reserved for the Anstruther young. "Go and talk to Richard," he said, and with a precipitancy that was more like a bird in flight than a girl running, Prunella went.

But as soon as she had gone the old doctor's smile vanished. Hands in pockets he stared gloomily out of the window. "A reprieve," he said aloud, and then growled like an angry old lion and sat down to do accounts.

I V

Prunella held the mouthpiece of the telephone in one hand and held herself braced against the wall with the other, for her body was so light now, like a balloon full of air, that she would have floated right up through the ceiling if she hadn't held on. "Richard!" she gasped, but only a sort of squeak came out of her, and she had to try again. "Richard! Richard!"

"Hullo," said Richard's sleepy voice, and then, in surprise, "Why, you aren't upset, are you?"

Sudden irritation restored Prunella's strength and sanity. "Of course I'm upset! We're all upset! Didn't you expect us to be upset?"

"I've told everybody over and over again," said Richard patiently, "that you don't start getting upset till a man's been missing for a month. That's the regulation time for not getting upset. I've only been missing two days, you silly idiots."

A month, thought Prunella. Another hour and I'd have been clean out of my mind. Then she suddenly remembered the horrible instruments and anæsthetics in the surgery. "Are you all right, Richard?" she gasped.

"Of course I'm all right," said Richard. "Aren't I always all right? But there's been a lot going on these last few days, one way and another, and I had a hot time, and got hit, and crashed in the sea, and bobbed about like one of those bloated rubber things kids have in the bath, till a minesweeper picked me up. All very stupid and wetting but quite harmless in this weather. . . . That's all."

His voice fell suddenly into a flat depth of weariness that somehow frightened Prunella. A lot more must have happened

155

than he had said to make him as tired as that. "Where are you?" she asked sharply.

"Out on the moor, at the Forest Ride."

This was a little fishing inn some sixteen miles away, much beloved by Richard and Stephen. But why go there? Why not come home?

"Why?" she demanded.

"I don't quite know," said Richard slowly, and his voice was caught up by a huge yawn, as though he were overpoweringly sleepy. "Yes I do, though. I started off by train yesterday, not being able to drive because of having my licence suspended, and it took ages, raids all the way, and at the place where I spent the night we got no sleep with Jerry and his cursed bombs. I just felt fed up and thought I'd come here and get a good night's rest before I faced the family. You know what it'll be; Uncle Charles thanking God, Stephen with a strong silent grip, Boulder's head shooting in and out of his collar like a tortoise's; families are a great strain on one in war-time." He yawned again. "I rang Stephen up and explained, and he thought you'd like me to ring you up myself, and I did, and I'll be over in the morning. Goodbye, Prunella. Darling little Prunella!"

There was a sudden deep thrill of tenderness in his voice that took the sting away from the fact that he might not have thought of ringing her up if Stephen had not told him to. She tried to answer it, but the words would not come, and then she found that he had hung up and gone away, and she was left leaning against the wall and could not get to him. Pushing herself away from the wall she ran down the passage to the little drawing-room that they seldom used, with the faded old chintzes and the framed water-colours, knelt down with her head on the sofa and cried with joy and pride and thankfulness, and misery because he was sixteen miles away and she could not get to him. She cried a great deal, and it was frightening because she could not stop. In the middle of it all the telephone bell rang again and then Grandpa's head came round the door. "This time," he said lugubriously, "it *is* Mrs. Anstruther's sixth."

Prunella raised her ravaged little face from her arms. "Well, go on, Grandpa," she sobbed breathlessly. "Go and deliver it. I'm all right."

He looked at her, went away, and came back with a glass of something hot and fiery. When she had obediently choked it down he sat on the sofa and pulled her curly head against his knee. "I'm not so sure you're all right," he said worriedly. "I don't like leaving you, Pru. That dratted infant! I may be hours."

Prunella choked down her sobs and rubbed her head against his knee. He had been very sweet to her, she thought, extraordinarily sweet considering that he could have no idea that she loved Richard. "I'm only upset because I'm so glad the Birleys need not be anxious any more. I'll go to bed early and I shan't even hear you come in. Go on, Grandpa. I expect Mrs. Anstruther is making a lot of fuss."

"I don't doubt it," said Grandpa grimly. "I never knew a woman who made more fuss over the normal processes of nature." But he got up and moved slowly across the room, and at the door he looked back at the little crumpled yellow figure on the floor. She had been so splendidly good all day that he wondered anxiously what the reaction would be. But she smiled back at him and called gaily, "Good-bye, Grandpa. I wonder, darling, will it be a brow presentation?"

He went out laughing. The little monkey! He didn't know how she managed to pick up these medical terms. He was always so careful what he said in front of her.

Left alone, her sobbing stopped by the fiery drink he had given her, Prunella found that she was not so gloriously happy as she had thought she was. Panic was upon her lest something should happen to Richard or to herself before to-morrow morning, and then they would never see each other again. His danger had driven the invasion alarm out of her mind, but now she remembered it again. It might come even yet, perhaps to-night, with guns roaring along the coast and salvos of bombs dropping down from the sky. One of the bombs might drop upon her, or Richard.

Suddenly an idea came to her. She jumped up and ran out into the garden and across to the garage. No, Grandpa had not taken the car. Mrs. Anstruther lived only just down in the village, and he had walked. She tested the petrol and oil, and there was plenty. She would drive out to the moor and see Richard, and then come back again. She did not want to stay long, only to see him and kiss him, in case either of them died in the night, and then she would come back and no one would know she had even gone. Richard might be cross, but she did not think he would, for he had said, "Darling Prunella!" in such a lovely way, lovelier than ever before. It was a great idea! She was happy now, gloriously happy, happier than she had known anyone could be on this earth. Thank you, God, she said, for bringing Richard back. I will try to be good for the rest of my life because you have brought Richard back. Then she raced across the garden like a tom-boy and burst singing into the kitchen to make herself a cup of tea. Sitting on the kitchen table, drinking the hot, reviving stuff, was a moment of wonder that she never forgot, for everything about her showed a strange illumination, as though bathed in the light of her inner joy. The cups and saucers on the dresser burned with colour, the saucepans winked and glimmered as though made of silver and gold, and the very cat, asleep in a patch of sunshine on the floor, was an object of almost sublime beauty, because Richard was alive, alive, alive, Richard was alive and Prunella loved him.

She went upstairs and changed her crumpled yellow frock for a flowery affair of white linen printed with red poppies and blue cornflowers, the brightest and gayest frock she had. Then she washed her tear-stained face and made it up very carefully, choosing a lip-stick that exactly matched the poppies, for Richard was always rather rude about it if her lip-stick clashed with her frock, and brushed her curly hair until it was a perfect riot of colour and light. It was odd that just a few hours ago the routine of living had seemed like a dull grinding machine, and now every tiny action that she performed, polishing her nails and slipping a pair of new white sandals on to her bare feet, was an exquisite thing, a thing of wonder, because Richard was alive and she was happy. Happy, happy, happy, sang her heart, as she bounded down the stairs and raced across the garden to the garage, it is lovely to be so happy.

She roared through the village much too fast in the doctor's noisy, clanking old car, bringing everyone to their windows to gaze in shocked astonishment at the brilliant madcap figure rollicking past, and out along the high road that had been traced by a giant's finger along the crest of the hill. It was a day of unclouded brilliance, with on one side of her the woods falling to the sea and on the other the lovely patchwork guilt of tawny shorn harvest fields, green pasturelands and ploughed fields of rose-red earth mounting to the blue haze of the moors for which she was bound. Once she saw a great crater like a wound in the hillside, and a strip of hedge with its green life stricken and blasted, and once a ruined cottage, showing where bombs had fallen, but to-day those scars could not touch her joy that was inviolate, because Richard was safe and she was going to him.

Then she left the hills and swept recklessly down through the steep winding lanes to an enchanted valley where the old gnarled orchard trees were heavy with rosy apples and a brown moorland river rippled over the boulders in its bed. She left a little town behind her, with its tall church tower and its triple arched bridge over the river, and began to climb upwards towards the moors, up and up through the woods and the steep fern-covered banks of the narrow lanes. This mounting towards the moors always exhilarated her and to-day, because Richard was there, it lifted her to the height of ecstasy. She roared up and up until a gate barred the lane and she had to stop and open it. This was the gate of the moors, the gate to heaven. When she had driven through she stopped again, even though she was hastening to Richard, and looked and listened as she always did.

The moors rolled all about her, washed with faint purple heather, tawny bracken and the enamelled gold of the gorse, sweeping gloriously to the horizon where the strange shapes of the tors broke like crested waves against the sky. There was no sound except the sigh of the wind over the heather and the faint tinkle of sheep-bells in the hills, but the quiet, immense silence did not seem empty. One did not need those groups of strange stones set endwise on the moors to remember that in the immemorial ages men had lived here, had worshipped and sacrificed to the sun-god at terrible blood-stained altars. One did not need to remember the ghostly legends, the fairy tales and folk lore that had been handed down for generations, to know that unfathomable mystery brooded over these haunted moors. One heard it in the sigh of the wind and breathed it in with the sharp tang of the bracken and wet peat, one saw it in the shimmer of the strange distance and felt it in every fibre of one's being. All that had ever been was still here, alive.

Prunella put her head down on her bare arms, crossed upon the steering wheel, and suddenly this terrible war seemed only a little thing. What had someone called it? "Just a spasm of pain in the long age of history." That was all. It might blast the lives of one generation, but what was one generation among the many that had passed over these moors in their turn? And the moors went on. They might be pitted with bomb craters here and there, but the heather and the grass would soon grow over them and future generations would not know what they were; perhaps the happy children of the age to come would call them fairy dells.

She lifted her head and went on, driving very slowly now because the road was rutted and so steep and she had to be careful. Far down below her she could see an incredibly green valley watered by the brown river, with small far-away cottages and farms set about with pines and scarlet rowan trees, and the low white-washed inn where Richard was staying. Looking down at the distant valley, so dwarfed by distance and looking almost too lovely to be real, she understood why Richard, newly delivered from death, had made for it like a fox going to earth. He might say that this country of his birth was only a museum piece, that it had not got his allegiance like the larger, uglier England, but in his heart she thought it had; and especially this valley. Richard was a fine sportsman, and he especially loved fishing. Mr. Birley had taught him to fish down there in the valley, in that brown brawling river. She knew, because he had told her so, that the happiest hours of his boyhood had been spent there. That enchanted valley made no claims upon him, bound him with no chains except the chains of his love, and so he liked it better than he liked the Castle.

She slid down the hill and parked the car outside the inn, but she did not ask for Richard there because she knew he would be by the river. She walked the short way, crossing another beautiful triple-arched moorland bridge and then pushing her way through a tangle of sweet-smelling bog-myrtle bushes, meadowsweet and purple loosestrife, to a small enclosed green lawn beside the river that was Richard's favourite spot for fishing.

But he was not fishing, he was fast asleep, lying luxuriously curled round on his side, his cheek on his hand. She dared not touch him, lest she should wake him up, so she sat down beside him, and waited quietly, and tried not to cry lest *that* should wake him up. It was absurd to want to cry now, when she was so happy, and she did not know why she wanted to. It was also exasperating, for the tears in her eyes made it difficult to see him properly; and she hadn't brought a handkerchief either. She rubbed her knuckles in her eyes, and then she could see again.

Curled round on the grass, in his rough brown tweed coat, with his brown ruffled hair like the plumage of a bird, it struck her strangely that he looked like some wild creature, like the fox she had thought of who had gone to earth, like a fallen eagle or a stricken deer. He looked so a part of the place where he lay, so much a creature of earth and air who might at any time melt into them. It was a queer, rather frightening fancy, making him not human, putting him somehow at a distance from her, and she pushed it away to look long and intently at Richard, the man whom she loved.

He was so big and strong, yet his rare gentleness came to the surface as he slept, softening the lines of his rather hard young face, making him look a boy again in spite of the deep lines of fatigue and the dark shadows round his closed eyes. "Sleep well, darling," she whispered, and she was grateful to the green turf he lay on and the sun that warmed him and the river that sang to him. They were being good to him, but then they had known him for so many years. For a whole hour she sat beside him and never moved.

And then he woke up, slowly and peacefully, saw her and smiled without a trace of surprise. He moved a little, held out his arms, and she crept into them. "You darling child," he said sleepily. "You darling pretty little child." And then he abruptly went to sleep again and Prunella lay as still as she could in his arms, her hand thrust inside his coat to feel the beating of his heart.

v

Nearly another hour later he woke up again fully and completely, aware now of life and its problems, especially of this problem of Prunella in his arms. He sat up, lifting her with him, and gazed at her in consternation.

"Silly little duffer!" he ejaculated. "Oh, silly little owl!"

"Aren't you pleased to see me?" asked Prunella, but she smiled as she spoke, because she knew that he was. She would never forget how pleased he had been to see her.

"I'm quite terribly pleased to see you," said Richard. "I was dreaming about you, actually, and then I opened my eyes and there you were. I think it was adorable of you to come, but awfully silly, for you'd have seen me to-morrow anyhow, and I haven't a doubt that all the old cats in the village saw you go by."

"No, they didn't," said Prunella. "The lanes seemed empty all the way. But I mean to go home now, Richard. I only just came to kiss you."

"Which, as a matter of fact, you haven't done," said Richard.

They kissed gently, but with a new depth in their feeling for each other. The hours of danger and suspense had changed the quality of their love. There was no childishness left in it now, and no cruelty. It was the full stature of the love of man and woman.

"It's eight o'clock," said Richard. "We'd better have supper, and then you must start back, or it'll be getting dark on the roads."

He pulled her to her feet and hand in hand they pushed their way out through the meadowsweet and bog-myrtle. Prunella looked back for a moment before they went up the road to the inn. While she lived, she thought, the scent of bog-myrtle and the sound of running water would carry her back to this place and this hour. She would never be nearer to Richard than she had been these last two hours. It had been as it had been on Beacon Hill, only lovelier; though then he had talked all the time and now he had slept all the time; but the sense of oneness had been the same. She had loved him during these last two hours with a selflessness that she might not be able to reach again, and in his sleep he had been dreaming of her.

But Richard, as they walked back to the inn together, was feeling uncommonly fussed and bothered about Prunella. He looked at her as she walked beside him, her gaudy dress crumpled, her curly hair tumbled and her bare legs scratched by the bog-myrtle bushes. She looked alarmingly fragile, her mouth a red gash in her exhausted little face. It was getting cold now on these high moors, and she shivered a little.

"Did you bring your coat, Prunella?" he asked her sharply.

"No," said Prunella, "I didn't bring anything. I forgot. Not even a handkerchief, and I want one, rather."

He gave her his, and groaned inwardly. She must have something to eat, or she might faint by the way, and then he must hurry her off. He couldn't have her driving that ramshackle car of the doctor's on these rutted roads in the dangerous twilight, not with all these Jerries about.

But it was difficult to hurry Prunella. She was exasperatingly fastidious, and she would not go to supper in the inn dining-room until she had washed her hands and her scratched legs and tidied her curls with her comb. And then the slow country meal seemed to take so long, and restored to brilliant happiness by hot soup she enjoyed it so much, and wasted so much time watching the cows going home for the milking, and talked such a lot, that Richard thought despairingly that it would be midnight before they'd done.

"And we've not been invaded yet," said Prunella suddenly and happily, laying down her spoon and making no effort at all to get on with her trifle. "Not even after all those trumpets and bells. Shall we be to-night, Richard, do you think?"

A change came over Richard. His heavy sleepy eyelids lifted and his dark opaque wild-bird's eyes looked across at her blazing with sudden light. His lips curved in an amused confident smile. The hours that he had lived through lately had been full of much that had been quite appalling but they had been full of a wild exhilaration and excitement too, and some of it communicated itself to Prunella. "Not to-night," he said quietly.

"What happened, Richard?" demanded Prunella breathlessly, elbows on the table. "What have you been *doing*?"

"A good deal, one way and another," said Richard.

"But what?" she whispered, her eyes as alight as his.

"Well—just the job," smiled Richard. "And it was a neat job, too, if brutal."

Then his reminiscent excitement died out, and his eyes darkened again, as though he were remembering chiefly the brutality. A queer feeling of doom was creeping over him now. During those long hours of danger and endurance there had come over him an unexpected fear and horror, a physical craven fear like an animal's and a sick horror of the things that he had to do, and would have to do while life or this war lasted. The fear and horror had taken him so utterly by surprise that they had shaken him badly. And he was stupefied with fatigue and his will seemed not to be functioning properly. . . . But Prunella continued to sit with spoon suspended, her eyes like stars, and he remembered that but for the things that he and others had done just lately there might have been no stars in her eyes to-night. There was comfort there, and his dazed thoughts fumbled for it.

"Hurry up, darling," he implored her.

She lowered her spoon and hurried up and they were finished at last and went out to the car waiting on the moor. It was as Richard had feared. The first stars were showing, it would soon be dark, and then the Jerries would be about.

"I must come with you, Prunella," he said flatly.

"But you can't drive the car," said Prunella. "Not with your licence suspended."

"But if I come with you I shall be there if anything happens."

Prunella stood looking up at him, her small face lifted, her hands childishly clasped behind her, the immensity of the evening sky behind her curly head. "No, Richard," she said. "You don't want to go home to-night."

He didn't. He wanted to stay in this peaceful place till he'd got a grip of himself again. And he wanted Prunella to stay with him so that he should forget his fear, forget his shock and horror at finding he could be afraid, forget the things that he had done and would have to go on doing, forget that he did not want to die, forget everything except Prunella and their love. If he could only go to sleep with Prunella in his arms then he thought he would wake up feeling himself again.

Prunella stood on tiptoe and put her arms round his neck. "I'm not afraid to drive home alone," she said. "Good night, darling."

Good night, good night, parting is such sweet sorrow. Only in war-time it isn't, it is bitter sorrow, even if the parting is only for a night. They clung to each other, and it was Prunella who said, "I can't go back, Richard. I'll stay here with you."

CHAPTER X

I

AUTUMN had touched the world with the tips of her fingers. In the mornings the valleys were always filled with mist and above them the slopes of the moors, covered with fading heather, were rose-pink. The hips and haws were scarlet in the hedges and here and there the green leaves had turned to pure pale gold. The gardens were filled with Michaelmas daisies and blazing dahlias, the blackberries were ripe and the children were gathering the sloes for winter-prick-wine. Threshing was in progress and in the centuries-old orchards, under the gnarled old trees, the cider apples were stacked in glowing piles. The rhythm of the autumn harvesting went on as usual, in spite of all, and the beauty of it stole into anxious hearts and brought its peace.

And with the peace came hope, for England still survived. Though the lovely harvest moon brought thundering death crashing from the sky, though great and lovely churches went down in ruins and whole stretches of the country-side crackled into flames, though the monthly death-roll went into thousands and no man knew what to-morrow would bring, yet England still survived. The mood of the country was changing almost imperceptibly from the flaming resolve to go down with all flags flying to the mood of grim endurance that fights on to victory. The worst was yet to come, they knew, the tide had not turned yet, but England survived.

There was confidence in Miss Brown's heart as with Moppet and Poppet, one on each side, she set out to take tea with Mrs. Heather at the lodge. It was a mellow, lovely day, with the wood pigeons calling in the woods and golden sunbeams slanting through the trees, and she was visited by a sudden glow of happiness. Such a glow was so unexpected in these days, like a visitant from another world, that she clutched it to her with astonished gratitude.

She'd a lot to be thankful for, so she recollected under its influence. The Castle was still safe, and much cleaner than it had been before she came. Boulder was more agreeable than formerly, and had informed her only this morning that, owing to her cooking, he now felt a lot better to what he did. The children were adorable, loved her increasingly and kept well. Richard gave them no more frights; he returned from his flights at the correct moment, won the D.F.C. and was more or less punctual in writing home. Stephen, toiling heroically in a Rescue Squad in London, was still safe; though she dared not let herself think about Stephen too much, for she loved him, and the thought of what he was doing, and of what the things he did might be doing to so sensitive and vulnerable a creature, robbed her of her sleep and sapped her efficiency. She fixed her mind upon the thought that now, to-day, he was safe, and let that suffice her. Above all, Mr. Birley was well, glowingly proud of Richard, proud, too, now, of Stephen, and completely dependent on her . . . and she loved him. . . . The complete hopelessness of her love, that gave her desperate pain at times, was eased to-day. Unrequited love was the most selfless form of love, she told herself again, and whenever Mr. Birley spoke to her, thanked her for something, showed her even by a smile or a gesture that he realised how necessary she was now to the Castle's life, she knew joy. They would never send her away now. She was part of the pattern.

She was very pleased to be going to tea with Mrs. Heather at last. Mrs. Heather was humble with a bygone humility, she knew her place, and it had taken her a long time to realise that "the lady" would like to come to tea with her at the cottage. But she had realised it at last, after a few broad hints from Fanny, and had issued the invitation, and Miss Brown had dressed herself and the children with care for what she realised was something of an occasion.

She wore her best white silk blouse with her dark-blue coat and skirt. She had polished her shoes until they shone like glass and her hat was dead straight upon her neat dark hair. She wore gloves, of course, though they only had to traverse a quarter of a mile of woodland between the Castle and the Cottage, and carried her handbag. Moppet and Poppet, trotting along beside her, wore pink, with sunbonnets, and were a sight for sore eyes. They were gloriously happy because mother had been invited to visit them at the Castle, and to-morrow she was coming for four whole days. Mother was coming and they were going to meet her at the station.

The windows of Mrs. Heather's cottage were a blaze of geraniums, as usual, and the shadows were deep and cool within the old stone porch before the front door. Miss Brown knocked, and as they stood waiting they all three let out a little sigh of pleasure. The historian in Miss Brown adored the Castle but the housekeeping part of her found it much too large, and Moppet and Poppet, though they disliked it less than formerly, still did not like it at all, but this little whitewashed cottage at the entrance to the woods was just the size that seemed right to the three of them. The children thought it was like the little safe warm house beneath the roots of the trees where Peter Rabbit and his brothers and sisters had lived, and Miss Brown thought that a residence of this size could be kept clean without undue exertion. Though they stood as yet only within the porch, they all three felt at home.

There was a printed notice nailed to Mrs. Heather's front door, "Enquire Within." It was for the guidance of tourists wanting to see the Castle, of course, but looking at it Miss Brown felt a queer thrill, as though those two words had some special meaning for her, as though within this cottage she would one day find the answer to some vital question. She lifted her hand and knocked again.

This time Mrs. Heather opened to them. "I was out the back," she explained. "Did I keep you waiting? Step in, my dears."

They stepped in, and enchantment gripped them, for Mrs. Heather's living-room was the setting of a happy life, and everything in it seemed to glow with the brightness of her own contentment. Gay rag rugs lay on the snowy well-scrubbed floor, bright cushions were in the old windsor chairs, copper pans winked on the mantelpiece, the geraniums blazed in the windows and a large ginger tom-cat with silver whiskers slept upon the hearth before the little fire of fir cones that kept the kettle boiling. A snowy cloth was spread on the table and cups and saucers with pink roses on them were set upon it, with a home-made plum cake, little round chocolate buns, home-made scones and bramble jelly and a small pat of butter. A year ago there would have been a large pat of butter and a bowl of cream. But not now. There was a war on.

But the absence of cream was the only sign of war in the flowery, sun-filled room, and it struck Miss Brown that it was in homes like this one that the idea of home would be kept safe. Homes like the Castle were faced by financial if not material ruin, and most of the small homes in the streets would go down into dust, but these little cottages hidden in the hills and among the tree trunks had more than a chance of survival. At the end of the war there would still be geraniums in their windows and gay rag rugs upon the well-scrubbed floors. She sank into a chair, pulled off her gloves, and felt more utterly at home than she had felt since she left "Sea View." "I should like to live here, Mrs. Heather," she said.

"There's many have said the same, my dear," said Mrs. Heather, pouring boiling water into a brown tea-pot the size of a beehive. She called everyone "my dear." She would have called the Queen herself "my dear" had that gracious lady had occasion to visit her. The words were not a mere form, for everything that lived was exceedingly dear to her.

"Now us be ready. Draw in, my dears."

She lifted Moppet and Poppet to two windsor chairs with cushions on them, and pushed them well in to the table, while Miss Brown divested them of their sunbonnets and tied the bib that she had brought in her handbag round Poppet's neck to protect the pink frock. Poppet was an untidy feeder. She ate always with one eye to the future, hurrying through the bread and butter lest the cake upon which she had set her heart should be grabbed by someone else before she got there. This led to spills.

"Now gently, Poppet," admonished Miss Brown. "Be a little lady."

Poppet, cramming scone and bramble jelly into her mouth with both hands, and squinting slightly because she had one eye on the fruit cake and the other on the chocolate buns, made no effort to be any such thing. Why should she? She had not been born a lady, and as ladylike behaviour, so far as she could see, completely destroyed all joy in life, she saw no point in striving after it.

Moppet disagreed with her. Moppet, these days, was trying very hard to be a lady. She had not, like Poppet, the independence of the artist. She liked to conform to her environment as much as possible.

There was a little garden of herbs and old-fashioned flowers behind the cottage, and when the children's hunger was satisfied they played here with the tom-cat, Nellie. Everything animate or inanimate, so Mr. Birley had told Miss Brown, is referred to in the West Country as "he" except a tom-cat, which is "she." Miss Brown and Mrs. Heather sat upon the bench outside the back door and watched them, Mrs. Heather at work upon the immense shapeless garment that she was still making for her grandson in the Navy, and Miss Brown sitting in the idleness that the sleepy peace of the little garden seemed to demand. It was a very private garden, walled in on three sides by the woods and on the fourth by the cottage itself, and in the centre of it, beside a huge lavender bush, there was a well that Mrs. Heather told her never ran dry. Miss Brown imagined that for the last hundred years the little garden had hardly changed at all. Year after year the daffodils and crocuses had given way to stocks and roses, and they to the dahlias and Michaelmas daisies that were blazing here now. Year after year the sun had distilled the scent of the herbs, the rosemary and lavender, the thyme and mint and marjoram, and year after year the bucket had been let down into the depths of the well and been wound up again full of the fresh clear water that never failed.

"You've lived here a long time, Mrs. Heather," was Miss Brown's opening remark.

"Since my wedding day, my dear," said Mrs. Heather, "and that's for most of my life."

"And all your children were born here," went on Miss Brown, angling for information, "and your husband died here, but the place has not altered at all."

"It don't alter," said Mrs. Heather. "They makes alterations at the Castle now and again, but I've never changed a thing here since the day I was a bride."

"Don't you feel lonely?" asked Miss Brown. "After having had so many children it must be lonely now they have all left you."

Mrs. Heather laid down her knitting. She did not often talk about herself, but she felt instinctively that there was some sort of link between herself and Miss Brown. Love of the cottage, perhaps. She had seen at once how much Miss Brown liked the cottage.

"I was born at Hatchett's Farm," she said, "that old farm that you can see from the Castle windows, down in the valley where the stream runs, an' where the old thorn tree is. Hatchett's Farm belongs to the Birleys; it always has done. From down there you can look up through the trees an' see the Castle towers right up above you against the sky. The first thing as I can remember, as a babby, was lookin' up one spring day an' seein' the Castle risin' above a mist of young green leaves. A pretty sight, it were. An' the next thing as I can remember is lyin' abed on a cold winter's night an' hearin' the gallopin' feet of the horse on the road that leads through the valley."

"What horse?" asked Miss Brown.

"The white one, dear," said Mrs. Heather placidly, "with the silver knight ridin' him. I never saw 'em but once, an' that was on All Souls' night, under the full moon, but I heard 'em time an' again, an' often in spring, where I'd been gatherin' king-cups by the stream, I'd wonder where they lay buried. Somehow I thought it were by that old thorn tree there, an' many's the time I've hung a garland upon it on All Souls' night an' said a prayer for him that he might rest easier. What if he did kill himself, poor gentleman, I've thought. Better for a Birley to die by his own act than yield himself to his enemies."

"Well!" ejaculated Miss Brown. She had never expected to hear a ghost spoken of in such a matter-of-fact tone, just as though he were the baker.

"But I hung no more garlands on the tree after I married Jim Heather, the forester," said Mrs. Heather, "I'd not the time. Jim was a proper man, though of a stubborn fashion, an' wooed me beautiful down there in the valley, an' fine I loved him; but after he brought me here I had no peace. Twelve childer us had; some died when they was little 'uns but there's some livin' to-day, though all gone their ways. I was seventeen when I married, an' I took it very hard. But Jim he were a proper man, of a stubborn fashion, an' he couldn't help himself."

Her voice ended on a note of matter-of-fact resignation, and Miss Brown tried to put herself in the place of that child of seventeen, the fairy-tale child who had hung garlands on a thorn tree and been wooed in the valley of the singing stream, when her body had been delivered over into the keeping of Jim Heather. Twelve children. She tried to imagine the birth pangs and the weakness, the grief when the babies died, the turmoil when they did not, the noise and overcrowding in the small cottage, the cooking and the mending and the scrubbing, the back-breaking hours over the wash-tub, the comings and goings of the virile husband with his mud-caked boots, his appetite, his incessant demands by night and day, the epidemics, the partings, the tragedy of the forester's death and the final loneliness. But imagination failed her. She wondered if Mrs. Heather had continued to love the man who had bound her in such iron service.

"You must miss your husband," she said tentatively.

"No, my dear," said Mrs. Heather placidly, "I can't say as I do. Not now. I loved him fine when we were courtin' for he were a proper man, tall an' strong, with merry dark eyes an' curly hair black as a raven's wing. I mind when I seen him first, fellin' a tree down there in the valley, swingin' the great axe as easy as you please, with his coat that was brown as the autumn leaves flung on the grass beside him. I hid behind a bush an' watched him, but he saw me an' pulled me out an' kissed me; an' then he never rested till he had me. But when the babbies started comin' 'twas hard to go on lovin'. I was not strong, see, an' I had bad times with the little things. An' then I thought to meself, well, we're one; he has me an' naught can alter the fact that he has me, an' he's as fine a man as God ever made, so I'd best cease complainin' an' let him do what he likes with what's his own. So I did, and then somehow I loved him again, I loved him more than the first time. I loved him dearly, so I did, an' I fretted sorely when he died."

"I think Mr. Birley told me he was killed by a falling tree in the woods," said Miss Brown.

"That's right, then," said Mrs. Heather. "November, it was, thirty years ago, with colour still on the trees. There was a terrible storm one night an' we sat by the fire, he an' I, alone together, for all the children were grown and gone from us by then, an' listened to the wind rushin' through the branches an' them creakin' and groanin' an' cryin' out like tormented creatures. An' Jim was terrible put about, for he loved his trees. Often I'd tell him he was like a tree himself, so tall an' brown, with his russet coat. Men do grow like the wild things they tend. Many's the time I've passed shepherd walkin' behind his flock, his child on his shoulder maybe, an' his dog alongside, an' thought how silly-like he looked, with the same blinkin' patience in his eyes that the sheep have. An' gardeners be the same, one with the earth they'll look at last. We be all one, ye see, closer nor what we think."

"You said he was afraid his trees would suffer damage," Miss Brown said, recalling her to the story.

"He was so," said Mrs. Heather. "An' then, as we sat there, we heard a crash, an' Jim jumped up with a sort of groan an' was out into the wild darkness afore I could stop him. Foolish he was, terrible foolish, but to hear one of his trees go down was the same to him as 'twould have been to me had I heard one of the childer fallin' on the stairs. He had to go to it. I waited a while, an' then there was another crash, an' the storm rose till it sounded as though all the waves of the world were breakin' on the cottage roof. I waited another spell, an' then I heard the owls cryin' so pitiful, as they will do when there's been a death. So I took a lantern, an' I put me cloak about me an' I went out into the woods, an' there I found him a-lyin' dead, with the second tree crashed across him. Just like a fallen tree himself he looked, in his russet coat, with his dark head layin' in the dead leaves. The shock turned me silly-like. I should have run to the Castle for help but I didn't. I just lay down beside him in the dead leaves an' spread my cloak over the two of us. Fine I loved him an' I thought maybe that way I should be dead too in the mornin'. But you can't die just for the wishin,' an' when they found us in the mornin' the life was in me still."

The sing-song voice came to a stop, but there was no sign of distress in her old wrinkled face, and her small gnarled hands, lying on the knitting in her lap, did not move. Yet the anguish of that night lived again in memory and it seemed to Miss Brown that the sun was darkened.

"No, you can't die just when you wish," went on Mrs. Heather. "You must bide the Lord's time, an' strange it is that the young an' the strong, those who love life, will be gone in a flash like my Jim, while the old or ailing, who'd be glad to go, must travel the road till the end."

"But you don't look as though you found the road hard going, Mrs. Heather," said Miss Brown. "You always look so happy."

"So I am, my dear," said Mrs. Heather. "But then, you see, I'm one of the lucky ones. I live in the woods."

"Live in the woods?" asked the puzzled Miss Brown.

"I can't say as I always cared for the woods," said Mrs. Heather. "After Jim died I hated 'em, for it was a tree that killed him. I was ill after he died, an' lyin' in bed with them trees sighin' an' moanin' round me I was like a mad woman, I hated 'em so. An' when I was about again I wouldn't go into the woods, I wouldn't even go down to the Castle because of the trees about the way. I just moped in the cottage, an' no good to man or beast I was, no good at all. An' then Mr. Birley's father, a very old man he was then, an' crippled with his rheumatism, had himself pushed up in his wheel chair to see me, an' talked to me straight. 'This won't do, Mrs. Heather,' he says. 'This won't do at all. Either you go right away from this place or else you go out into the woods an' make friends with 'em again. One or other you must do, Mrs. Heather,' he says. 'An' you must pull yourself together. You're not the first woman to lose the man she loves,' says he, 'nor you won't be the last with life what it is.' Well, I did not want to go away for I'd been born an' bred in this place an' it was all the world to me, an' I loved this cottage, too, that Mr. Birley had promised should be mine for life. So I did as Mr. Birley said. I did it that night. It was moonlight an' starlight an' I went out into the woods all quiet with the hard frost holdin' 'em, an' down into the valley where Jim had wooed me. I walked up an' down on the road where I'd heard the horseman gallopin' when I was a child, an' I looked at the farm where I'd been born, an' that thorn tree where I'd hung the garlands, an' the bush where I'd hidden when I first saw Jim, and the woods all about, an' the frozen stream, an' the old Castle where so many had lived an' died towerin' up white in the moonlight above it all. Very still was the earth with the hard frost, no voice of bird or leaf or water, no colour nowhere, only the darkness under the trees an' the moonlight like a shroud. Dead it was, with the death of winter, an' I felt dead too with the joy slain in my heart. I put out my hand an' I took hold on a branch of the old thorn tree there beside me, an' I looked at my hand that was thin an' white with the sickness I'd had, an' me grown old, an' I didn't see no difference between my hand an' the bare branch; like white bone they looked, the two on 'em. An' sudden I loved that tree because it was white an' wasted with the frost as I with my sorrow. An' the Castle, that was white too, white as the bones of the dead man an' his horse that lay not far away, an' the stream an' the woods were still under their shroud. White shroud, black night, I thought, they make us one. Livin' we seem different, an' we kill each other, as a tree had killed my Jim, an' we hate as I'd hated the trees, but dead things don't hate; with death comes oneness, an' that's love."

Mrs. Heather stopped and Miss Brown could find nothing to say. She thought this a gloomy tale and found no food for satisfaction in it.

"An' then, my dear," went on Mrs. Heather, "thinkin' of the tree an' not of myself, breakin' away from myself as you might say, seemed to make the tree come alive. Believe it or not, but that branch grew warm under my hand. Maybe 'twas just fancy, but I thought as I could feel the sap arisin', pulsin' like heart beats. An' I grew warm, too, warm an' joyous like a young thing once again. An' 'I remembered that the spring was comin', with the brook ripplin' an' the birds singin' an' the trees full of livin' leaf. An' then I see as death weren't death at all but a sleep an' reconcilement. There's war in the autumn woods, with the wind tearin' the leaves from the trees an' the trees screamin' out loud in their anger, an' then there's frost an' stillness, an' then there's the spring with the sweet wind wooin' the new buds from the trees. So 'tis with men, I thought, for we're all alike, men an' trees an' all that lives. Livin' we seem different, we don't see that we're all one, but death teaches us better an' when we wake again 'twill be to love."

"Some love now," said Miss Brown softly. "There are some who cannot hate."

"They've seen, dear," said Mrs. Heather. "They've seen right down to the bare bone an' the livin' spirit that's the same. Some way or other they've been through a sort of death, as you might say, an' woken again. Some know, many know, but just knowin' don't make you happy. You may know there's sun outside a shuttered house, but you're still in the dark, you don't see till summat breaks the shutters open an' you cry aloud for joy."

Miss Brown suddenly remembered that day when sitting on the seat outside the Free Library she had felt herself one of a multitude. She had not exactly seen then, the house had still been shuttered, but surely that flashing moment of delight had been like a chink of light between the shutters. "I can imagine what that seeing might be like," she said softly.

"Yes, I saw that night," went on Mrs. Heather. "I don't rightly know how to tell of what I saw, me never havin' had much schoolin', but I was happy, knowin' I'd got somethin' I was meant to have, somethin' that had been lost an' was found, an' I've been happy ever since, an' I've loved the woods because it was from a tree that the comfort came."

"What did you *do* afterwards, Mrs. Heather?" asked Miss Brown. "How did you live after that?"

"No different from before, my dear," said Mrs. Heather placidly. "I just cooked an' washed an' ironed like I'd always done, an' took the visitors round the Castle."

"But you must have thought differently," persisted Miss Brown.

Mrs. Heather pondered. "Maybe I did, my dear. I think I thought about life as I'd thought about Jim. It has me, I thought, an' naught can alter the fact that it has me, an' if what I knew down there in the valley, with the sap risin' in the branch under my hand, be life, then it don't stop at death an' it be the grandest thing God ever made; so I'd best cease complainin' an' let it do what it likes with what's its own. . . . Life's very like a husband you know, my dear; it makes you bring forth fruit."

Miss Brown was shocked. She blushed a little.

"Do you say all this to the tourists, Mrs. Heather?" she asked a little anxiously.

"Oh no, my dear," Mrs. Heather hastily reassured her. "But as I tell 'em tales of those old men of the Castle I thinks to myself, 'tis all one thing, they an' the dead men an' the old walls, an' they belong to each other because they was made out of the same bone an' the same spirit, an' God's hand holds 'em all. I don't know of no way to show 'em more clearly than just tellin' 'em the tales, an' thinkin' in my own mind that to be one an' love each other is man's inheritance that do be lost out of the world."

"And yet men hate," said Miss Brown bitterly.

Mrs. Heather seemed undisturbed by this. "Men'll learn," she said placidly.

"But look what they do while they're learning!" cried Miss Brown in despair.

"Man's of a stubborn fashion," agreed Mrs. Heather, but she still refused to put herself out about it. Though Miss Brown had been touched by Mrs. Heather's story, she yet felt a little irritated by this placidity; yet humble at the same time, for she knew that it is only their inferiors who find the saints exasperating.

The children came running back with posies of flowers clasped in their hot hands. "For mother," they shouted. "To put in mother's room."

"Say good-bye to Mrs. Heather," said Miss Brown. "We must go home and make up mother's bed."

As they went back through the woods the children were chattering like sparrows. Mother was coming. Her image had grown a little dim during the long summer, but they still remembered her as the source of all comfort and joy. And she was coming to stay with them for four whole days.

II

That very same evening the Baxter men, Mr. Baxter, Fred and Terry, ate their supper in the deepest gloom, though it was their favourite meal of fried pork and pickles, strawberry jam and an extra allowance of sugar in the strong stewed tea prepared for them by Mrs. Baxter to comfort them because she was leaving them for four days. But it did not comfort them. They masticated fried pork in a gloomy silence and eyed Mrs. Baxter's suitcase, already packed in readiness for the morning, with disfavour.

"It'll only be your breakfasts you'll have to see to for yourselves," encouraged Mrs. Baxter from behind the tea-pot. "Mrs.

Bridges she'll run in to clean up of a mornin', an' Mrs. Potter she'll run in of an evenin' to cook your tea, an' the time'll soon go. Only four days."

Her cheerful voice dropped a little flatly. Only four days of Moppet and Poppet, her two little angels, only four days' respite from the titanic struggle of keeping the family respectable under present circumstances.

Keeping the family respectable had always been something of a struggle, with so many mouths to feed and Dad perpetually out of work, but now the struggle had assumed the proportions of a nightmare. Mrs. Baxter looked about her. Most of the windows had been destroyed by blast and were boarded up, so that they lived in a perpetual twilight. And there was no gas; they were eating their cooked tea by the light of a couple of candles stuck in saucers. And there was no water either. Every drop that she needed for cooking and washing up had to be fetched in a bucket from a quarter of a mile away. But those were minor inconveniences compared to the fact that the lavatory in the yard at the back had been blown clean away; and now they had to walk right down the street and share one with five other families. But even that was nothing compared with the horror of the nights spent in the shelter, those sleepless nights of screaming, thundering din; and theirs was a bad shelter, overcrowded, lice-infected, damp, filthy. England, that from the days of Ethelred the Unready onwards had never been ready for anything, and never would be, had not been ready with proper shelters when the Blitz came. Mrs. Baxter fought down the nausea that swept over her at the thought of the night that would soon be upon them. She could take it, she told herself. It was not getting her down. No, it was *not* getting her down. To reinvigorate herself she looked at her kitchen, still spotless, and her young sons, still cleanly. It was taking long daily hours of washing, and doing the boys' heads with a tooth-comb every day, to keep them so, but she had not been beaten. Respectable the Baxters had always been, and respectable they would be while she could keep upon her feet and hold her eyelids open.

Mr. Baxter pushed his plate away, his pork only half finished, swung round his chair to the little fire made of smashed-up furniture collected in the streets that Mrs. Baxter had lit to fry the pork over, and opened a two days' old evening paper.

"Can't you fancy your pork, Dad?" asked Mrs. Baxter.

Mr. Baxter shook his head.

"A nice bit of pork, too," mourned Mrs. Baxter, and cut what he had left in half for Fred and Terry.

Dad always went off his feed when he'd been given the sack; not that he'd exactly been given the sack this time, only when he had arrived this morning at the block of offices where he worked as a lift man it hadn't been there any more. It had quite upset him. Given him a nasty jolt. He looked very poorly to-night, she thought, very thin and sallow, his shoulders more bowed, his moustache very straggly and drooping, the whole air of him hopelessly dejected.

It was a relief to look from him to the rosy freckled faces, with bulging cheeks and bright eyes, of her two rapscallion sons. Upon them the Blitz seemed to have no harmful effects whatsoever; it went off them like water off a duck's back. They enjoyed the nights in the shelter, roaring out the choruses of patriotic songs, laughing at the drunks, falling into sudden depths of sleep, apparently only lulled by the guns, and awaking at the scream of a bomb to sing and laugh again. And by day life was almost as exciting as by night, for there was no knowing whom you might meet in the streets. Fred had careered round a corner on his bicycle and fallen off slap at the feet of the Queen. Terry, messing about happily inside a bomb crater, had looked up to see the King standing on the edge and laughing at him, and had hastily scrambled out to wring his Sovereign by the hand and assure him with great kindness and condescension that he was "taking it." The Prime Minister was often to be seen stamping doggedly around, very angry, but relaxing a little, smiling and waving his hand when the people cheered him. A grand mix-up, it was, while between the leaders and their people there tightened and held the bonds of mutual trust that has been vindicated.

Mr. and Mrs. Baxter were not unaware of the glory that was round about them. This surging to the heights of valour had not left them cold; if it had Mrs. Baxter would have ceased her fight to keep the boys' heads clean, and Mr. Baxter, upon finding his flats a heap of ruins, would have betaken himself to the nearest pub instead of stumping off immediately, as he had done, to the Labour Exchange to try again. But at their age, after a lifetime of struggle, they were too tired to feel any exhilaration. Mr. Baxter felt nothing but a huge and awful lethargy, and Mrs. Baxter wondered for how much longer, but for the respite of the four days that were coming, she could have gone on sharing the lavatory with the other five families. The one thing that she had

176

always feared, for herself and her family, had been the loss of respectability. In these days of death and destruction it was still her only fear, but sharpened to a spear-point of agonised intensity.

The sirens wailed. All over the great, sprawling, battered and tormented city echoed that eerie wailing of impending doom. Only a noise made by electricity yet somehow demoniacal, horrifying, and as usual Mrs. Baxter felt for a couple of minutes that she could not breathe, and choked over her tea. "Seems as though I minded the sirens worse than I minded the bombs," she muttered. Fred and Terry wasted no time on speech, they just reached for the last fragments of bread and jam and crammed them in. Mr. Baxter got up and began piling the crockery neatly beside the sink. "'Urry," he commanded his family briefly.

They raked out the bit of fire, put on their coats, and poured what was left of the tea into an old Thermos, and Mrs. Baxter found her knitting. Sometimes, when her reason seemed tottering, she did a bit of knitting in the night. Then they blew out the candles, opened the door and stepped out into the darkened street.

And immediately, the wind being in that quarter, they were met by a whiff of the over-used lavatory, and something seemed suddenly to break in Mrs. Baxter; she who had prided herself upon the fact that she could take it to the end. Her fingers closed painfully upon her husband's arm. "I can't, Alf," she whispered. "Not again I can't."

"Can't what, girl?" he asked her gently.

"Face that shelter." Her breath came in quick, panic-stricken gasps. "The smell an' filth, an' the rats an' the drunks. 'Taint decent."

Mr. Baxter drew her back within the shelter of their door. "Think a minute, girl," he said. "It ain't safe to stay in the 'ouse, an' you don't want to risk your life just when you're off to see the kids in the mornin'. Just one more night, girl, an' then you'll get a bit of rest."

But it was no good. "It ain't decent," reiterated Mrs. Baxter, and she was sobbing now, with a hysterical note in her sobs that her husband had never before heard in her rare weeping. He saw it was no good. "Then we'll stay 'ere, you an' me," he said. "You go on, boys. You go on quick! Off with you!"

Fred and Terry, standing outside on the pavement, bundled up in their shabby little overcoats, their eyes popping with astonishment at this unwonted display of emotion in their mother, turned and made off. Their father anxiously watched their small scampering figures, fitfully lit by the light of the moon that was now hidden, now revealed by the scurrying clouds, until they had turned the corner where the shelter was. Safe; at least as safe as they could be. He loved his children and thinking of them there was a little smile on his lips as he shut the door and turned back to the darkened kitchen, where the last faint glow from the raked-out fire showed only the figure of Mrs. Baxter standing before the hearth, her clenched hands pressed to her face, fighting her sobs.

"There, there, girl," he said to her. "Sit down an' we'll 'ave another cup-a-tea."

Mrs. Baxter watched him with a growing tender astonishment as he relit the candles, made the fire anew, put the kettle on and made fresh tea. It was the rule in their class that the man did not help his wife in the house unless she were "bad," and Mr. Baxter had always conformed to that rule; though during those times when the babies had been coming he had decided that she was "bad," and had put on the kettle himself, on days when another man would have ignored her dragging movements. In the quarrels that they had sometimes she would suddenly remember that, and see to it that they were reconciled again as quickly as might be.

"I'm not 'bad,' Alf," she said to him now, sitting by the fire in astonishing idleness while he poured out the tea.

"It won't do you no 'arm to 'ave a bit of rest," said Mr. Baxter, and pulled up his chair beside her. They sat with their hands curved round their hot cups of tea, and Mr. Baxter cleared his throat but couldn't get hold of what he wanted to say. It was so long since they'd sat like this, idle, quiet, alone together without the children.

"Pity the tea's runnin' short in the country, an' tea 'bout the best comfort there is these days," said Mrs. Baxter.

Mr. Baxter cleared his throat again with immense effort and spat into the fire. " 'Tis comfortin' bein' together," he got out at last.

Mrs. Baxter opened her mouth in astonishment, but she did not immediately reply, for suddenly the roar and tumult seemed all about them and speech was impossible. But later on there were uncanny intervals of quiet, and then they spoke to each other.

"Don't be feared, girl," said Mr. Baxter. "This is a lucky 'ouse. All these weeks there ain't nothin' 'appened to it 'cept the winders goin', an' the privy out the back."

"I ain't feared," said Mrs. Baxter. "I ain't never been feared of nothin' 'cept us not bein' decent."

"We'll never not be decent, girl," said Mr. Baxter, "not whatever 'appens." He put his cup down and scratched his head, struggling to express himself. "What I mean is, we can't 'elp it if the privy blows away. That's our share in the blinkin' war, that is. If we does our best to be decent without a privy then we *are* decent, that's wot I ses."

But Mrs. Baxter shook her head hopelessly. She could not see it in that light.

"That's a real nice woman wot cares for Moppet an' Poppet," she said later on, in another quiet interval. "Kind she is, writin' every week. Askin' me to stay, too."

"You should 'ave gone for the 'ole week, like she asked you for," said Mr. Baxter.

"I wouldn't leave you for a 'ole week," said Mrs. Baxter. "Nice fuss you've made over me goin' for these four days."

"Don't like bein' without you, girl," said Mr. Baxter.

They sat in silence as the guns roared. They felt very close to each other. There was the scream of a bomb not far off, and a thundering detonation. They looked at each other and smiled. "This be a lucky 'ouse," said Mr. Baxter when the noise ceased, and put his hand over his wife's.

"That's a kind woman that 'as Moppet an' Poppet," repeated Mrs. Baxter. "An' the boys are old enough to look after themselves. I dare say we've been 'as 'appy as most."

"'Appier," declared Mr. Baxter stoutly.

They said very little more. "'Ow it do make me back ache!" said Mrs. Baxter once, as the fiendish noise smote upon her, and Mr. Baxter grunted. Then they were silent, their bewildered thoughts slipping backwards over the past. . . . Courting days. Their first home. The births and deaths of babies. In work. Out of work. Good luck. Bad luck. But always decent and respectable. Quarrelling sometimes, but always reconciled again. . . . Happier than most. It had all seemed to take long at the time, but in retrospect it seemed so very short. "A thousand ages in Thy sight are as an evening gone."

They had just time, when there came not far away that sound as of a colossal sheet tearing, as though the very heavens were being ripped open, to turn quickly to each other, as they had turned when they had first met each other, when they had first kissed, when they had first lain together in the same bed, and then it was over. The final agony was very short, as short as life itself.

CHAPTER XI

I

Mr. Holly, these days, was having a very varied existence. His experiences as the guardian of the train that linked London with the West Country had always been of a lively nature, but now they were so lively as to be positively startling. "I don't never know what'll 'appen next," he said frequently to Mrs. Holly. From the moment when he had found Mr. Isaacson prostrate upon the floor of the guard's van life had been, in his own words, "one blinkin' thing after the other."

But how Mr. Holly was enjoying it! He was one of the most important men in England just now, and he knew it. In spite of the rationing he was waxing fatter than ever upon the knowledge, and Mrs. Holly was hard put to it letting out his waistcoats and his braces. He was as Jove in his world, and his world just now was full of lightnings and thunders, a world of gods and heroes among whom he was the mightiest of the mighty and the envy of the brave.

Part of his exhilaration was due to the fact that though his duties were the same as they had always been, the care of the train, the guardianship of the mails, the comforting of the passengers, they were no longer prosaic duties but tasks that demanded for their fulfilment the very utmost that he had to give. They demanded courage, intuition and an overflowing compassion. Of all these things Mr. Holly was capable. He gave and gave again, got fatter than ever and had to be measured for a new suit.

The train, for instance. In old days it had been just a mechanised affair of wood and steel and steam that seemed to more or less look after itself. Mr. Holly, as it wound upon its way, had frequently dozed a bit. He never dozed now. The train seemed to him now a living creature of bone and blood and sinew, a beloved creature that looked to him to save it from death; alert and watchful he sat in its tail, intent upon its every movement, intent upon every danger that threatened it from bombs and machine-gunning and wrecked railway tracks. He and the engine driver had grown very wily. They had learned to send it dashing for shelter to a tunnel, and keep it panting there like a fox in its lair till the baulked Jerry had gone off again, and to decide quickly what to do in a hundred different emergencies and dilemmas. When the eager panting creature suffered injury in any part of its long serpentine body, he felt it as though his own child had cut its knee.

And then the mails. They had long ago ceased to be mere bags full of letters. They had become to the men who handled them as the flame that the vestals guarded or as the treasure upon an altar; sacred things. "Get out the mails!" was the cry in emergency. It was a point of honour to save the mails. Mr. Holly had risked his life to do it, and there were men who had died that a girl in Cornwall might get a letter from her lover in London wishing her a happy birthday.

And the passengers. Their lives were in Mr. Holly's hands and he was both awed and elevated by the trust, but not worried at all; he was too fat to worry. No pleasure-seekers these days, except a few parents visiting their children, but men in uniform, women in uniform, taut, cheery, resolved, their lives as golden pieces in the nation's treasury. But it was the homeless who were Mr. Holly's chief care; thousands of them to be transported out of London to somewhere where they would find a roof to cover them, something to lie down on and something to eat. The stream seemed never-ending, and if he hadn't been so fat the sight of them would almost have got Mr. Holly down. Pitiful they were, clutching bundles of odds and ends salvaged from the ruins of their homes, bewildered, stumbling with fatigue. Up and down among them Mr. Holly strode, red-faced, cheery, huge of stature, his stentorian voice booming encouragement. He had always been pitiful to passengers in distress, and with Mr. Isaacson his pity had taken the form of most practical and efficient assistance, but nowadays his pity had deepened to a great stream of godlike compassion that left hardly a single refugee upon his train uncomforted. That was the way those days. The greatness of the horror could be measured against nothing but the greatness of the spirit of the common man. As the evil mounted so, from the trivial faces of human beings, there looked out, to confront it, the eyes of God. Mr. Holly could take it all right, and, what was more, he could have a jolly good time in the process.

"An' wot's the matter with you, eh?" he demanded of a woman and two little girls on Torhaven station.

He was off duty for a bit and was just off home for a nice bit of 'addock and a bite of cold 'am before a good night's rest. The train had gone on, in charge of another guard, and the stream of passengers had practically disappeared. There were only a few people left on the station, among them a demure-looking little woman in a dark-blue coat and skirt with two little girls clinging to her hands, one of them holding a teddy bear. They were examining the few people left on the station with anxious, puzzled faces, trying to make them someone whom they were not. Mr. Holly knew the signs. They had come to meet someone and the someone had not arrived. Only nowadays, of course, when someone did not arrive, the anxious puzzled expression was over-laid with one of blank panic.

Mr. Holly did not like to see this expression upon the faces of children. He loved children. The grief that Mrs. Holly had lost her first was a grief that had never quite healed. He looked down into the pleading blue eyes upturned to his and thought irrele-vantly how shining was their fair hair and how satin-smooth their skin. The perfection of their stainlessness smote upon him, as he had been smitten sometimes by the sight of virgin, un-trodden snow. The pity of it that it must be marred and trodden under. The pity of it.

"Mother's just missed the train," said the demure little woman firmly. "She'll come to-morrow instead." But her firm tones lacked conviction, and Mr. Holly's hearty, "That's right, then," must have lacked conviction also, for the smaller of the two little girls suddenly began to weep.

She made so much noise, and made it so suddenly, that Mr. Holly, who had been bending down to look at her, leaped upright as though a squib had gone off under his nose. But the uproar relieved the tension of the situation, for fortunate are those who can express their grief. Mr. Holly and the demure little woman smiled at each other, pitifully yet with amusement, and Mr. Holly felt in his pockets for a penny. Its production was a suc-cess. The roars stopped immediately, as the small creature dived for the chocolate machine, and once more voicing the soothing West Country phrase, "That's right, then," Mr. Holly strode off home.

Yet the couple refused to be banished from his mind. The

older child had not cried, and her small face had blanched wanly as she watched him walk away, her eyes still pleading with him to produce her mother from that platform. Well, he hadn't done it. He had achieved many wonders in this war, but there were some things that were beyond even Robert Holly.

But he was still thinking about them as he walked up the suburban road where he lived, a very neat road where neat little houses stood each in a trim bright flower garden. The houses had grey stucco walls, grey slates, bow-windows to the sitting-room and the front bedroom, and front doors with coloured glass in the upper panels. Nearly every sitting-room window had an aspidistra in it, reposing upon a small bamboo table covered with a velvet cloth, and all the window curtains were bright and gay. Most of the window panes were protected with strips of adhesive tape to keep the glass from flying when the bombs fell, arranged in varying patterns of squares or diamonds or triangles, according to the individual aesthetic taste of the owner. There were streets and streets of these houses in the hinterland of Torhaven, behind the old harbour and the big white Victorian houses on the cliffs, running up and down the hills like endlessly unfurling ribbons. They were ugly, but nowadays, by reason of their frailty, poignant. There were few who could pass them by without a catching of the breath. Up till now only a few bombs had dropped on Torhaven, but one could only suppose that there would be more to come, and the frail little houses stood waiting for them gallantly with their flowers, their bright curtains, their coloured glass and their decorative window strappings.

Mr. Holly, however, puffing and snorting up the hill, did not catch his breath from anything but obesity. He had the sense not to concern himself with bombs that had not fallen yet. He'd enough to do dealing with the ones that had, and he weighing fourteen stone and not as hasty in his movements as one would wish to be with a war on. He lifted the latch of the front gate, walked up the narrow path of grey granite chips between his autumn dahlias, opened the front door and bellowed, "Mother!"

Mrs. Holly, always called "Mother" by Mr. Holly because of that baby who had been born thirty years ago and only lived an hour, squeezed herself through the kitchen door and inserted herself into the passage. She entirely blocked the passage, for she was even broader than Mr. Holly, though not so tall. Her face was round and rosy and smiling, her eyes dark brown, merry, bright and kindly, her shining black hair untroubled with grey. She wore a black silk dress with red roses on it, a purple cardigan, large dangling green earrings, a string of artificial pearls round her neck, high-heeled shoes upon which her great bulk tottered most perilously, and a large white apron. In a sense she cared about fashion as little as did Miss Brown, for she had no time to bother about the mode, or to see that her garments matched each other, and was concerned only to be clean and gay. Yet she never looked blousy, she was as fresh and consoling and cheerful to the eye as a full-blown peony in the early morning. . . . And she was a superb cook. . . . Mr. Holly embraced her with appreciation and backed her into the kitchen.

In the kitchen the saucepans shone like silver and the windows winked in the sun, and there was a huge pot of yellow marigolds on the snowy tablecloth. On the table, besides the 'addock and the 'am, there was tea, jams and cakes and pickles made by Mrs. Holly, and a huge steaming dish of baked beans. Other housewives might find themselves handicapped by the food shortage, but not Mrs. Holly. When she appeared at the grocers with her merry eyes shining, her beads tinkling and her earrings swinging, her hat jammed hastily but jauntily over one eye, and unfailing good temper writ large upon her smiling countenance, that worthy dived beneath the counter and brought up a little packet of something or other that he had been saving for her.

Mr. Holly removed his coat, washed his hands at the sink, and sat down. Mr. Isaacson was already in his shirt sleeves, getting down to it.

It is possible that good food had been as instrumental in accomplishing the spiritual salvation of Jo Isaacson as the Hollys' kindness. Thoughts of suicide do not flourish in an aroma of baked beans and belief in God is strengthened, not weakened, by a well-cooked ham. Mrs. Baxter had been a good cook too, but not nearly so good as Mrs. Holly, and she had been cruelly handicapped by lack of means. Her hams had been well cooked, but they hadn't been a nice bit of ham to start with; not like this one. In an incredibly short space of time Mr. Isaacson handed up his plate for more.

Mrs. Holly, as she refilled it, smiled indulgently, as though Mr. Isaacson were a small and greedy boy. If his contact with humanity upon the railway had saved Mr. Holly from having his perceptions blunted by fat and good living, the child she had lost had performed the same office for Mrs. Holly. Motherhood had been quickened in her with her child, and turned compassionate by her grief, and now she poured it out liberally upon every unfortunate creature who came her way, including Mr.

Isaacson and the stray cat without a tail who sat before the fire.

She'd not had an easy time with Mr. Isaacson, and if her compassion had not been strengthened by the conviction, shared with Mr. Holly, that in a world gone mad with destruction everything that could be salvaged must be salvaged, bones and chocolate paper and immortal souls, it is possible that after a reasonable time had passed she might have looked about her for another lodging for him, and given herself a bit of rest from those eccentricities in Mr. Isaacson that she did not particularly appreciate. There was the drink, for instance. You can't wean a man from the drink all in one day, and though good food was having a certain amount of success in conquering the craving for it, Mr. Isaacson did frequently return home at night in a state not approved of by Mrs. Holly. She had difficulty in getting him to bed sometimes, and as he usually chose the nights when Mr. Holly was away for being extra merry, the neighbours talked. And then Mrs. Holly was not musical and couldn't see a lot of difference between the noise Tibby the cat made on the roof and the noise Mr. Isaacson made in his bedroom on his violin. And nor could the neighbours, who talked again. And then she could have taken in refugee children from London if Mr. Isaacson had not been filling up her only spare room, and she would have liked that. She wished she could push Mr. Isaacson on to some other woman to look after; it was, she felt strongly, some other woman's turn now; but she was determined not to do it until she could find a woman capable of carrying on Mr. Isaacson's rehabilitation as expertly as she was doing herself. And then, as she would say to Mr. Holly, we can't pick and choose in this world, and if the Lord had seen fit to send her Mr. Isaacson to care for, rather than a nice little boy and girl, she'd best get on with it. Both she and Mr. Holly were deeply religious. They were Wesleyan, crossed with Baptist, with a dash of Plymouth Brethren on Mr. Holly's mother's side. It was a good combination. They never missed Chapel on a Sunday and sang fit to lift the roof off.

"Many children on the train, Father?" Mrs. Holly asked.

"'Undreds," said Mr. Holly. "An' two on the platform wot took my fancy. Fair-'aired, an' there to meet a mother wot 'adn't come. The little 'un, she hollered as I've never 'eard a little 'un holler before. Wunnerful the row a little 'un can make. This is a tasty bit of 'addock, Mother."

"Gone up in price," said Mrs. Holly. "Shockin', wot one pays for an 'addock these days. Why didn't the mother come, Father?"

"There's many," said Mr. Holly grimly, "wot won't leave London no more."

Mr. Isaacson abruptly became a gentleman. He laid down his knife and fork together, instead of spread-eagled sideways, and refrained from wiping his mouth on the back of his hand. A queer dignity crept over him, and his voice when he spoke was quieter than usual, with a touch of music in it. These sudden transformations did sometimes take place in Mr. Isaacson, and they always made Mrs. Holly feel most peculiar. They happened, she noticed, whenever anything touched him very sharply, as though the touch released something pent up in him, something deeply hidden that yet still existed because it once had been. She was in awe of Mr. Isaacson then. There was a kingliness about him that she did not understand.

"Were the children alone?" he asked Mr. Holly gently.

"There was a woman with 'em," said Mr. Holly. "Nice little woman she was."

"And the child who cried, had she a toy to comfort her?" asked Mr. Isaacson.

"A teddy bear," said Mr. Holly. "An' I give 'er a penny wot stopped 'er 'ollerin'. You should 'ave seen 'er dive for the chocolate machine." He laughed reminiscently, and handed Mrs. Holly his cup to refill. "'Ave some more 'am," he encouraged Mr. Isaacson.

But Mr. Isaacson, though he had eaten only moderately as yet, seemed to have finished. "If Mrs. Holly will excuse me I'll go upstairs," he said. He got up, pushed in his chair, bowed to her, and left the room with a graceful easy stride quite unlike his usual loping, dogged walk.

"Queer chap," marvelled Mrs. Holly.

"'E was Somebody once, I shouldn't wonder," said Mr. Holly, and poured his tea into the saucer. "'E is still when anything's put 'im out."

III

Alone in his room Mr. Isaacson sat by the window, looking out at the distant wooded hills that rested so tranquilly against the sky, above and beyond the long sprawling lines of the little gaily coloured suburban houses, so distant to-day in the blue autumn haze that they looked like the outlines of another country. Far up among them, folded within their peace, was the old Castle. In imagination he could see it among the blue hills like one of those distant towns in a Van Eyck picture, clear but yet unearthly beyond the busy foreground, an inviolable celestial city. That old Castle always drew him now with a painful persistent longing that dragged at him, pulling, pulling, as though the whole hope of his life lived within its woods. He had never known anything like that persistent pull, unless it were the persistent lifting, lifting, of the *Andante of the 9th*. He trusted neither of them. Though, no longer in hell, he could play the *Andante* again he still thought it was a lying cheat, promising what it could not perform. And he felt the same about the Castle. In the person of Stephen it had promised so much; yet when he got there, and in the deep peace of the woods had seemed so near to fulfilment, it had most cruelly cast him out in the person of that woman whom he loved. It made no difference to the intensity of his feeling that he knew his love to be a crazy thing, without foundation of knowledge or even probability; he loved her and she had run from him at the mention of another man's danger as though he no longer existed. It had been a cruel wound that she had dealt him. He had walked straight back to Torhaven, drunk himself besotted and vowed he would never go back to those woods again.

And now Mrs. Baxter was dead and in the shadow of them Moppet and Poppet wept.

He had not the least doubt that those two children had been Moppet and Poppet, in charge of Miss Brown. Nor did he doubt that Mrs. Baxter was dead. She had been good to him, and sitting in the Hollys' gay kitchen the conviction of her passing had fallen like a cloud upon the brightness of it. May God have pity upon her, and upon those who killed her. May God have pity on us all. Strange how in moments of emotion one prayed still, though faith in God was a childish toy, set aside long ago. Prayer was so instinctive a thing, and as fair and shining as the *Andante* with its beautiful betrayal.

But what about the kids? Should he go to them at the Castle he'd vowed he'd never get within a mile of again? Did they need him at all? Surely not. They were surrounded by kindness and by this time they would have forgotten the old fiddler who had long ago amused them with his tunes in a far-away London kitchen.

Then he remembered the conversation he had had with Mr. Holly in the guard's van. "You felt you 'ad to keep your eye on 'em," had said Mr. Holly. "Any father'd feel the same." Mr. Holly had thought then that the children were Mr. Isaacson's own, and in a sense he had not been mistaken, for in London Mr.

Isaacson had always been a second father. It might be that they looked to him for something or other even now, something connected with that old home that had gone for ever. Yes, he must go to them. He must face another repulse from that woman he loved, he must even brave that butler if he could think of no better way of attracting the children to him than ringing the front-door bell. He would wait a day or two, for them to get the news of their mother's death. He would go on Saturday, when they would be home from school.

His decision taken, unreasonable joy descended on him. In imagination he saw again those towers among the blue hills, far up above the hum of the busy town, the towers of a celestial city that was calling, "Come this way."

IV

Pratt the gardener slowly perambulated the vegetable garden, and Moppet and Poppet perambulated in his rear, for they found him a comfort to them. They wanted comforting, for mother was dead.

Everybody always found Pratt very comforting. He was stout, with a large red face, a broad smile and a rolling gait that was very soothing to watch. In his corduroy trousers and brown coat, with earth on his hands and in the creases of his smiling face, he looked a part of the land he tended. He never seemed to do very much work in the garden, beyond rolling around it spade on shoulder, yet under his care it blossomed with an astonishing luxuriance. It was his competence, combined with his good-natured refusal ever to put himself out about anything, that made him so comforting. He cared only that his vegetables and flowers should grow; the crimes and failures of men were to him mere irrelevancies, and watching him one was inclined to share his view; if the earth continued to bring forth her fruit in due season then all was well with the earth, and who was man that he should think himself of more importance than that permanent and blessed thing, the solid earth?

Moppet and Poppet did not reason about Pratt, they merely trundled along behind his broad brown back and were comforted by the feeling of safety that its sheer solidity gave them. For safety had been rudely torn from their world and they were terribly afraid. Mother, who had always been the centre of their life, was gone, and if she, hitherto the most permanent thing in existence, could go, then everything else could go too. Everything might fall away and leave them quite alone. Nothing seemed certain now except Pratt's broad back.

Miss Brown said that heaven was certain. She had assured them over and over again that mother and father were not really dead but had merely gone away to this other country where the three little children already were, leaving their bodies behind them like a suit of clothes, and so Moppet and Poppet must be good little girls and not cry their eyes out, and Miss Brown would look after them always; they were her very own little girls now and she would never let them be taken away from her. But Moppet and Poppet were not much comforted because they did not know where or what heaven was. They did not know where to look for it or how to find a point of contact with it, and Miss Brown's explanations were so vague that they doubted if she had much idea either.

"I'm off home for me tea," said Pratt from the recesses of the toolhouse, in which his perambulations had finally landed the three of them. "You childer would be best indoors along wi' Miss Brown."

But Moppet and Poppet, standing in the toolhouse door side by side and gazing sadly up at him, shook their heads. They loved Miss Brown, and they were glad that she wanted them to be her own little girls always, but she could not show them where heaven was and so she was no use just at present.

"Go 'an play in the woods, then," suggested Pratt. "There's nuts i' the woods." He picked them up one in each hand, for they were blocking his way out of the toolshed, and set them down on the long path between the lavender hedges that led to the woods, and then rolled off to his tea.

The woods? They had always been afraid of the woods, and they had still never ventured into them alone, but Pratt seemed to think the woods would be a good place for them, and the birds who had woken them up in the early mornings when they first came, and whose singing had seemed to pull their hearts right out of their bodies, came from the woods and went back to them again. And the trees outside their bedroom window were always calling to them to go and find their hearts where the birds had hidden them. Perhaps it would be a good thing to go. Certainly they seemed to have no hearts inside them at present; where there had once been two merrily ticking clocks there seemed now nothing but two aching voids. They would go. The huge vague terror caused by their mother's death was so immense a thing that their little fear of the woods was lost in it. They were now no more afraid of the woods than of anything else.

Hand in hand they trotted down the path. It entered the woods beside a maple tree that was a blaze of scarlet, lighting the way, and across the entrance there drifted the fragrant blue smoke of Pratt's bonfire. They had to push through the smoke with arms across their eyes, and when they were through it seemed to drop behind them like a curtain cutting off their retreat, so that they had no choice left but to go on.

They were in the deepest and the most mysterious part of the woods on one of those dark still autumn days when not a leaf stirs unless it is to leave its home in the branches and float down silently to the ground. The winter winds and rains were coming and the woods knew it, yet against the grey sad background they spread themselves in a beauty that was like a shout of triumph in the face of death. The bracken was tawny, the leaves of the nut trees yellow, the bramble leaves were touched with scarlet, and the mosses and lichens upon earth and tree-trunks shaded through every imaginable colour from deepest crimson to palest gold. Overhead the leaves were a mass of darkness against the clouded sky, but the great tree trunks held it far off and distant, like an uplifted doom that they would not permit to fall. Under the massed darkness the two little figures trotted, hardly conscious of it, seeing only the golden toadstools and the scarlet moss-cups on the fallen twigs. They stopped sometimes to pick a spray of moss like a miniature fir tree, or a green fern glowing on a tree trunk, and the littleness of these things stole away some of their fear.

They came to a place where the path forked and because they did not know which way to turn, they stopped to listen. When they had gone out for walks with their mother or Miss Brown they had often run on ahead, and then when they did not know which way to go they had stopped to listen for the voice that called, to the right, to the left. In their experience, when you did not know which way to go, there was always a voice that called.

But now they heard only the birds, not the victorious chorus that had woken them up in the summer but a soft mooted cooing and fluting that were like the murmuring of sorrow. It was lovely to hear but it did not tell them anything, so they went on standing still and waiting. And then from out of the flutings and murmurings a single voice detached itself and cried aloud in joy. As the bright colour of the leaves against the grey day so this joyous voice, too, against the sorrowful autumnal murmuring of the birds, was an affirmation of triumphant faith. The children knew no more than before where or what heaven was, but unconsciously they had made their contact with it. They turned to the right, from whence the voice called, and ran on.

And presently it was not just an isolated cry but a definite thread of music that one could catch hold of, like the end of a coloured thread that they could pick up and wind into a ball as they followed where it led. On and on they ran, the tune growing more and more joyous, the woods burning ever more gloriously about them, so that the greyness and the sorrow vanished right away, and then they turned a corner and saw a man sitting on a fallen tree trunk with a fiddle tucked beneath his chin. He heard the snapping of twigs beneath their running feet, heard their joyous cry, put down his fiddle and held out his arms, and in one wild rush the little girls flew into them.

They had always loved Mr. Isaacson, but never so much as at this moment. Because he had been with them in the old life he seemed to them now like mother, like home, like all the old familiar things that they thought had fallen away for ever. Not all Miss Brown's tenderness and careful explanations had comforted them like the feel of Mr. Isaacson's old coat against their cheeks and his strong bony arms about them. They sobbed, and they laughed through their sobs, and nestled against him with the soft thrusting movements of young puppies or lambs who seek again the shelter of their mother's womb against the rigour of a pitiless world, and the universe seemed to steady about them and safety came back, and the aching voids where their hearts had been were filled again. . . . Thank God, thought Mr. Isaacson, that children are so easily comforted.

v

Ten minutes in the woods before tea had become a habit with Miss Brown. She had come to find it almost as refreshing as tea itself. Things did not go wrong in the woods, as they often did indoors. The life of the trees was without mistakes. Why can't you communicate your good sense? Miss Brown asked the trees that grey afternoon. Here, with you, I ought to be wise, yet I'm no better, really, than I am indoors. . . . Look at the way I behaved that afternoon.

Walking along this particular path Miss Brown never failed to remember how deplorably she had behaved to that battered man who had asked her for her friendship. She had tried to give it, and then, at the news of Richard's danger, she had brutally run away from him without a word of apology or farewell. And when she had got to the Castle Mr. Birley had, naturally, not wanted her. She had run from a man who needed her to one who did not. I was stupid as well as cruel, she thought; and in this perfect setting of the woods. If I'd had Mrs. Heather's wisdom that day I'd have known we were one, that man and I, and I'd have been gentler. I wish I could live that afternoon over again and do it better. Some people say one lives human life over and over again until one gets it perfect; one ought to be given the chance to live certain scenes in one's life over and over again, reliving them like scenes in a play until one no longer blunders. She looked about her at the glory of the autumn woods. Oh, to get the drama of man's living right at last. The scenery was perfect, the great lights in heaven and the mighty arc of the sky, the woods and waters and the jewelling of leaf and wing and flower. Such a setting was surely not designed for such a perpetual blundering. . . . I wish, thought Miss Brown, that I could live that afternoon over again.

Quite unconsciously she had come in her walk to the fallen tree where she had sat with Mr. Isaacson; and there he was. She stopped dead, rubbed her eyes and looked again. Was there some extra magic abroad in the woods to-day, that she was being given her second chance? But things were not quite as they had been the other day, for Mr. Isaacson was not alone but actively engaged in comforting Moppet and Poppet. And he was doing it much better than she had been able to do. She saw that and was humbled.

"It's because I knew 'em in London," explained Mr. Isaacson. "I've been like another father to 'em." He had looked up and seen her, and had seen that she was humbled, and instantly given her what comfort he could. He moved himself and the children further along the tree trunk, too, so that she could sit beside them and not be shut out from their family love. For that was what it was, and Miss Brown recognised it as she sat beside them. In Mr. Isaacson the children had found again what they had lost.

"Please forgive me," she said to him, and he nodded to her, smiling, for he knew of what she was thinking. He, too, had the sensation that they were playing the previous scene over again, and that this time they were getting it right.

"What's for tea?" demanded Poppet suddenly of Miss Brown.

She had cried her grief out, she had been comforted, and now she found herself uncommonly hungry. If she looked to Mr. Isaacson for spiritual consolation, she was well aware that bodily comfort proceeded from Miss Brown.

"Bread and butter and honey," said Miss Brown, "and biscuits with sugar on the top, and Mr. Isaacson will come back to the Castle and have nursery tea with us."

"What'll Mr. Boulder say?" enquired Moppet.

"Mr. Boulder," said Miss Brown bravely, "has nothing to do with nursery tea."

Mr. Isaacson laughed. He no longer felt afraid of Boulder. He most mysteriously no longer felt afraid of anything. The thought of nursery tea with these children and this woman whom he loved gave him a sense of firm ground beneath his feet that he had not had for years.

CHAPTER XII

I

MR. BIRLEY looked up from his writing to find his younger great-nephew standing before him. "I've had my tribunal," said Stephen, "and I've got a spell of leave to come and tell you about it. They were sympathetic and I'm to go on with the work I'm doing now."

"Glad to see you," said Mr. Birley. "Sit down." And he put the stopper in his ink bottle and leaned back in his chair, the tips of his long fingers pressed judiciously together, unconsciously taking up the attitude that he had always adopted when in the past he had had to lecture the boys upon their misdemeanours. But Stephen, taking the chair upon the other side of the writing table, did not take up the tense expectant attitude that had been his in those far-off days; he leaned back easily in his chair, one leg crossed over the other, and smiled at Mr. Birley. The Stephen who had left the Castle an over-sensitive boy had come back a man; and a resolved and hardened man who, though he would respect his uncle's opinion, would no longer be wounded by it. . . . He was incredibly changed. . . . Mr. Birley removed his finger-tips from their judicial position and laid his hands humbly on the arms of his chair. He was now, he recognised at once, in the presence of a man who was his equal.

"The fact that you went to the tribunal tells me that you are still a pacifist," he said. "Somehow I was expecting the London Blitz to smash your pacifism."

"But why, Uncle Charles?" asked Stephen. "I was still undecided when I went to London. I went there to see war at first-hand and really make up my mind about it, and after a few days of digging the dead and the dying out of the ruins of their homes I made it up quite easily. War is the most hideous evil that ever existed and I'll fight it with every ounce of strength I have until I die."

"We won't argue," said Mr. Birley in his lecturer's voice. "We've argued too often and too bitterly in the past. I consider your point of view to be demonstrably false but I recognise your right to it. It is for the freedom of a man's mind that we are, after all, fighting. It has always been my conviction, as well as yours, that a man's first duty is the keeping of the faith, whatever that faith may be. I have never deplored the fact that individual faiths differ so violently, jostling against each other like the chariots in a chariot race, for that jostling is a testing in which the unworthy beliefs go under while those worthy of a man carry him thundering in to victory."

Stephen smiled again, for by this time he and Richard had all Mr. Birley's little lectures well by heart. "And harnessed to the chariot are those furious horses fear and pride," he said, "and to learn how to control them is the second duty of a man."

"A knowledge which you have gained in these last few weeks," said Mr. Birley. "I am proud of you, Stephen. I did not know you had it in you."

Stephen flushed at the unexpected praise. Fear? Pride? Certainly, ringed round with fire, with death at his right hand and all hell let loose about him, he had learned to control physical fear; and that other fear that had always dogged him, the fear of censure, had completely perished; if he could not think as other men did at least he could suffer as they did, and the grand high pride that came of equal suffering had done to death the niggling despicable pride that in old days had been so wounded by other men's criticism.

> ". . . our strength is now the strength of our bones
> Clean and equal like the shine from snow
> And it is the strength of our love for each other."

In the gallery once, on a day that now seemed centuries ago, he had read of that strength of love and longed for it; and in the London Blitz he had found it, and found it through such a trivial incident.

"An odd thing happened——" he said to Mr. Birley, and then

stopped, flushing again. One could not tell these things. Put into words they sounded so unutterably silly.

"I should be much obliged if you could tell me of it," said Mr. Birley with strange humility. "I should be glad if you could tell me of yourself and your work. I feel most painfully out of things. . . . An old man, taking no part. . . . And you and I have never been as intimate as we ought to be."

Stephen smiled and began again, quite easily now, for any sort of need in another seldom failed to draw the perfect response from him.

"The first week or so was hell," he confessed. "I thought I'd break, not just physically, but mentally. I was more afraid than I knew one could be; not afraid of what was happening, but afraid of breaking. It was not so bad when things *were* happening, there was no time then for anything but working like a demon, the bad times mostly came when one was supposed to be resting. One couldn't sleep, of course, one's body ached too much and thoughts whirled madly and one saw things; the grotesque dead bodies, the injured, the filth and stench of it all. The kind of death one sees in peace time, a body decently laid out, with flowers about it and the eyes closed, is one thing, but death in battle is quite another, it's hideous and horrible, and when the dead are little children it drives you mad; you can't forget it."

"Nor should you," said Mr. Birley fiercely. "And hatred of their murderers is righteous hatred."

"But I don't hate their murderers," said Stephen. "Those who kill and injure are killing and injuring themselves. What I hate is myself, because the humanity that's me can do these things. I've never loathed myself as I have since the war broke out; somehow seeing how bestial man can be shows one how despicable one is oneself."

"Aren't you proud of yourself, too, that you did not break?" asked Mr. Birley. "And proud of your country that she had not broken either?"

"Yes, of course," said Stephen. "It cuts both ways. One can loathe oneself and be proud of oneself at the same time. And I'm happy because I know now that I shall never go to pieces; nor will humanity; we'll win through."

"You spoke of something particular that happened," said Mr. Birley. "There always comes, I think, a sort of peak in suffering at which either you win over your pain or your pain wins over you, according as to whether you can, or cannot, call up that extra ounce of endurance that helps you to break through the circle of yourself and do the hitherto impossible. That extra ounce carries you through 'le dernier quart d'heure.' Psychologists have a name for it, I believe. Christians call it the Grace of God. . . . Something odd often happens at the peak."

"It wasn't odd," said Stephen. "It was just ordinary. A whole row of houses had been blown to blazes, one of those rows of mean little poor houses that mostly seem to bear the fury of it all, and the neighbours thought that there were a man and woman buried in the ruins of one of them. We started working in the early morning, by the light of a blazing building up the street, getting the rubbish off them. It wasn't difficult, for the house had been a small frail one, and there weren't many of us on the job. We were nearly at the end of it when the other chaps were called off to help with something more urgent down the street, and left me to carry on alone for a bit. I was at what you call the peak. It had been an awful night and I kept being sick, bomb-stomach they call it, and I'd the sort of backache that makes you feel you're breaking in half. I was terrified that I'd conk out. And I kept seeing things; a dead body where there wasn't one, a bit of an arm or leg that turned out to be only a splinter of wood; I wondered if madness hadn't really got me this time. And then I tripped over something and fell on my face on a pile of rubbish, and I tried to get up and I couldn't. It was awful lying there, knowing I was done. I'm broken, I thought; failed; I knew I should. There's a man and woman lying here beneath me and I can't get them out because I'm broken. And then I thought, I'm *not* broken. No man's defeated till he says he is. I'll not say I am. And I began to pull away bits of brick and stuff with my hands even though I couldn't get up. And then somehow I got on my knees and began scrabbling like a dog does when he's after a bone. And then I was on my feet and I could use my pick again, and then I seemed to have broken away from my own weakness and it didn't seem any time at all till I'd got through to the man and woman."

"Alive?" asked Mr. Birley.

"They were dead. At first that seemed bitter, after the struggle I'd had to get them out. I got the rubbish and stuff off them. They weren't pretty to look at, and I was turning away to find the chaps with the stretchers when something made me look at them again. It was their attitude. They had been thrown together so that it looked as though they'd turned to each other as they'd died. It was dawn now and the light of it washed over them as they lay. They were hideous, with their staring eyes, but there was beauty in their attitude, a sort of love, as though in their last moment they had been reconciled to all that is. I leaned over them, looking at them, and the blood from a cut on my hand fell on the woman's face. And I was reconciled, too; one with them, with everyone, loving with such power that I felt as though the strength of all that I loved was mine too. If that's to be the end of it all, I thought, this reconcilement, then nothing matters. I went with their bodies to the mortuary and I know where they're buried, and I'll never forget them. Whatever happens I'll not be afraid again, for when you've once pushed through the place of torment to the peace beyond, you know that you can do it again. You know there's a strength somewhere that you can call upon. You've confidence."

Mr. Birley looked curiously at this inconceivably changed young man. Was this the Stephen who had disliked getting his hands dirty, who had shunned gardening because it made him ache in the middle? The dirt was ingrained on his hands now and the long sensitive fingers were calloused, with broken nails. He had lost most of his beauty. His bright hair was dulled and receding already at the temples, fatigue and the unhealthy conditions under which he lived had lined and stained the clear skin, and he moved stiffly and heavily, as the immensely weary move. That look of lightness and ease that had been his great charm was destroyed now in his physical body. Yet it still lived in him somewhere. He was reconciled, as he had said, at home in the house of life as he had once been at home in the narrow world of the Castle, and his eyes, with their direct clear glance, were as hard to meet as ever by one who did not retain, as he still did, the distinction of having never yet compromised with himself. Odd that Roger, that gross and unscrupulous rascal, should have had those same eyes. Though the sins of the body had got him down he must yet have retained, at some desperate cost of battle, his inner integrity.

"One sees why he drank," said Mr. Birley suddenly. "A pacifist at that date could not retain the respect of his neighbours by clearing up the debris of a blitzkrieg at peril of his life. A lonely business. He kept the faith but he drugged the loneliness. And then he got the gout and drugged that. Strong-minded though he was, he must have lacked your strength, that extra ounce of endurance we spoke of, and not he but his pain was the victor. He didn't win altogether. Drink and drugs are a humiliating confession of failure."

"Who on earth are you talking of, Uncle?" asked the bewildered Stephen.

"Roger," said Mr. Birley. "It suddenly struck me that you are more like him than like your mother. . . . But you have the extra ounce. . . . This is the first time in your life, Stephen, that I've seen you with dirty hands. Not much hot water for washing, I presume, and the sanitary arrangements probably a little primitive. These things must have borne hard on your fastidiousness."

"My aristocratic pride has been well curbed," agreed Stephen ruefully. "Every kind of pride has been well curbed; the men one works with see to that; they've not much use for aristocrats. Richard with his leanings to the left would feel more at home in my present surroundings than I do, yet I believe Richard has every modern convenience at the aerodrome."

"By the way, Richard's just been transferred to that new aerodrome on the coast, not thirty miles from us," said Mr. Birley with satisfaction. "He'll be home more often now."

"Perhaps," smiled Stephen.

"And your tribunal was sympathetic, you say?" asked Mr. Birley.

"Very," said Stephen. "I'm merely to go on with the work I'm doing. And reconstruction in the intervals of raids. I'm half an architect, you see. I'm well paid. Three quid a week."

The smile they gave each other had grim amusement in it. A Birley wielding a pickaxe for three pounds a week! Shades of their ancestors!

II

Stephen wandered round the beloved old garden, recapturing a faint echo of the joy he had felt when in his schooldays he had come home for the holidays for the first time. There would never be a happiness like that again, but because of his intense love for this place every homecoming, under whatever conditions, would have its joy.

It was November, but there was a warmth in the pale sunshine and a softness in the silvery sky that were like spring. There were still a few late chrysanthemums in bloom, and violets under the Castle wall. The smell of wet fallen leaves was pungent and pleasant and there was no sound to be heard but the cawing of a rook in the woods below. He sat on the low south wall and looked out over the valley, the house hidden from him by bushes of laurestinus still carrying clusters of starry flowers. The autumn gales had stripped the leaves from the trees and laid bare the strong lovely curves of trunks and branches and the exquisite tracery of delicate twigs. The misty sunshine brought out the colours of the bare wood, colours that had lain hidden for so long beneath the canopy of the leaves, browns and greys, amethyst and pink and saffron, fading one into the other to make for the earth a veil of pale soft colour that was surely the loveliest garment that she wore through any of the seasons. It was incredible, thought Stephen, that the same small country could hold the horror he had lately lived through and this peace; incredible but blessedly true. He realised that if the rest of life had to be a perpetual turmoil of struggle—and it was difficult to see how it could ever be anything else for any man or woman alive to-day—this place would be the quiet background of his life, the refuge of his homing thoughts, the thing that kept him sane.

A beloved background, but not more than that. Somehow in the last few weeks his feelings towards the Castle had changed a little. It had always been the centre of his life, its traditions his most sacred possessions, but now, though he loved it no less, there were other things he had come to love with a greater passion. In old days, when he had thought of England, it had always been the pastoral country of his birth that he had thought of, the Castle and the men who were his ancestors. But now the thought of England brought side by side with a vision of green fields and woodlands the thought of steep streets lit by flame, the roar of traffic and the clash of machinery, grey-faced workers hurtling backwards and forwards in the tubes, brave slatternly women, sobbing children, drunks and prostitutes, and the toiling sweating men with whom he worked. Once he had felt he had nothing in common with this England, now it was part of the stuff of his life, nearer to him than breathing, closer than hands and feet. He had moved, he realised, nearer to Richard's point of view, and he was glad, for Richard was right. Richard! He had always loved him, even worshipped him as a small boy less proficient at games than Richard was, but lately it had been increasingly difficult to keep in sympathy with each other. But now it would not be so difficult. He longed for Richard. Sitting on the wall he dreamed of a happiness that he and Richard would yet have together.

But it was not Richard who came to him, it was Prunella, and a Prunella quite extraordinarily pleased to see him.

"I didn't know you'd come home, Stephen," she said happily.

"I came to see Miss Brown about the eggs and she told me you were here."

Eggs? Stephen smiled. It was very refreshing to come to a part of the country where people were still preoccupied with eggs. And a rush of painful happiness swept over him, because he loved her and she was pleased to see him. In London he had hoped that other things were submerging his love of Prunella, but at sight of her he was robbed of this hope. It was no good. He would never love anyone else as he loved her. His new sense of union with everything had brought her nearer to him than ever. The old longing for her rose up again, nearly choking him.

But though she was so pleased to see him she held herself aloof, self-contained and a little challenging, her hands thrust into the pockets of her coat, her golden head held a little arrogantly. She reminded him suddenly and painfully of a young stag at bay. She was on the defensive, and he had never seen her on the defensive before. She was afraid, and unhappy, and the vivid colour in her strained little face did not deceive him at all.

"What's the matter, Prunella?" he asked sharply.

"Nothing," said Prunella. "What should be the matter?"

"Something's always the matter when women load themselves with make-up like that. And you look shockingly tired."

"There's a war on," she reminded him. "You look tired too. Dead beat."

Abruptly and bravely, as though consciously taking a risk, she came to him and put her hands on his shoulders, looking up at him, searching out the changes in him as Mr. Birley had done. He knew that she was deliberately and generously refusing, for their friendship's sake, to let this unknown trouble get between them. Impulsively, before he could stop himself, he flung his arms round her and pulled her close to him, fear for her driving him to the only sort of union with her that he could seize hold of at the moment.

"What's the matter, Prunella?" he demanded again. Yet even as he asked he knew, her body yielding its secret to him because he loved her. He remembered that summer morning when she and Richard had come driving back from the moor together in the doctor's old car, deliriously happy, gallantly good to look upon, equally devoid of either explanations or excuses. Where Prunella had been, how she had found Richard, had been questions which no one had been able to ask because the two of them had been so absurdly happy. He had left that morning for London stunned by their happiness, too numbed by it even to feel the sorrow of leaving home. . . . And now here was Prunella in this trouble.

She stayed quietly in his arms, her hands still on his shoulders. "I didn't know you still loved me, Stephen," she said. "I thought you'd stopped loving me ages ago. Oh dear, what a mess! You love me and I love Richard. It's silly, isn't it?" She spoke in puzzled bewilderment, almost like a little girl who had broken her doll.

"Duffer, of course I didn't stop loving you. I'll always love you," said Stephen, with the impatience of his pain. "Tell me, Prunella."

"But you know," said Prunella wearily. "You know from holding me like this, just as I know that you love me still. One knows so much more about people if one hugs them. So one shouldn't hug them. It's silly. I'm going to have a little baby, and it's Richard's." She finished childishly, almost pettishly, and pulled herself away from him.

They sat together on the wall, and to Stephen the soft colours of the winter trees and the starry flowers of the laurestinus were lost in a sort of mist of crimson rage. Jealousy and furious anger, primitive and ugly, had hold of him. A moment ago he had longed for Richard, but now he hated him, his hatred all the greater in reaction from the longing. Richard was a careless, selfish beast. Richard knew quite well what sort of a girl Prunella was; an ignorant and generous child; if he'd had a spark of decency in him he'd have been more careful of her. His rage mounted until it seemed to take possession of him like an evil spirit, part of him, himself. Get away, break free, he cried to himself, wrenching at his will, and he dragged away from it just as during that night in London he had dragged away from his physical weakness and gone on digging for those buried bodies. And as then, so now. The red mist parted and he saw them again, lying together in that attitude of reconcilement, and it seemed to him that all hatred fell away from him for ever.

Prunella watched him with compunction. "You're the last person I ought to have told, Stephen," she said sorrowfully. "I don't know what made me do it. You seemed to pull it out of me, somehow. I haven't told anyone else but Grandpa. I didn't tell him, only of course he saw. It's very trying, in some ways, living with a doctor. But he's been very sweet to me."

"I should hope so," flashed Stephen angrily, for he blamed Dr. Maxwell too.

"But he needn't have been," said Prunella, "because it was my fault, not Richard's. It was all my fault. I'll tell you, Stephen."

But Stephen, when she had told him, continued to curse the old doctor in his heart. Prunella, after the shock she'd had, should not have been left alone.

"Don't be afraid, Prunella," was all he could find to say. "Human beings are always groping for oneness with each other, any and every sort of oneness. Many of the ways we try are futile, stupid, but the thing that's drawing us is all right. It's life, and that's good. You'll live more deeply because of this, have more to give, and that's all that matters."

"I'm not afraid in the way I expect you think I'm afraid," said Prunella. "Not of the village talking about me, or being ill, or anything like that. I'm just afraid, like I've always been afraid, of losing Richard. You see, Stephen, if Richard finds out he'll feel he must marry me, and he'll make me marry him, for I can't hold out against him. But he won't go on loving me, Stephen, for he'll feel he was forced. And then I shall have lost him as utterly as though he had died."

"So you've not told him," said Stephen.

"No," said Prunella proudly. "And I've made Grandpa promise not to tell him, and you must not either."

"No," promised Stephen, and looking out over the woods he marvelled at the perpetual paradox of human life. Longing for him she must not have him lest she lose him. It was a mystery that this world could not solve.

"But what will you do now, Prunella?" he asked her. "What will you do? Richard is to be stationed quite near here, you know. He'll be over often."

"Grandpa and I," said Prunella quietly, "are just waiting for a bit. We'll see what to do soon. One does, you know."

"Yes," said Stephen. "One does."

She got up to go, standing in front of him boyish and straight, her hands once more deep in the pockets of her coat. "I'm glad you still love me, Stephen," she said. "It's selfish of me to be glad, but I am. I've been telling you about things almost as though you were my mother."

She smiled and was gone, leaving Stephen to recover as best he could from the unconscious cruelty of her final stab. To have her thinking of him as a mother was ridiculous, an intolerable insult to his man's pride. What was missing in him that he had not been able to make her love him as she loved Richard? Something was missing, some spark of virility that Richard had and he had not, and no amount of doing a man's work and bearing a man's burdens would give it to him. Bitterly he realised he would never be loved as Richard was loved. Respected, yes, perhaps held in lasting affection, perhaps even one day reverenced, but not loved with that fiery love that seemed to him now the greatest treasure life had to offer. Well, he had much. He knew now that there was something in him that knew how to break away from defeat, and he was reconciled, and at home in the world.

III

That night, when darkness shrouded the Castle, Richard sat by the reading lamp in his little room at the aerodrome, and chewed the end of his pen. Writing letters was always anathema to him. Either he didn't know what to say, or if he did know what to say he didn't know how to say it. But this was a letter that must be written, and written soon. He had already kept Prunella waiting far too long. And he must really try to say what he felt, difficult though it was, for if he left it until they met again something might have happened to one of them and then it would be too late. He grinned ruefully at the confusion of this thought and then coiled his legs boyishly round the legs of his chair as he bent to the labour of composition. There was a raid on at the town on the coast not many miles away but the crackle of the guns and the distant crash of bombs did not disturb him any more than the wind in the trees at home would have done. This was his night off, for the dawn patrol was his. A strange attentive quiet seemed to gather about him as he wrote and the words came to him more easily than he had expected, his sprawling boyish hand-writing covering the pages with surprising speed.

"Darling Prunella," he wrote, "will you marry me next time I come home on leave? And will you forgive me for being such an age asking you? When I think about it I can't really forgive myself, because I've loved you ever since that day last winter when I was on the terrace and you walked in under the archway in a green dress, looking like a dryad, or Celia in the Forest of Arden, or something not to do with this world at all. That's why I love you, I think; because you're not such a clod of earth as I am myself. And because you're like that I can't forgive myself, either, for what happened on the moor. And now I want to say something that's frightfully important. I'm not asking you to marry me because of what happened on the moor but because the thing I want most in the world just now is to have you for my wife. That's the truth, Prunella. Good Lord, what a conceited letter I'm writing! As though I expected you to accept me gladly, instead of turning me down as I deserve. Well, it's true. I don't expect you to turn me down. I know you love me, even though I've been such a cad. You see, when I first loved you I didn't want to get married, I didn't want to settle down at the Castle or to be tied down to anything at all, not even to you. I hated the Castle and the sort of boring orderly life it stood for. I wanted to cut loose from it all and go to the North Pole, or fly the Atlantic upside down, or explore an unknown desert, or some crazy fool thing like that. And yet I felt I had a duty to the Castle, and the fight between that feeling and the longing to cut loose gave me the queer fear of being tied down. At least I think it did. They say that fear comes from holding on too hard to something that you don't want to give up, and I held too hard to my freedom. And so though I always loved you, Prunella, I did not want to love you, and I thought if I married you I'd make you a rotten husband. But the war has changed all that. That time when I was missing I got a nasty jolt. I'd thought myself the devil of a fellow, afraid of nothing, and I discovered then that I could be desperately afraid, a coward, shamefully afraid to die. Of course most of us flying chaps are afraid pretty often, and most of them don't mind owning it. 'I *was* in a funk,' they'll say, and laugh, and get on with it. But my fear did not seem to be the natural sort of thing that theirs was. It was a morbid sort of thing, the crawling fear of the imprisonment of death, of being pinned out of sight beneath some revolting marble cross. I suppose it was just part of the old fear of being tied down. The humiliation of finding out what a coward I was at heart, and the fear of my fear, if you know what I mean, in case it should make me do something despicable one beastly day, got me down absolutely. I was so frightened that I just bolted for home, for the little stream on the moors, like a rabbit with a ferret on his tail. Well, then I knew that home meant something to me after all. Every living creature must have somewhere to bolt to. The foxes have holes and the birds of the air have nests. Doesn't that come in the Bible somewhere? I never seem to listen to the lessons in church. Yes, it does. But the Son of Man has not where to lay his head. But he was wrong there, for he had. He had that garden. Lying there by that stream I knew I loved this bit of earth that was my inheritance after all; loved it with the love of all the men of my blood whose hole in the earth it had been. I began to feel about the Castle more in the way that Stephen feels about it. Stephen is right after all, I thought. And then I fell asleep. And then I woke up and you were there, and you were a part of it all, and we fell asleep together as though we'd been married for years. Later, at supper, I had the horrors again, and it was to try and recapture the peace of the time by the stream that I was a selfish brute and let you stay with me. Well, I'm all right now, Prunella. I've been in some even tighter places since then, and I've learned that there's unfailing strength somewhere that's yours if you learn how to make that extra push that controls your will and your fear. And that conflict between wanting to cut loose and wanting to do my duty by traditions and things seems over. Those two points of view can be reconciled, I think, if one keeps the balance true between them, and keeping a true balance, though it's about the most important thing we have to do in this world, seems to me just a question of getting that mastery over one's will. It's taken me a long time to feel like this; having this confidence and feeling at home in the universe as I felt at home beside the stream has come only gradually, and so I've been a long time asking you to marry me, because before I asked you I had to feel more hopeful of making you a good husband. Well, I think I can, so I'm not afraid of asking you to marry me. I expect I'll be restless sometimes but I know that I can be faithful to you. And I love you, Prunella. I think I love you equally with the England I'm fighting for, the England of the woods and hills as well as of the towns and mines and factories. Life is good, Prunella, and especially with you. Life is fine and grand and I love it to the depths of my soul."

His letter finished, he made his way through the darkness to the nearest letterbox and posted it, so that Prunella should get it at the first possible moment, and then he went to bed and slept like a child, lulled by the distant tumult as though it were the wind in the trees at home.

IV

It's good, he thought, as his plane taxied along the ground and roared up into the cold crystal air of dawn, to be keeping one's eye on one's own bit of country. It had been an odd twist of fate that had stationed him at an aerodrome so near his home, so that the bit of coast that he was patrolling this morning included his own bit of coast, with the little rocky bays set about with peaceful harbours and small towns climbing the cliffs.

What a morning, thought Richard. Was there ever anything so lovely? The sky shaded through saffron to green and ultramarine, and then to deep blue overhead, veil upon veil of heavenly colour dropping about him. Far up in front of him was a gorgeous mass of cloud all purple and crimson and rose-pink, with towers and battlements of pure gold, like a great city floating the sky, and over it there trembled one last star, like a lamp upon the highest tower. . . . Civitas Dei. Avalon. The cloud-capped towers, the gorgeous palaces. . . . He laughed for joy at the sight. Now and then he would fly through a smaller cloud that broke over him like a silver spray all lit with gold, and lose sight of it for a moment, and then it was back again, not quite the same, for the sun was building with the clouds to make this city of peace, but lovelier than ever.

He flew into a flock of gulls, disporting themselves at an astonishing height, and immediately they were all about him, wheeling, gliding, beating around and about, their great white wings feathered with gold cleaving the flitting skies. Other birds were afraid of a plane, but not gulls. They seemed to be always wanting to show this queer bird-man that they could do much better than he could. "Who'll get there first?" he cried to them, but even as he spoke he had outdistanced them; they fell away below and he went on alone. It would be fun if one could really get there, thrilling to explore the stoneless streets of that city, lit by the star upon the tower, to hear the trumpet at the gate and see the watchers on the wall, and then set off again like flying pursuivant from city to city of the country of the sky, to see the red suns and the yellow suns, with their planets of lilac and blue, and all the festoons of the little stars like sprays of diamonds in between. That would be the unblazed trail, if you like. What a universe! And he belonged to it. It was home. There was no corner of it where he would feel himself a stranger.

What a row he was making in this great clear quiet sky. Yet the pulsing of the motors seemed a part of the riotous pulsing of his own blood, and the wing-tips to left and right seemed slowly rising and falling with the rhythm of life itself. He was exhilarated as never before, happy as never before. Had it been he who had once been so full of mockery, letting it down like a veil between himself and others so that they should not get near enough to him to bind him with their claims? There should be no more of that. He was free of that fear, now, free of the fear of fear, of the fear of death. He would be able to give now, to the uttermost, and he would be more gentle now because his conflict was over and he was at peace. One was oneself when one was at peace, oneself and utterly happy. "If it were now to die 'twere now to be most happy." Who had said that, his own mind remembering something or that trumpeter at the gate? But death was nothing, a nonentity, a lie, a cheat. It was life that mattered, life that was glorious like a great wind bearing you along, life and not death that plucked your soul from your body, like a feathered seed from a withering plant, and swept it away to a new birth. You knew that with absolute certainty once the fear of death had fallen from you.

His first joyous climb upwards had lasted only a few minutes, though it had seemed like a hundred happy years, and now he dived down, as was his duty, and flew lower over the coast. There was the sea like a spread counterpane of opal silk, reflecting the colours of the sky, fretting with a line of white foam the golden sand that edged a small red town, a town so dwarfed by distance that it might have been taken from a child's playbox and set there upon the verges of the sea. He flew on and then turned a little inland and beneath him were the winter woods, the green pasture lands dotted with sheep, the farms folded in the hollows of the hills. This was his own country and his new-found love for it made his heart leap up in joy. Now for a brief moment he could see Beacon Hill with its sentry on guard. Was it, perhaps, Stephen, keeping watch over their inheritance on land, as he in the air? And there was Applegarth Church, and the Castle among its woods, poised upon the precipice over which Richard his ancestor had plunged to his death rather than yield to his enemies, and leading to it the road that the giant's finger had traced along the crest of the hill. It was old, centuries old, deeply sunk between its hedges. Many times had the men of his blood passed and repassed along that road, men in armour, men on horseback, men tramping in doublet and hose, men marching to the wars with pennons flying, men riding to court or camp, or down to the coast to fight for England on the sea. He could see the very harbour from which they had sailed, not used very much now, its fishing boats rocking at anchor and its old houses climbing the steep cliffs, white walls flushed by the dawn and wet roofs glistening. How important they had been, those ancestors of his to whom he had scarcely ever given a thought. Each a link in a chain. Each generation the foundation stone on which the next would build. How clear the light was now, amazingly clear, like the atmosphere in a Flemish landscape. One could see everything. One could even look back into the past and see those marching men. Good-bye, good-bye, he cried to it all, to the woods and the fields, the Castle and the church, to the marching men on the road and the sentry on the hill, good-bye, good-bye. And then he flew on. Yet he had not really said good-bye, for he carried it with him in his heart.

He had just turned back again over the coast when he saw the column of earth shoot to the sky. Three Jerries, a bomber and two yellow-nosed Messerschmitt fighters, the sun glinting on the chromium of their engines, had swooped out of the lovely dawn-flushed clouds and were attacking the little town and harbour by the sea from which long ago the men of his blood had set sail for the seven seas. The brutes! The little town was of no importance now; only the fishermen used the harbour, and the people who lived in the old white houses had no protection but their frail rubble walls. The rage seemed drumming in his veins in time to the rhythm of his motors as he soared up and then dived, man and machine one vengeful entity together as they screamed down, like a hawk out of the sky. Three to one, but it didn't matter. He felt only a glorious exhilaration. He steadied the plane, flicked over the catch on the gun button from "safe" to "fire," and pressed the button. He felt the exciting trembling of the plane as the gun answered and the fight was joined. This would be a grand fight, the best he had had. One last quick clear vision was his of the dawn sky, the city built out of clouds, the beautiful clear landscape lying so defenceless beneath him, and one last quick thought of the ugly country of the factory chimneys and the grey-faced men in the streets that were all one thing some-how, a thing called England, and then there was no time to think of anything but what one had to do. That bomber must be kept over the sea, where his bombs could do no harm. Climbing, diving, escaping, attacking, thinking intensely, daring to the uttermost, every nerve and thought and muscle working together like oiled machinery, the last ounce of available strength tapped and used, the whole mechanism of a man keyed to the highest point of efficiency and unified in a blazing flame of selfless courage. Glorious and perfect living, just for a moment or two. Worth while having lived if only for this.

The bomber was reeling off over the sea, flame licking out along his fuselage and smoke pouring from his tail. Thank God he'd got the bomber. The little town was safe. Only the bright yellow-nosed fighters were left, furiously enraged, more tenacious than most Jerries, and hard to keep at bay because his plane was now a bird with a wounded wing. The tracer streaks seemed all about him, there was blood on his hands and his mind was moving now most damnably slowly. The cockpit was full of cordite fumes and it was infernally hot. But one did not give in. Better to crash to death than to yield to one's enemies. Over the Castle wall and down over the precipice. Better that than give in. Think, think, you fool; but he could not think and there was a hideous scorching pain somewhere in his body. He had been fighting for hours, for years, for ever, yet the last thing he saw clearly was the face of the little time-piece in the cockpit registering a fight of just ten minutes. He had lost control and was plunging down. Fear again, fear just once more, and then no more of that for ever.

CHAPTER XIII

I

A COLD grey sky and a hard frost after a fall of snow held the woods in utter stillness, no cry of a bird, no stir of wind, and the Castle waited brooding on its precipice. For what? wondered Miss Brown, standing on the terrace steps and pulling on her gloves. Haven't we had enough yet? The house seemed to sigh behind her, and in the cold hard grey light the old walls and the frost-bound bushes in the garden, and the poor plants all stark and cold, seemed to move a little closer, as though the whole place were gathering itself together to withstand a further blow. No, not yet, she thought. We are not at the peak yet. It's the same with places as it is with nations and individuals, the pain must reach its height before the tide can turn, and it is just then that a place will show its quality. What nonsense, she said to herself, I'm thinking of the Castle as though it were a person. It isn't. It's only stone and mortar. . . . Just behind her, in the doorway, somebody sighed, yet when she looked round there was no one there. . . . I'm getting fanciful, she thought, and walked briskly across the garden and out into the woods, searching in her mind for a platitude to steady her. Troubles never come singly, was the one that occurred to her. Yes, that was what she was feeling. No nonsense about an old Castle crouching down like a living thing in pain, but just the age-old human conviction that when you have just had one blow you must prepare yourself for another. It is only with blow upon blow that the metal is shaped.

Was it only three days ago that Richard had been buried in Applegarth churchyard? They seemed like three centuries. It was only three days ago that the little church had been packed to the walls, the mourners for Richard kneeling even out in the porch and down the path to the lych-gate. The men and women from the little town, who felt that their homes and lives had been saved by his fight over the sea, had come with their children to join the ranks of the village folk, and Richard's friends. Yet if there were many mourners it had not been a mournful funeral. The packed congregation had sung "I vow to thee my country" until they nearly lifted the roof off, and the streaming sunshine of that day had lit the union jack that covered Richard's coffin, and the piled flowers about it, to a riot of blazing colour. As they had stood singing in the sunshine the thing that had happened had seemed to Miss Brown glorious, fitting and quite perfect. . . . Until they had gone back to the empty shell of the Castle and she had been confronted with those three silent men, Mr. Birley, Stephen and Boulder. She had not known what to do with them, for they had seemed as empty as the Castle. It was as though Richard had been their life's blood and now they, like the Castle, were bled dry. Their sheer lifelessness had taught Miss Brown, if she had not known it before, the meaning of the word desolation.

It had been a relief to her, distracted as she was by her love for them that could not be expressed, when Mr. Birley had asked her if she would leave them for a week or so and go and look after Dr. Maxwell and Prunella. "Mrs. Heather will come here to be with the children," he had said, "and you can pay us a visit every day, if you like, to see how we're getting on, but I'd like to feel that Dr. Maxwell and Prunella had you for a while. To send you to them seems to me the best thing that I can do for them just at present."

That had caused Miss Brown a thrill of pride. Nothing that he could have said to her, short of telling her that he loved her, could have pleased her more. She was in the pattern this time and no mistake, the mainstay of not one house but two. Instantly she had packed her neat suitcase, issued fluent but clear instructions to Mrs. Heather and Fanny, put on her hat and coat and betaken herself to the little grey house above the village where Prunella was ill in bed, ousted a most unsatisfactory nurse and taken entire and competent charge.

Prunella had taken the news of Richard's death very quietly, but next day she had given birth to a very tiny dead baby and now she was ill, not dangerously, but more ill than she had ever been in her life before. She was very good and quiet in her illness, did exactly as she was told, and smiled and said thank-you childishly and sweetly when things were done for her. She had not mentioned Richard once, had not indeed mentioned anything at all. "Stunned," said the old doctor. "Shock. The whole thing has been wiped out of her mind."

But Miss Brown knew better. Prunella had forgotten nothing that had happened. She had a letter under her pillow in Richard's handwriting, and when Miss Brown moved Prunella on to her other side she moved the letter too, so that Prunella could tuck her hand under the pillow and keep it on the letter. Prunella's peacefulness was simply due to the fact that she thought she was going to die. She had never been really ill before, she was unaware of the extraordinary toughness of the human body, and she thought that this abysmal weakness must surely be death. She lay there patiently waiting for it. Miss Brown did not undeceive her. All too soon would come the day when Prunella would realise that she was getting on very well indeed.

But Miss Brown hurried as she went back through the woods, just in case that knowledge should have come while she was out and Dr. Maxwell be unable to deal with what would happen then. Though for that matter would she be able to deal with it? Would any one? Stephen, perhaps. It was Stephen who had told Prunella that Richard was dead. It was Stephen who dealt with everything nowadays.

She reached the lodge, empty now because Mrs. Heather was in charge of the children at the Castle, but still with that "Enquire Within" notice hanging in front of the geraniums in the window. She stopped for a moment and again she had the feeling that one day, inside that cottage, she would find the answer to something. Some sort of answer the place had already given her to the how and why of living. "With death comes oneness an' that's love," had said Mrs. Heather of the lesser death, physical death, and it was the same with the greater death, the death to self that she had described as "breakin' away from myself." But that had not been a very satisfactory answer because she had only had it on hearsay from Mrs. Heather. She had not discovered it for herself. Perhaps one day, inside the cottage, she would.

Two small fair heads bobbed up behind the geraniums. Moppet and Poppet were inside the cottage. Mrs. Heather must have told them where to find the key and they were playing "house" there. So absorbed were they that they did not see her. She smiled and went on.

It was Saturday afternoon and Moppet and Poppet, with Teddy, were playing at being Peter Rabbit and his brothers and sisters in their home under the roots of the trees. They were happy, for they always felt at home in this little cottage, and utterly unaware that this was the most important day in their lives. To-day, for the first time, they would lift their small hands and knock at the invisible door between this world of time and space and the other that recks not of them, and the sigh, the breath of another life that came through the crack, would colour their thoughts until they died.

The Peter Rabbit game palled at last and in spite of their thick overcoats, their boots, and their little scarlet hoods, they felt the room grow chill. A frozen twig kept tapping at the window, calling, "Come out, come out." They went out, locked the door carefully as Mrs. Heather had bidden them, hid the key under a stone and went stumping along hand in hand up the deep old lane that led to school. They stumped just to keep warm. When they got to the place where the lane reached the crest of the hill before it dropped down again to the village they would turn back, run all the way home and have tea with Mrs. Heather in the warm housekeeper's-room.

But at the top of the lane they stopped, looking up at the steep bank that towered above them. They had lost their fear of the woods since that day when Pratt had told them to go inside, and they had heard the voice calling and had found Mr. Isaacson. The woods were beautiful, they had discovered, and deep in their heart you found yourself in the arms of a father. But they were still afraid of what was over the tops of the hedges. The green fields went on and on until they came to an end in a line against the sky over the edge of which you fell into that terrifying thing called space.

But to-day it seemed that something out of the ordinary was happening over the tops of the hedges. A strange light was flooding over the cold grey sky and it seemed to come spilling over the edge of the high bank they were looking at and dropping in fiery flakes at their feet.

"What's over there?" wondered Moppet, and she looked at Poppet with wide questioning eyes that asked, "Shall we?" And Poppet nodded.

It seemed a simple thing to do, just to climb a bank and look over the top, but it was a great decision and it took great courage, for they really were mortally afraid of space. Yet they felt impelled to do it because the light that came spilling over the top of the bank was so very lovely, and they could not see where it came from unless they climbed.

Scrambling and slipping on the steep frosty ground they tugged at tussocks of grass and the long trails of ivy and periwinkle and pulled themselves slowly up and up. They were hot and panting, with scratched hands and faces, when at last they got there, parted the bare twigs of the bushes that grow at the top, and looked through into such a blaze of glory as they had never seen before. The world of green fields that rolled along until it came to that abrupt and frightening end against the sky had vanished and in its place was a great shimmer of silver white. And the frightening horizon line was no longer in the distance, it was here with them, just this row of little trees on the top of the bank that they were holding on to, and beyond it the shimmering white melted imperceptibly into streaming gold that swept up and over them in a great arc of light. Light. Light. Space was light. Space had moved and come flooding right up to their feet and it was not frightening after all, it was just light.

Sunset over the snow in the country. How were Moppet and Poppet to know that that was all it was? They'd never lived in the country before. They'd never before been so blinded by this virginal stainless glory that they could distinguish no objects at all but only light, light, light. They pushed their way through the tree trunks and went forward, blinking, ecstatically happy, blinded with light, soaked with it, drunk with it, and presently they were running because children when they are happy cannot stay still. They ran downhill, on and on, and they would never have stopped had not Poppet tripped over something and fallen headlong on her nose.

Most astonishingly she did not yell because while still in a prostrate position she saw something of absorbing interest. . . . Footsteps in the snow. . . . Now here was another new thing to a London child, for in London the snow was always cleared off the pavements at once and one did not see footsteps, or if one did it would be just the dirty brown mark of a great boot, not these tiny dainty tracks like the prints of dancing fairies.

"Look! Look!" cried Poppet. "Little children made them! Little children made them!"

Moppet bent to look, and she measured her own small foot against the tracks, and they were certainly the tracks of children, two children, one smaller than the other, about the sizes of herself and Poppet, only these tracks were lighter and airier than hers and Poppet's. The check in their headlong run had more or less brought her to herself now, and she was able to look about her and see where they were. They had run right down to the bottom of a long sloping field. To their right was the snow-powdered dark mass of the Castle woods and to their left the church tower, with snow on its head, rose up out of a hidden hollow and soared towards the sky, and the tracks of the children came from the woods and went towards the church.

But Poppet was not herself yet, she was still in another country. With a queer little cry, rather like a bird's cry of joy, she put her feet in the print of the other little feet and ran on the way they went. And Moppet trundled after.

The airy footsteps went through an open gate and right down another field, and through a second gate and under the yew trees into the churchyard, and in and out around the graves, old ones and new ones, and a very new one where there was a pile of flowers under the snow. The children who had made the footprints had danced as they ran. Poppet knew they had because as she ran she danced too, the joy that had been left behind in the footprints getting right into her and bouncing her up and down like a robin on a swinging branch. She did not know that these were graves that she was dancing round, she just knew that she was happy because the other children had been happy.

But Moppet, trundling after, knew that these were the graves of people who had gone away to the other country, as her father and mother had done, leaving their bodies behind them like suits of clothes. But she did not feel at all afraid because she too felt the happiness that came from the footprints. That day in the woods, when the voice of the violin had cried out so triumphantly against the sorrowful autumnal murmuring of the birds, she had known that the other country existed, and now she knew that it was a happy place.

The footprints ran out of the churchyard another way and turned back again towards the Castle woods, and Moppet and Poppet went with them. It was lovely not to be afraid of the woods any more, even though they were held so very still by the hard frost. It was getting dark in the woods, for the sun had set, and they were running through them by a path they did not know, but they did not feel lost because the footprints were so clear in the gloom and they trusted them utterly.

And suddenly they were scrambling steeply uphill, and looking up through the leafless trees they saw the old grey Castle towering up above them in the twilight. They were glad to see it, for they no longer disliked it. It stood to them now for warmth and shelter. They looked up gratefully at the tower above them, Stephen's tower with his window up in the sky, and down below it Mr. Boulder's window, and below that again the locked door, with the ivy growing over it, that was never opened.

But to-day it had been opened, and two little girls were going in. They wore bunchy frocks of blue and rose-pink and queer little caps on their fair short hair, and one carried a doll dangling from her hand by one arm, and the other carried a book, and Moppet and Poppet wanted to catch up with them more than anything else in the world. They ran and ran, but when they got to the door it was shut and locked and the ivy was growing over it again.

Yet they were not too badly disappointed. Though they realised that they could never now catch up with those other children, yet that glimpse they had caught of them had made it certain that those footsteps in the snow had been real footsteps, made by real children, and that fact made them somehow happier than ever. And they felt proud to think that they had danced so fast that they had very nearly caught them. The long run through the fields and the churchyard and the woods must have taken just no time at all. Time, like space, had seemed to disappear this afternoon.

Hand in hand, rosy from their run in the cold, they went round to the front of the house and climbed the steps to the dark porch, where they nearly fell over That Dog lying on the mat. They bent down to pat his great head, for they knew he was very unhappy. For the last few days he had been lying in the passage outside the closed door of Richard's room, refusing to eat anything or be agreeable in any way, but this morning he had stalked down to the porch and lain there, his great bulk stretched across the threshold of his home as though he were taking care of it. He had not moved all day, although now and then he had raised his great head and bayed deeply and angrily, as though the enemy were already at the gate. Moppet and Poppet knelt down beside him and caressed him with their warm fat hands and Poppet kissed him on his great domed forehead. He put out his tongue and languidly and politely returned the salute, then dropped his head on his extended paws, sighed and closed his eyes. He had liked these children, but he did not really want to be bothered with them now. He was old and very cold and the vital spark was burning low. And once more he had seen the marking of blood upon the door and the eldest son had died in battle. He, The Dog, had lived for centuries in this place, and many times had he seen the marking on the door, but never for a son so fair to look upon and so beloved as this one had been. And now there was doom in the air, and the enemy at the gate, and once more the exile of his people. And he was old and the vital spark burned low. He did not want to be bothered longer with these alien children, and when Moppet in her turn bent to kiss him he growled and flicked his ears.

Moppet and Poppet went hand in hand up the oak staircase. It was very dark now, for the night was coming and the lights had not been lit yet, and the gallery and passages were full of whispers and dark shadows. They knew, as they had always known, that this place was full of people whom they could not see or know, who were there by night as well as by day, as though they had no watches and paid no attention to time. But the unknown no longer frightened them. The unknowable woods had held comfort, and space had turned out to be a great white shining light, and if the people who didn't bother about time were anything like the two little children whose footsteps they had followed in the snow then they were happy people, not so different from themselves, and one was never afraid of happy people. In the years to come they would forget what they had seen, or thought they had seen, to-day, but they would always keep a half-remembered memory that once they had knocked at an invisible door, had seen a beam of light and heard the breath of a sigh; intangible things that had yet set their mark upon life even till death.

"What was written in the little girl's book?" asked Moppet, her hand on the door of the housekeeper's room, where they were going to have tea with Mrs. Heather.

"The little girl's book was 'Peter Rabbit'," said Poppet with conviction.

But Moppet, opening the door, shook her head. She did not think it was.

"Though I walk through the valley of the shadow of death I will fear no evil."

It was Mrs. Heather speaking. She was sitting by the blazing fire reading aloud to herself, her bible on her lap. The lights were lighted and the curtains drawn and a grand tea waiting on the table. "Come in, my dears," she said, and took off her spectacles and put her bible down on the table between the buns and the pot of honey. The children ran to her, warmth and love and joy all about them.

III

In his study Mr. Birley laid down his pen, unable to see any longer, and sighed irritably. He could not switch on his light because it was after blackout time and the curtains were not drawn, and the curtains were not drawn because, though he had rung the bell three times for Boulder, his summons had not been answered. It would have been easier, of course, to have drawn his own curtains, but that would have been bad for discipline. It was Boulder's business to draw the curtains and Boulder must draw them. Discipline must be maintained.

It was one's salvation just at present, the habitual discipline of mind and body that made one able to work and eat and dress and undress, go to bed and get up as usual even though life was drained of its virtue. When one is old the young are the future. One lives in them, for them, life is purposeless without them. When they die the future dies too, leaving the old without hope. . . . Richard. Prunella. Richard. . . . Mr. Birley wrenched his mind away from the thought of them and bent low over the sheet of figures on his desk, trying to make them out in the fading light. Owing to the destruction of house property in London, they had lost close on five hundred pounds a year. Other investments were dwindling too. As far as he could see they were more or less ruined. Not that it mattered. Nothing mattered. . . . Only that grave piled with flowers under the snow and a young girl's life perhaps wrecked for ever. . . . Savagely he pushed the bell for the fourth time. Where the *dickens* was Boulder?

The door opened and he turned round, casting his pince-nez from him, to administer the deserved reproof. But it was not Boulder, it was Stephen. "I found Boulder in a dead faint in the hall," he said laconically. "He's coming round now, and sent me to draw your curtains." He drew them across and switched on his uncle's light. "I should say, Uncle Charles, that Boulder is pretty ill. He looks it. I daresay he's been ill for months, only we haven't happened to notice it."

He spoke with bitterness and self-scorn. He couldn't recall that he'd ever paid much attention to Boulder, nor could he remember that during the last few days he had said a single word of sympathy to him, though Boulder had known Richard longer than he had. There had been a beautiful Chinese bowl in the hall once, but none of them had ever noticed it very much until one day a curtain blown by the wind pushed it over and it lay shattered at their feet, when they suddenly remembered that it had been priceless. He had felt the same reproach, a thousandfold intensified, when he had seen Boulder lying huddled at the top of the stairs that led up from his pantry to the hall; this was ours, without price, lost now; for the unseeing eyes and the casual acceptance may God forgive us.

Mr. Birley strode into the hall and peered through the dusk at Boulder sitting on the edge of a chair, choking over the brandy that Stephen had administered. "I 'eard the first bell, sir," said Boulder apologetically, "an' I started upstairs, an' then I took a queer turn, an' the next thing I knew the bell was ringin' again an' Mr. Stephen was givin' me brandy." He held the glass a little away from him in his shaking hand and looked at Stephen almost venomously. "Our best brandy, too," he mourned. "You should 'ave given me the cookin' brandy."

"Sorry, Boulder," apologised Stephen, drawing the hall curtains. "I just took the first that came to hand."

As the lights shone out Mr. Birley gathered in his pince-nez and adjusted them to look at Boulder with real attention for the first time in years. What he saw horrified him. "Where's Miss Brown?" was his instant reaction to the situation.

"We've lent her to Dr. Maxwell," Stephen reminded him.

Mr. Birley sighed. The world was full of troubles just at present and not the least of them was the fact that the invaluable Miss Brown could not be everywhere at the same moment. But Stephen's mention of Dr. Maxwell told him what he should do next, and he crossed to the telephone.

"No, sir! No, sir!" cried Boulder sharply. "Don't send for the doctor, sir. It ain't nothin'. It ain't nothin', sir."

But it was too late. Mr. Birley had got the doctor's number and the doctor was at home. Boulder listened to the one-sided conversation in dumb despair. Dr. Maxwell would be round in the morning. In the morning he would be sent to the hospital. Mr. Richard was dead, and he would be sent to the hospital. His world crashed about him in utter ruin. He got to his feet and stood swaying. "Thank-you, sir," he said.

"Go to bed, Boulder," said Mr. Birley kindly from the study door. "Fanny and Mrs. Heather will look after us to-night. Go to bed and get a good rest."

"I am perfectly recovered, sir, thank-you," said Boulder stiffly. "I should prefer to continue my duties."

"Just as you like, Boulder," said Mr. Birley, and closed the door and returned to his accounts.

Boulder went to the curtains that Stephen had pulled and pulled them again, rearranging them in their correct position. Stephen stood by the fire and tried to think what to say, and suddenly he remembered, for the first time since Richard had died, that he was now the master of this house. This beloved place belonged to him, it was his own. It was his until he died, and if he married it would be his children's after him. At first a shock of revulsion swept over him, for his inheritance had been bought at too dear a price, then it was followed by that queer feeling of lost identity that comes sometimes at times of shock or strain or weakness. Who was he, this man standing here in this old room lit by the dim shaded lights, the quiet night gathering veil upon dark veil beyond the walls? And who was that other man, treading cat-like through the shadows, alone with him in this place? Overlord and serf. Knight and man-at-arms. Master and servant. They had been together here for so long now, working out an ever-changing pattern that had yet in its essence been always the same. And now, with a flash of premonition, he knew that it was over. After so many centuries the pattern was broken and the epoch ended. He, the master, must find a new way to live, had indeed already found it in that oneness of labour in London, but what of the servant? What could Boulder do?

"Thank-you, Boulder," he said, when the last curtain had been for the last time disposed in its immemorial folds.

Boulder came and stood in front of him, shooting out his cuffs. "Anything you require, sir?" he asked. He looked as usual now, except for the agony in his eyes.

"It's been a long time," said Stephen confusedly. "I mean, it's been a long time that you've been here. All my life."

The ghost of a smile twitched Boulder's lips. "Longer than that, sir," he said. "I was 'ere before you were born. . . . Before Mr. Richard was born."

A hard grating noise came into his voice at the mention of Richard. He could not endure to speak of Richard, or to think of him, unless he had first taken to himself a stony hardness that shut down upon emotion like stone upon the waters of a well.

But Stephen, when he said "all my life," was still not quite certain who he was. He was still trying to think what he wanted to say to Boulder when Boulder left the room and went downstairs.

He went to his pantry, locked the door and sat down with his head in his hands, while his mind dragged itself painfully over the sequence of events that had brought him to this abysmal hour. Mr. Richard had been killed. Grief had weakened him. He had had a worse attack of pain than usual and had fainted in trying to answer Mr. Birley's bell. The doctor had been sent for. To-morrow his illness would be discovered and he would be sent to the hospital. At this point fear broke over him, his deep unreasonable fear of being separated from the place and the people with whom alone he had always subconsciously believed that salvation lay. With them he was saved, apart from them he was damned. The hospital stood to him for the full horror of uselessness and desolation, loneliness and death. He felt almost drowning in his fear and from the depth of it cried out upon his God. "Gawd, Gawd, let me die to-night. Let me die to-night. O Gawd, let me die to-night." There was no answer at all. Only silence in the gathering darkness.

IV

After dinner Mr. Birley went back to his accounts. Stephen, his offer of help having been curtly refused, went slowly up to the gallery, Argos deserting his post at the front door to follow him. How idiotic, he thought. Uncle Charles shut up with his grief in the study, Boulder in the pantry, Argos and I here. How idiotic. Just now I'd find it easier to speak of Richard to a perfect stranger than to Uncle Charles, and so would he. Why on earth? There seemed no answer, unless it was that in speaking to a stranger of one's grief one lifted it a little away from the place where it lay so painfully against one's heart and placed it with the universal sorrow of the world in which all strangers shared; and with sharing ceased to be strangers.

The gallery was dimly lit and utterly quiet, the sea-green curtains unstirring, the painted faces of the dead men just white blobs in the gloom. He sat down to read a detective story, in the dim hope that the puzzle of it would keep his mind off Richard, and Argos flopped at his feet, lying without movement until a low deep throbbing in the night made him lift his head and growl, the hair standing up all along his spine.

"Only Jerry going over," said Stephen, and pulled Argos's ears. But Argos would not be pacified, and would not lower his head until the night was quiet again; and even then he growled spasmodically, and his great body twitched as though with pain.

But his restlessness had communicated itself to Stephen, and he threw down his book. That had been Jerry going over, and in a few hours' time they would hear Jerry coming back, and for them the time between would probably hold only the peace of a still winter's night, but for men and women and children living in one of the big towns on the coast there would be thunder and fire and destruction, and for some of them a violent death such as Richard had endured. He slipped behind the curtains into a window recess and opened a window. Already, far away, he could hear the boom of the big guns, the rattle of the pom-poms, and see a glow that crept ominously up the star-lit sky. For a little he listened and watched, sick at heart, then closed the window and went back into the room.

The sound was so far-away that the closing of the window made it non-existent, and to step back through the sea-green curtains was to step from the present into the past. He wandered restlessly round the gallery, looking into the faces of the dead men hanging round the walls; only now they did not seem dead, they seemed most painfully alive, waiting for something, waiting with sorrow, resignation and illimitable patience. Men in armour, men in jewel-encrusted doublets, men dressed for hunting, for war, for the sea, for love, for hate. But their faces did not vary so much as their clothes. They were all of the same breed. He looked with stabbing pain into the eyes of Richard, then into his uncle's eyes, and at last, with a slight sensation of shock, into his own.

To his fancy they were all alive to-night, but old Roger was more alive than any of them. There he was, apart from the others, with his strong, gross humorous red face, his gouty hands, his direct glance and his beautiful fastidious clothes, his coarseness and his integrity, his strength and his weakness, his laughter and his pain; a man who had kept the faith but could not keep away from the drink, a man who had accepted the loneliness of independent thinking and then drugged it because he lacked that extra ounce that would have made him victor; not an enigma any more but just a very typical human being. Looking at him, Stephen loved him, and pitifully wondered what the end had been. A rather horrible end, probably, a terrible paying of the price for the lack of that extra ounce, the slow dissolution of a diseased and pain-racked body. How, in the end, his body must have revolted him, that man with the clear eyes and the fastidious garments, how he must have loathed himself and his own failure. . . . Happy are they who die as Richard had died, quickly, at the peak of glorious achievement. . . . Yet something you did, Roger, Stephen cried voicelessly to him, something you gave to life, you made a garden and you kept the faith, and something of you is quickened in me, who am the last of us all.

He to be heir of the ages, he, unworthy. Suddenly the longing for Richard swept over him again, intolerably. It was no good trying to read, no good wandering round and round the gallery like this. He'd go out for a while before he went to bed. Perhaps out there in the bitter night, under the frost-bound trees, the stars overhead, he'd feel nearer to Richard, who had never stuck under a roof if he could help it. Calling to Argos he walked to the top of the stairs and then looked back, his hand on the switch that would plunge those men on the walls into darkness, to look at them once again. He loved them all. They had built well, giving some of them much, some little, but all of them something, some jot of courage, some spark of beauty to the pattern that they had made. Good-bye, good-bye, he said to them, good-bye and thank you for anything I have that is worth while, and he switched out the light.

Down in the hall, lit by one dim lamp, he put on his coat, and then went outside. Argos would not come with him but stretched himself out again to lie in guardianship across the threshold of his home. It was a glorious night of stars and moonlight. He would go down through the woods, he thought, to the valley below where the old thorn tree grew, the valley that he saw from the window in his tower and loved so well.

It was almost as light as day down on the road between the leafless trees, and the crisp snow gave back the shining of the moon with clean and equal light. He walked quickly in the direction of Hatchett's Farm, where Mrs. Heather had been born, and fought the bitterness of his grief. He knew he had not been wrong when he had thought a few days ago that, in spite of their mutual love for Prunella, he and Richard would soon achieve a friendship they had not known before. No, he had not been wrong. The experience and suffering of the war would have given to them both a clearer vision and their outlook would have approximated more nearly. And now he would never have that friendship. Just on the point of blossoming it had withered and died. In that, to him, lay the bitterness of Richard's death. Had theirs been a perfect comradeship the loss of it would not have been so hard to bear as this loss of a might-have-been. The frustration of life is bitter but not hopeless, for while life lasts the thing longed for may yet in some way come to one's heart, but the frustration of death, that beating against a closed door, is agony, for the closed door cannot open. Never. Never. The bitter word seemed sighing in the silent woods. Was Prunella saying it yet? Had she awakened yet to the knowledge that she must stay on the wrong side of the door? Was not her frustration greater than his? He began to think about her, the adored Prunella. What could he do for her? What would Richard have him do? She would never love him, or any man, as she had loved Richard. That first love had gone deep with her, and she was faithful, but in years to come, if she lived, she might marry him for old affection's sake, and, in the old phrase from the Bible, "to raise up seed unto his brother." She'd not give him the love he wanted, that every man wanted, it would be a poor sort of second best, but then did not half the world subsist on second-best? And he loved her, and her second-best would mean more to him than another woman's whole devotion. And he believed that he could give her what she wanted. It had hurt intolerably to be told that she had talked to him as though he was her mother, but perhaps that kind of confidence was just the thing that she had missed and needed most. But all that was far away now. It would be a long while before he could dare to speak to her of love. There was nothing he could give her now except the friendship he had hoped to give to Richard, and perhaps some of his own perpetually growing faith that life is too great a thing to be contained by this world only; there is another where the broken friendships are knit up again, and the broken loves are mended. One had to believe that nowadays, or go mad. One had to believe and work.

That was another thing that he could do for Richard. While he had life he could work for the grey-faced men in the streets, the workers in mines and factories and offices, the slatternly women and the dirty children of the slums, whom Richard had thought of so constantly and who had become now so much a part of his own life. He could make houses for them, take his infinitesimal share in the building of a new world that would not be unworthy of its foundation of blood and tears.

It was so still in the frost-bound woods, deathly still. They seemed waiting. He stopped in his restless pacing and waited too, his hand gripping a branch of the old bare thorn tree that grew beside the road. Blanched by the moonlight they looked so alike, his hand and the tree. It struck him that the raid on the distant town must have been quickly ended for the woods had been silent like this for some while now. It was deathly cold, and he shivered. He must go home. Crazy to tramp about in the night like this. He must go back to his room in the tower, and get into bed, and lie through the long cold night staring into the dark and remembering all the impatient words he had spoken to Richard throughout their life together, all the sympathy withheld, all the anger, all the understanding that might have been and yet had not been. But somehow the branch of the old thorn tree held him and he still stood there, waiting. It held him as though it were alive, as though it were a hand that held him, his brother's hand, as though Richard stood beside him and said, stay here with me for a while longer. I must be mad, he thought. First I thought the portraits were alive, now I think this tree's alive. "Let me not be mad, sweet heavens. Keep me in temper, I would not be mad." But he did not leave the tree, he held on to it still and cried out to Richard in his heart, "I'm sorry. I'm sorry."

Was that a horse's hoofs upon the road? No, it was distant firing. The returning raiders were being chased. Thank God for that, so long as they did not jettison their bombs. How clear the Castle was in the moonlight, standing up stark and white above the leafless trees. And now there came the drone of the great engines and evil bat-like shapes that blotted out the stars. He turned his face to the sky, watching them. God, how he hated them! Not the men in the machines, suffering creatures made of the same bone and spirit as himself, but those shapes of evil that enclosed them, imprisoned them, tortured them. Powers of darkness, let go of us, leave us alone, give us peace, give us rest, go back again to the slime from which you came.

With the first fearful explosion the tree let go of him and he fell flat on the ground from sheer force of habit. Under the snow against which his face was pressed he could feel the very earth quake and shiver in outrage. Another explosion came, and another, then silence. So swiftly were the raiders gone that by the time he staggered to his feet again the sound of their engines was a distant hum that only intensified the frost-bound stillness all about him. The bombs, he thought, had fallen almost on top of him, yet when he looked he could see only one crater close at hand, in the open field beside the stream. Still swaying and stupefied he looked on and up, and saw the Castle standing up against the stars in stark ruin. The south-west tower, where was his own room, with Boulder's just below it, had simply disappeared, and the gallery and the hall below were shattered. The further end still stood but behind its windows there showed already the glow of fire. But it was not his habit to stand still and stare when this sort of thing happened. He had learned not to.

He started running, strongly, swiftly, and already there surged in his body and brain the vigour and skill of ten men. One thought was uppermost in his mind. . . . The children.

CHAPTER XIV

I

"GRANDPA, I've walked right round the garden," called Prunella from the little drawing-room. "I'm well."

He stood in the doorway looking at her where she sat on the sofa by the bright fire, with her feet up, stitching at a pair of very small pyjamas for an evacuated child. She looked a wraith-like creature, all hair and eyes, but she had not broken beneath her trouble and she had picked up the burden of living again with determination and grit. He was immensely proud of her. "Good," he said.

"If you're going out this morning will you drive me to the Castle?" asked Prunella. "I want to say good-bye to Stephen. He's going back to London to-night."

"No, Prunella," said her grandfather firmly. "It's only three weeks since the raid and the Castle's a horrid mess. It would upset you to see it."

"I don't feel as though anything could ever upset me again," said Prunella. "Compared with what has happened, everything else will be only a pin-prick."

"Can't Stephen come to you?" he growled.

"He could, but I don't want him to," said Prunella. "Why should he be perpetually sent for to me? I'll go to him this time. I want to show him that I'm grateful."

"Ready in half-an-hour," assented the old man. "And for the love of heaven put a hat on. It's beastly cold."

He went out, closing the door softly behind him, and Prunella put down her work and leaned her swimming head against the cushion behind her. If only Grandpa would give in without argument. Nothing is more exhausting, when you are not well, than having difficulty in getting your own way. She *must* show Stephen how grateful she was. She *must*. Only she knew just how much she owed to him.

It had been Miss Brown who had told her she was going to get well. She would never live through a moment like that again.

She remembered it with a dreadful vividness, and lying on the sofa by the bright fire lived through it again for the hundredth time. It was odd how one had to go on re-living terrible moments, on and on, as though they would never be over.

"I must leave you, Prunella," Miss Brown had said one morning. "They're in dreadful trouble at the Castle. I must go to them."

"What trouble?" Prunella had asked indifferently. So determinedly had she turned her back on life that the things that happened in it had no longer seemed to matter to her at all.

"Two of those bombs you heard dropped on the Castle. Mr. Birley has been injured, and Boulder and Mrs. Heather and Argos are dead."

"Stephen?" Prunella had asked quickly. Yes, it had seemed to matter what happened to Stephen. Even in the dim borderland where she had been wandering it had mattered very much.

"He's all right," Miss Brown had said with pride. "He was wonderful. He saved Mr. Birley's life and he got the children out without a hair of their heads being touched. But I must go to them, Prunella. You're all right now. You're doing splendidly. Your uncle and the maid can look after you now, and you'll be up in no time." Then, seeing the fear dawning in Prunella's eyes, she had added hastily, "As soon as he can get away Stephen shall come to you."

But he hadn't been able to come until the next day, and until he came she had fought her way alone through her abysmal hour. The fear of death is bad, and Richard had drunk of that cup, and she had drunk of it in her fear for him, but the fear of life is infinitely worse. Death is soon over, but life goes on so long. When you are not yet twenty it feels as though it would last for ever. Inexorably the huge weight and length of it had closed down between her and Richard like an iron door. While she had expected to die too, she had felt him near to her, but on that awful morning she had felt him infinitely far away. The thing that she had feared had happened. She had lost him, she had lost her life, and yet she lived. How *could* she live? Through the rest of that day, and through the night that followed, she had cowered before the spectre of life in the very abyss of fear. How did one live in this fear and pain? How ever did one *do* it?

And then Stephen had come, grim-faced, his eyes red-rimmed with sleeplessness, and for the first time in his life too exhausted to be gentle with her. "What's the matter, Prunella?" he had asked her roughly.

The matter? Lying flat on her back in her little white bed in a dreadful stillness she gazed up at him, her eyes widening in her small pinched face, and he had seen the naked fear and astonishment in them. He had seen that look in so many eyes lately, not the fear of death but the fear of life. Is it like this? Is it true that it's like this? Oh God, if it's like this what do we *do*? He had instantly pulled himself together to grapple with her fear.

"It's all right, Prunella," he had said a little wildly. "I tell you it's all right. Life's not this little bit of existence you're plodding through now, it's the whole thing, all that is. It's the breath of God, words that he spoke, a song, a stream of white light that goes back to him again. Life is good, Prunella. Life is fine and grand and we should love it to the depths of our souls."

Memory had chimed in her weary mind. "That's what Richard said," she had murmured, " when he wrote asking me to marry him."

"Did he ask you to marry him?" Stephen had demanded sharply.

"Yes. He wrote a letter the day before he died."

Stephen had smiled. "Did he? Well, that's all right then, isn't it? You've got him now, haven't you? He proved his love by giving you himself in every way that he could. Nothing can take him from you. You've got him more completely than if he had lived."

"No," had said Prunella. "There's a sort of door between us."

"You only think so," Stephen had flashed back at her. "Separateness is only an illusion, a sort of curse on us because of sin. We refused to be children of God, we wouldn't be brothers of each other, and so there was egotism and the hell of loneliness. But it's only an imaginary hell. You can break out of it if you break away from yourself. Richard's as near to you as I am, part of the sun that's shining on you and the air you breathe."

He had spoken quickly and passionately, as unlike himself as he could be, and had gone away as roughly as he had come, stumbling with fatigue, and left Prunella in a condition of bitter rage. What was the use of talking in that large, lofty, grandiloquent way? Stephen had always been so understanding but now he did not understand at all. He was hateful. He understood less than Grandpa with his platitudes about time healing all things and life not being ended when you thought it was, and all the rest of it. No one understood. She didn't want to feel at one with the air and sunshine, she wanted Richard, Richard, Richard, his sleepy voice, his smile, his dark eyes kindling as he looked at her, the touch of his hand and the feel of his arms about her. She just wanted the two of them to be together with all the rest shut out.

But her rage against Stephen had helped her, dragged her a little way up out of her weakness and despair, given her energy, set her mind at work. Because he had spoken with such unusual roughness his words had stuck in her mind, stuck like barbed arrows, but stuck. Now, three weeks later, sitting on the sofa, she could think of them without anger and even hold to them as to a life-line. It had been selfish to want to keep Richard to herself, the rest of the world shut out, selfish to want, as she had wanted on that summer morning months ago, to set sail with him in a little boat for a place where there was no more war. That was escapist, and people poured scorn on the word escape nowadays. If what Richard and Stephen had said was true and life was the sum of all that is, and glorious, then one did not escape from it, one gave to it, one gave love to beauty and worship to holiness and courage to devouring fire, one gave even those one loved to justice and truth, and then through the power of some strange mystery you weren't separated from them any more, they were yours, the barriers went down and you escaped from what Stephen called the curse of separateness. She had not lost Richard. She had only to love him to have him for her own. And he loved her. Stephen had said that he had proved that by giving himself to her in all the ways there were, and that was true, and now nothing that this world could do could spoil his giving. She had been so terrified in the old days that to possess him would be to lose him, but that was a paradox that only held good for this world, the other country turned it the other way round, she had lost him and so she possessed him for ever, and all her fear was gone. . . . She remembered that Richard had always liked her best when she was not afraid.

Suddenly she began to cry, bitterly, miserably. It was no good. This living in two worlds at once, the one a part of the other because the same life flowed through them both, this struggle to live in time and eternity together was so dreadfully difficult. It pulled one in pieces. For a little while one could see the way to live, one could breathe the air of another country, one could escape from oneself and know peace, and then one was back in oneself again, stifled by one's grief, shut in, despairing.

But not hopeless despair. Through it all one's mind clung on to the truth of what one knew, and at the peak of it, when one could not bear it any more and cried out, give me something, just something, memory came and the little things that it gave fitted themselves together into a sort of pattern that one felt had meaning. . . . That heavenly green-gold evening on Beacon Hill when Richard had told her he wanted by any means, even death, to make his country happier, and the other lovely evening when she had found him in a hollow of the moors and had lain in his arms beside the stream, closer to him than she had been even during that night at the inn. And then that battle and that death in the dawn-lit sky. A trinity. Two evenings and a morning, all with the same setting of the beautiful country that had made the body of this man. Patriot, lover, warrior, and at those moments perfect as all three. That threefold memory enshrined the very soul of the man, not a memory so much as a vision of something that for ever lived, the promise of an order of being in which the conflict was reconciled and all things fell into order as the pattern was made plain. . . . And when in her dream she had stood with arms outstretched against the closed door she had heard trumpets sounding on the other side.

She sat up, dried her eyes and looked at the clock. She must put on her things and go and say good-bye to Stephen before he went back to that hell on earth of the London raids. He had been good to her, just how good she was only now beginning to realise. She supposed that his friendship was the best thing that she had left in this world. They must always be friends. They had been through so much together. They knew more about each other than anyone else would ever know.

II

"On the whole I should say you were lucky," said the cheerful government official who had come down to investigate the damage. "No one dead but the two old servants and the dog, and they killed instantaneously as far as one can know. It might have been a great deal worse. Yes, you've been lucky." He leaned back in his chair, crossed one leg comfortably over the other, and lit a cigarette. "Lucky and plucky," he added kindly.

Lucky? The grim-faced young man who sat at the other side of the table looked a little startled. Lucky? Boulder dead. Mrs. Heather dead. The dog Argos dead. Uncle Charles in a nursing home, lamed for life. This room in which they sat, the study, the only habitable portion of the Castle left, the rest of it destroyed by fire and explosion. Every beloved treasure gone, every book, every picture, even the tattered flag of Simon and Stephen the Crusader. The whole of the precious past destroyed in a night.

Lucky? He lit a cigarette, too, with hands that trembled a little, and said, "Yes, compared with what others have suffered, we're very lucky."

"Well, I think that's all," said the cheerful official, and gathering his papers together he stood up. "You will in due course receive what compensation can be given under the new government scheme. It won't, of course, be adequate. One realises that the restoration of a place like this is an impossibility."

His official voice was suddenly tinged with a very human sorrow. So much was shattered in England now that could never be restored; by the end of the war the list might include most of the monuments that linked one with the past.

"It's the end of this place," agreed Stephen. "But the past is, after all, the past. Thank you very much. Good-bye."

The official's car roared away through the woods and he was alone again in silence. Thank God for silence. One had not realised, in the old days, what a blessed thing it was. . . . Silence.

He pulled himself together. He was dropping off to sleep again. It would be heaven to lie down on the camp bed in the corner of the room and sleep till doomsday, but there was no time. At night, when he ought to be sleeping, he could not do it, he lived over and over again that night of the fire, and his fight to get the children and Uncle Charles to safety, and by day there was no time. He angrily stubbed out his cigarette, propped his head on his fists and wondered what he still had to do to-day. It was three weeks since the raid, and this evening he must catch the night train back to London. He looked at his watch. Eleven o'clock. He must see Prunella and say good-bye. He must see Uncle Charles at the nursing home and say good-bye. And he had promised to take Miss Brown to the nursing home too; she was now living with Moppet and Poppet at the lodge until she could decide what to do with herself and them. He must say good-bye to her, and thank-you. . . . Awfully good to them she had been. Rotten that she should be thrown out of employment like this again. . . . At five o'clock he must be here to pack his bag, that a taxi would take to the station. Then he must ride Richard's horse Golden Eagle down to Oakdown where Richard's friend Tim Jackson lived, their M.F.H., who was to have him. And then he would walk the rest of the way to Torhaven. Then—that was the end. The end of life as he had always known it, the end of this particular pattern that he had loved. Yet he must go on. Go on, go on, he said to himself. For some reason or other you're important, necessary, vital to something new. If not, why weren't you in your room that night of the raid? Why did the thought of Richard drive you outside? Why did the thought of Richard keep you from going back? Why do you have to live on? Richard knows, not you. Your job is to do the next thing, and live.

"Stephen?"

It was Prunella standing in front of him, grief and weakness gallantly disguised by the way she held her body tautly upright, her head back, her hands in the pockets of her coat, by the bright orange scarf she wore twisted round her throat, and her vivid make-up. . . . She was like a flame in the desolate fire-blackened room. He hardly recognised her for the same woman as the desperate sick creature he had last seen.

"My God, Prunella, you've got the guts!" he exclaimed, and his heart leaped triumphantly to greet her courage. She had the extra ounce. She'd won.

"You've picked up a lot of inelegant phrases since you went to London," Prunella teased him. "I've come to say good-bye, Stephen, and thank-you for being such a good friend to me, and if you've got your car handy will you run me down to the church?"

"It's handy," said Stephen. "I've given it to Bob Hatchett at the farm, but he's not fetched it yet. . . . Ought you to go to the church, Prunella?" he asked anxiously.

"I ought," said Prunella steadily. "I'll go and look at Richard's grave later, by myself, when I'm well, but before you go away we ought to go to the chapel together and decide where his tablet ought to be put. All the Birleys who die in battle have a tablet. He must have one, too. Fetch the car, please, Stephen."

Silently and obediently Stephen fetched it and tucked her up in it. He couldn't think of anything that Richard would have detested more than a tablet to his memory, but on the other hand he supposed there was nothing he would have wanted more than to have Prunella do what she liked, so he made no protest.

"You see, Stephen," said Prunella as they slid away through the winter woods, "I want us to do things together now. Poor old Mr. Birley may not live very long, and then you won't have anyone but me. But I'm half a Birley, aren't I? Richard asked me to marry him, and I had his baby, though the poor scrap died, so I should say I was half a Birley."

"I should say you were entirely a Birley," said Stephen, "and a great credit to the family." They smiled at each other and a small flutter of happiness was born in him somewhere. He wondered if the second-best that he hoped Prunella might one day

231

give him would not be a more satisfying thing than he had thought.

"Are you going to stay here, Prunella?" he asked her. "Wouldn't it be a good thing if you went away for a bit?"

"No, it wouldn't," she said stoutly. "It would be cowardly to go away. There'll be talk about me in the village because of what happened and I must face it. And I must look after Grandpa; that's my job. And I love this place, it's my place. If Hitler does anything awful to us in the spring I'd like to have it done to me here, where I belong. And you'll come whenever you get leave, won't you? Though the Castle's gone you can stay with Grandpa and me, or at the lodge or the farm."

"I'll come when I can," Stephen promised.

"Perhaps one day you'll come back from exile like the other Birleys did," said Prunella. "Come back as a famous architect, build up the Castle and live there again."

"Perhaps," he said, "but I don't think so. Whatever sort of world we have when this hell is over it won't have landed gentry in it. That's all over. There'll be more important building to be done than the repairing of old castles. I expect this one will just become a ruin like the others, with ivy growing over it and birds nesting where the great hall used to be."

She moved nearer to him, her shoulder pressed against his. "Never mind, Stephen. However far away you go you'll remember it always like it used to be. Lately I've thought that memory isn't just recollecting what's past and over but slipping out of time and seeing it still alive. You'd say that time and death are just illusions like separateness."

They reached the lych gate and walked under the old yews to the church porch.

"Jolly unpleasant illusions," said Stephen grimly. He was haunted, this morning, by that ruined castle of his, and it was Prunella, to-day, who was the stronger of the two. She was making her supreme effort. By her visit to Stephen, and this that they were doing together, she was trying to pick up their two lives out of the ruins and bind them firmly in the new pattern of work and memory and friendship that they must make. Patriot, lover, warrior, had been the man who had gone, and he had lit her life with his own flaming colours, artist, comrade, man of peace was the man who had come and with those quieter colours the pattern would be quite different; but she would bend her whole strength to make it beautiful.

"Nice to be an architect, Stephen," she said, as he pushed open the heavy old door. "When this war's over you'll be wanted more than any one. I'll draw out your plans. I can draw a little, did you know? I'm not clever, but I can do things neatly with my fingers."

"I think you're very clever," said Stephen. "Especially at rebuilding."

They sat down in the Castle pew while the sun illumined for them the loveliness of the Birley chapel.

"*That's* still there, anyway," said Stephen with a breath of relief. "I once heard Uncle Charles say that this was the shrine of the soul."

"Our soul?" asked Prunella. "The family's soul?"

"Yes."

The light seemed to burn a little brighter. It lit up the warrior angels of the old carved screen, the Spanish crucifix on the altar, the memorial window to Stephen's father, the tablets on the walls, the exquisite tomb of the Crusader, the comic monument to Harry Birley and his multitudinous family, and the empty space on the north wall that had lately frightened Prunella so much.

"That seems to be the place, doesn't it?" she said, pointing it out to Stephen. "And the sun will shine full on it."

"But what can we put on it?" asked Stephen. "All the usual texts and verses seem to have got a bit hackneyed, somehow, and Richard would have loathed the lot."

"I know," Prunella answered. "Something that Keats said, and that I quoted to Richard once on Beacon Hill, and that he liked. 'Patriotism is the glory of making by any means a country happier.'"

"That'll do," sighed Stephen with relief. "That's satisfying. That goes deep."

He talked learnedly and almost happily for a few minutes about the different kinds of stone and lettering and Prunella acquiesced a little wearily. She had made her great effort and it was spent. She had wanted to make Stephen happier and she'd done it. Now she just wanted to go home and lie on her bed and howl.

". . . it seems to hold the light," Stephen was saying upon the subject of some stone or other. "Just as the Crusader is holding it now. Look."

She roused herself and they both looked at the white austere figure of the Crusader lying bathed in the light from the south window.

"It's a perfect thing," muttered Stephen. "So utterly simple. And the horror of old Harry's monument next door sets it off to perfection."

They got up and stood beside the tomb, looking intently at the steel-clad figure with the sheathed sword, his shield for a pillow and his dog at his feet, his visor raised above the watchful eyes, the grim set mouth, the winged and eager nostrils, his hands set palm to palm in prayer.

"Not a word to tell us anything about him," said Prunella, running her finger along the worn ledge where once the tale of the Crusader's deeds had been set out. "Yet one feels one knows him. Do you know, once when I was riding with Richard below Beacon Hill we looked up and saw a man and a dog on guard at the top, and I said, 'That's the Crusader and his dog from the church.' Richard laughed, but I thought it was a nice idea."

Stephen thought so too, then, looking at her, he saw how tired she was and slipped his arm through hers to take her home. Their footsteps clanged on the stone aisle as they went out, and the door creaked as they closed it. Then deep quiet fell upon the old church and the sunbeams played over the vigilant unstirring figure of the intercessor on the tomb.

III

"Miss Brown wants to see you. I brought her with me in the car and she's waiting downstairs. May she come up?"

It was four o'clock. Stephen had said good-bye to Mr. Birley and stood at the door.

"Of course," said Mr. Birley placidly. "The admirable Miss Brown. I have not seen her since the accident."

Stephen went slowly downstairs. "The accident." What a placid sort of way in which to refer to the irretrievable disaster that had overwhelmed them. But during this last week, when Mr. Birley had risen above the pain and prostration and drugged semi-consciousness of the first fortnight and returned to possession of himself, serenity had been his chief characteristic. Told that his right leg was permanently crippled, and his heart, overstrained by years of endurance, in a most precarious condition, he had said calmly that he had endured illness before and could endure it again, and that the men of his family seemed mostly to end their lives in invalidism, and he saw no reason why he should not do the same. He was quite clear as to what he wanted to do. The Castle being now uninhabitable, he would go into rooms at Torhaven with a male attendant. He was, he had said, glad that Stephen, after rescuing Moppet and Poppet, had dashed back and dragged him from beneath the debris of his wrecked room just five minutes before the floor collapsed. The other way would have been too easy a death for a man who had had too easy a life. Now he would have time to make his soul.

Stephen opened the door of the waiting-room. Miss Brown was sitting very upright upon the most uncomfortable chair she had been able to find and was gazing with disfavour upon some dust on the floor that the housemaid had overlooked.

"He'd like to see you, Miss Brown. His room is No. 3 at the top of the stairs. I'll wait for you here, shall I?"

"No," said Miss Brown. "You take the car and go back to the Castle. You've so much to do. I must go to the butcher when I have seen your uncle, and then I'll catch the bus."

"You'll be all right?" asked Stephen. Miss Brown was not quite herself, he thought. She looked almost too precise, too neat and controlled.

"Quite all right," said Miss Brown. "And it is absolutely necessary that I should go to the butcher. I see no reason why he should overcharge for the joint just because it has been bombed in the larder. There is no way now, of course, of ascertaining what it *did* weigh, but I am convinced that it did *not* weigh what he says it weighed."

Stephen smiled as he left the nursing home. Miss Brown was very refreshing. Thinking that she was not quite herself to-day must have been just his imagination. They'd miss her. He hoped his uncle would be all right with that male attendant.

Miss Brown, however, walking quietly upstairs, had other views for Mr. Birley's future that quite excluded the necessity for a male attendant. Her heart was beating as she knocked at his door but it was with no sign of trepidation that she entered, sat down by his bed, her gloved hands folded demurely upon the black bag in her lap, and smiled at him with her cool refreshing kindness. Admirable little woman, thought Mr. Birley. Capable, controlled little woman. He knew he was looking a shocking sort of scarecrow, and this was the first time that she had seen him since the raid, but though her eyes were pitiful she remained unemotional, and made no agitating references to what had happened.

"Glad to find you better, Mr. Birley," she said cheerfully. "Moppet and Poppet send you their love."

"Tell me about the young ladies," he said. "Not shell-shocked at all?"

"It doesn't seem to have had the slightest effect on them," said Miss Brown. "Until the fire got a hold that part of the house escaped, you know, though Mrs. Heather, being so old, died of the shock of the explosions. And then Stephen got them out so quickly that I think they were scarcely even frightened. They talk more about the two little girls whom they met in the woods the evening before than they do about the bombs. And then at tea-time that same evening Mrs. Heather happened to read them the twenty-third psalm and they went to bed with the idea in their heads that fear is unnecessary. Mrs. Heather and the two little girls, whoever they were, seem to have armoured them well beforehand."

"Most fortunate," murmured Mr. Birley. "And Boulder and Mrs. Heather and Argos were all old, and would have felt the destruction of the Castle cruelly. They were mercifully dealt with. It's about yourself, Miss Brown, that I am most concerned."

"Why should you be?" said Miss Brown. "Stephen gave me your cheque and I want to thank you for it. It was most generous of you, and it will more than keep me until I find fresh work. I hope to find some way of keeping Moppet and Poppet with me, or near me. An uncle is taking the Baxter boys but no one seems anxious to have the little girls."

"You are not so afraid now as you were that day I first met you," smiled Mr. Birley.

"I am not at all afraid," said Miss Brown. "The pattern re-formed for me once, and it will re-form again. My life must have been spared for some reason or other, mustn't it? If I had not been with Prunella I would have been at the Castle, probably down in the hall mending that hole in the sofa cover, a thing I've been meaning to do for ages. Then I would have been killed too. You taught me to believe that these things are not chance."

"Someone obviously has need of you," agreed Mr. Birley, and stifled a yawn, for he was getting tired.

Miss Brown had reached the most important moment of her life, that peak of experience to which all else had tended, and her gloved fingers tightened their pressure on the shabby old bag in her lap; but Mr. Birley, dizzy and bewildered now with the effort of talking to her, saw no change in her.

"May I ask you something?" said Miss Brown in exactly the same matter-of-fact tone in which she was accustomed to enquire if he would prefer mutton again this week, or beef for a change.

"Certainly," said Mr. Birley.

"I don't like to think of you in rooms, in the care of a male attendant," said Miss Brown. "You ought to have a home. I would count it the greatest joy that life can give, the greatest honour, to make a home for you. I would be your housekeeper, your nurse, your wife, or all three, whichever you liked. In whatever way I could serve you I would be happy."

The room seemed to Mr. Birley to turn upside down, to swing through space, to turn a somersault, and then slowly to right itself. Was the admirable Miss Brown subjecting him to a proposal of marriage? Horror seized him, astonishment, bewilderment, mirth, dismay, and then again, overwhelming the other emotions, horror. He groped feebly for his pince-nez, lying on the table beside him, put them on and looked at her. There she sat in her neat dark blue coat and skirt, her hard hat dead straight upon her dark head, her hands still quietly folded. But her whole being was in her eyes. Though he still lay on his back and she still sat demurely on the edge of her chair her spirit lay at his feet, pleading and unashamed. His quick observation could not fail to know that, yet it was almost impossible to reconcile such an utter abandonment with the modesty and self-control of a woman like Miss Brown, and the measure of it was the measure of her love. It was the worst situation in which Mr. Birley had ever found himself and he was without the strength to deal with it. He felt the small fraction of independence still left to him slipping away and was too weak to stretch out a hand to save it.

But Miss Brown saved it herself. She had seen his dismay at her suggestion, she felt his burning pride that would hate to submit to the care of a woman. Quickly, before his weakness should deliver him into her hands, she made her supreme effort and dealt herself what she felt at that moment was her death blow.

"I should be happy to make the sacrifice," she said.

Mr. Birley clutched at the word "sacrifice" that, like a life-line, she had thrown to him, and looked at her again, his weakness now blinding his observation. Her eyes looked quite dull now, without the blazing light that he thought he had seen in them. She had spoken with a prim smugness. Of what outrageous fancies is a sick man capable, he thought. He must be feverish. The good little woman had spoken merely from a sense of duty. He broke into a sweat of sheer relief.

"You have made an uncommonly generous suggestion, Miss Brown," he said. "But I should never allow you to make that sacrifice you spoke of. Never. But I shall not forget it, and I shall be eternally grateful to you."

Miss Brown got up with the air of one who has just accomplished a duty, smiled at him and held out her hand. They shook hands cordially and she left the room. As she went downstairs she knew that she had done a quite appalling thing. She, the woman, had proposed marriage to a man immensely her social superior. It was enough to make her mother turn in her grave. But she had had to do it, because he could not have done it, and there had been just the possibility that he might have preferred what she had offered him to what he had in fact chosen, and everything she had and was, not merely her dignity and modesty, would not have been too much to fling away to give him what he preferred. But in any case she was too numbed to feel any shame. She felt as though she was, in very truth, dead. What would life be without him? What would life be without Stephen? What would it be without that lovely life in the Castle that she had shared with them both? Nothingness. When a woman has lost husband and son and home all at one blow there seems just nothing left.

She shivered as she stood on the doorstep, for the chill damp of coming thaw was in the wind. She was cast out again, for the second time in her life. Well, she was not afraid this time but she was most desperately unhappy, and once again she asked herself, as she had asked outside the Free Library, "What do I do? What do I *do*?"

Suddenly she remembered the butcher. There was still something that she could do for Mr. Birley and Stephen. She would not have the men she loved overcharged for their joint when they were in such trouble. It was outrageous. Indignantly she turned up the collar of her coat and hurried off to do battle for them.

I V

By the time he had finished his tea Mr. Birley had quite recovered from the shock of Miss Brown's proposal. Good little woman, she had done what she considered to be her duty. For one awful moment he had thought—well, never mind what he had thought—she had shown him in the nick of time that her proposal had been made from a sense of duty and not from— well—inclination was the word he chose, for he shrank from a stronger one. He dismissed the incident from his mind and lay back to watch the last cold light of the winter's day trembling over the sea.

It was most astonishing to be so happy. He could not expect this strange peace to be always so deeply felt, he was aware that he had grim battles ahead, but while it was so strongly with him he would make the most of it, draw it deeply into his soul like air into his lungs, have it with him, he hoped, in some degree until the end of his life.

He had read once that there is a certain deep happiness that is experienced only by those who have lost, almost literally, everything. He now experienced the truth of that statement. His home had gone, his possessions, his health and nearly all his independence. He could not see that he possessed much at the moment except his immortal soul . . . and this happiness.

It was impossible really to analyse this peculiar joy, for it was a spiritual thing that defied analysis. Yet a few things he could say to himself about it. Fear had gone, for one thing. He had dreaded the dependence of invalidism and had fought hard against it; now it had come upon him and it was just as detestable as he had thought it would be, but he had yielded to it and was atoned. He had expected that only death would rid him of the conflict and the fear but the acceptance of his own mind had been mightier than death.

And then there was a change now in the way he thought of Richard. He did not now, as in the first days of his grief, think of him as lost. He remembered that day when he had thought he would gladly endure all the torture that there was if he could see Richard soar to perfection. Well, he had done that, and he did not now think his grief too high a price to pay for it. Richard had been perfect in his death, and like Prunella he found in that flowering something immortal. It rang true. That clashing of a man and his fate, like flint on tinder, had lit a flame, and by a willing acquiescence in Richard's death he did his part in destroying the power of this world to put it out. Here was another reason for happiness, and the bitterness of his grief was past.

"Having nothing, yet possessing all things." That great paradox slipped into his mind and brought him round again to the thought of the joy of loss, enclosing within its circle the thought of the fear and bitterness that had been vanquished by his acquiescence, reminding him of how, and at what cost, it had been won. The flinging away of what he possessed had been forced on him by circumstances, yet among his dim memories of the first two weeks of his illness, when his body had been fighting for its life, was one of another sort of fight, a titanic struggle of the spirit with an unseen adversary. He had been fighting to keep what he had and his adversary had been fighting not only to take it away but to wrench from him a glad acquiescence in the robbery that should rank as highly as a mighty giving. Sometimes he had fought, and sometimes he had fled, down there in the valley of the shadow of death, but always the relentless adversary had pursued him and grappled with him again. And at last it had seemed that he had prevailed in the fight, that he had not yielded his will, that he was victor; yet even in the moment of his triumph, as he felt his adversary departing from him, he had cried out in despair at that departure that was as the going from him of all the treasure of the world, and had yielded himself; and the adversary had turned back and bent over him and stretched out his hand and touched his thigh, so that like Jacob he would halt upon that leg until he died. He had woken up to the agony of his injured leg, but in his soul he had said, "I have seen God face to face. . . ." If you could say that there was no more to say.

He thought very much of Boulder in these days. That Boulder had escaped from the misery of a slow dissolution, while he had not, seemed to him just. He imagined that that unattractive, disagreeable little man had suffered enough and given enough, filled up the full measure of what a man can give to life in this world, and gone on to give again. He, Charles Birley, was still here; unnecessarily, some might think, but he knew quite well what he had to do. He had to be victor over his pain, not vanquished by it like old Roger. He had, while his strength lasted, to go on with his work and chronicle from an invalid's chair the mighty deeds of men of action that the love of life might be kindled in those who read. He had himself to love life, to give to it courage and yet more courage, to worship it in all its manifestations, and when he had given all that he could, when his will had broken in his hand, when the mind was a chaos and both sight and sense had left him, he would yield the essential spark of his being without fear, for life is God and life is love and in that final hour the Lover of the Lord shall trust in him.

CHAPTER XV

I

MISS BROWN'S misery was a good deal eased by a stormy interview with the butcher. The strength of character that was the iron framework of her gentle shyness always gave tradesmen quite a jolt when they fell foul of it. They did not discover it until they offended against her sense of rectitude, and then they were so taken aback that they invariably got the worst of the argument.

As the Birleys' butcher did upon this occasion. Miss Brown triumphantly restored eight halfpennies (the butcher had regained a little prestige by paying her in halfpennies) to her purse as she walked down the hill to the bus stop at the harbour. . . . She must remember to give them to Stephen before he left, for they were Birley halfpennies.

The harbour was sheltered from the wind and the light lay softly on a sea of smooth grey silk. The gulls sat motionless upon the sea wall, like birds carved out of mother-of-pearl. A tall man was standing on the curb playing his violin to a group of four children and a mongrel dog. One child wore a scarlet cap and another a bright green scarf, and the light that gleamed upward from the sea seemed to have got entangled in the dog's golden plume of a tail. It was a pretty scene. Children and dogs always loved Jo Isaacson. They knew that he had loving-kindness. Miss Brown knew it too. That day when he had had nursery tea at the Castle had been the first of several such tea-parties, and once or twice when he had been in funds he had taken her to the pictures, unspeakably proud and joyful at being able to pay for a little pleasure for her, and through those meetings she had come to value Jo Isaacson's kindness at something that approximated fairly close to its worth. The full worth she could not know without knowing the full story of what he had suffered without himself becoming brutalised. But she appreciated now, even more than before, the fact of his sensitiveness. She knew that only a man with greatness in him could have carried it unscathed through the fire. She had grown very fond of Jo Isaacson. The sour smell of his shabby old clothes no longer repulsed her; only made her long almost with desperation to get at them with a wash-tub and a hot iron. Mrs. Holly no doubt did her best but in Miss Brown's opinion she did not look after Jo Isaacson quite as well as he deserved.

What was he playing to those children? She drew a little nearer and then she heard. Oh, dear God! That thing with the whispering leaves that he had played outside the Free Library, the thing that promised shelter in the heart of a wood. Miss Brown felt almost sick with the sudden pain. Jo had promised her that shelter all those months ago, and she had found it, together with a perfection of love and service, but for how short a time. As she came up to him her eyes were blinded by a sudden rush of tears.

He instantly stopped playing, shooed off the children and the dog like a lot of chickens, and turned to her in something approaching panic, for he had never seen her look like that before. That day outside the Free Library she had scarcely shown her trouble. She must be in worse trouble to-day; or else she felt that she knew him well enough now to honour him with a share of her grief.

He slipped his arm through hers and they walked up and down beside the sea wall, and he talked a little to give her time to recover herself.

"It was good of you to write and tell me what had happened at the Castle," he said. "Thank God you weren't there that night. It was you I thought of first—you and the kids—then young Mr. Birley—and old Mr. Birley—grand old fellow."

Miss Brown sighed, but she did not speak. She would never be able to talk much to Jo Isaacson about Mr. Birley and Stephen, but she did not mind when he talked of them to her, because he always did it with unerring sympathy. She felt that he understood a little of her feeling for them and respected it. She was grateful to him now that he did not speak with pity of Mr. Birley; that absence of pity was a subtle compliment to the man she loved that she appreciated.

"As a matter of fact I'm waiting for the bus to take me to the Castle now," went on Mr. Isaacson. "I thought I'd like to go and have a look at it, just on my own. It means a lot to me, that place."

"Yes," said Miss Brown. She knew that it did. The importance of the Castle in both their lives was one of the links between them. "I'm waiting for the bus too," she went on. "When you've looked at the Castle I'll give you nursery tea at the lodge. I'm living there with the children, you know, until I see what to do next."

"Any ideas about the 'next'?" asked Mr. Isaacson, and the grip of his hand tightened a little on her arm.

"No," said Miss Brown. "Except that I'd like to keep the children with me if possible. No, I've no ideas. I'm just back where I was that day in London when I heard you playing in the street."

"You are not back where you were," said Mr. Isaacson decidedly. "You are a great deal further on. You have lost your fear."

Miss Brown smiled. "If I have that is partly because of you," she said. "Whenever I feel afraid I think of what your music made me feel that day—I can't exactly describe it—sort of leaning back against a multitude."

Mr. Isaacson hesitated, then came to a decision. "I'd like to tell you something," he said, bringing them to a standstill beside the harbour wall, looking out to sea. "If it hadn't been for you, that day in London, I think it likely that I'd have done away with myself."

Horror seized Miss Brown, cold horror that started in her toes and crept up through her body to lay an icy hand on her heart. Brought up as she had been she looked upon suicide as a sin.

"Jo!" she gasped, and was unaware for a moment or two that she had for the first time addressed him by his Christian name. Then she became aware, and blushed, and the rush of heat coming on top of the rush of cold made her feel most peculiar.

"Well, I must have moved on a bit further, too," said Mr. Isaacson, "for I can't imagine myself contemplating such a thing again. 'Henceforth I'll bear affliction till it cry out itself, "Enough, enough," and die.' That's what has got to die; the affliction, not ourselves; we're of too much value, even useless sort of chaps like me. That sounds conceited, but, you know, when someone has saved one's life, as you saved mine, one comes to put a new value on it."

"But how did I save your life, Jo?" gasped Miss Brown.

"Just by having a use for me," said Mr. Isaacson. "I thought if you had, well, maybe life had."

The bus arrived, and they got in, and all the way home Miss Brown sat marvelling at the fact that apparently she had unconsciously done for Mr. Isaacson exactly what Mr. Birley had of deliberate intent done for her. . . . Made him feel again that he had his place in the pattern.

They parted at the lodge, and Miss Brown went inside to get tea ready, and Mr. Isaacson went on alone through the woods.

He left the higher road and struck down through the trees to the road below, that led through the valley of the singing stream past the thorn tree to Hatchett's farm, so that he could be quite alone while he looked for the first time upon the ruin of the thing that he had loved.

Until that afternoon he had not been able to bring himself to go and look at the ruined Castle. To his great astonishment he had felt the tragedy as though it were his own personal loss. The Castle had always called to him, drawn him with the attraction of an enchanted place that stood on its little hill inviolable beyond and above the turmoil of daily living. Well, he'd been wrong about that, for the turmoil had engulfed it too. He'd been right to put no faith in it. It was a cheat like everything else; and now he must look at it, realise what had happened, once more pick up the dead body of a dream and shove it discreetly away out of sight.

As he reached the lower road, he braced himself to stop and look up. There it was, a fire-blackened ruin, a skeleton of dead bones upon a frozen hill. While all around it stretched the silence of the winter woods. The sky was lowering and overcast and it was bitter cold with the damp cold of approaching thaw. The snow had a dirty look, and the colour that sun can woo from winter trees was missing, they looked black and twisted and sinister. There was no beauty anywhere. The whole place looked utterly dead, and, tarnished by the thaw, rather horribly corrupt.

Mr. Isaacson shivered and turned up the collar of his shabby coat. Desolation seized him and there came with it the rather dreadful thought that the ruined Castle up there was a symbol of England herself. Great and glorious had been her history, this throne of kings, this rock, this fortress, and great had been her finest hour with the love of her people flung about her as the summer woods had wrapped themselves about this Castle on the hill, but was she doomed now, doomed like this Castle? Mr. Isaacson, to his own great surprise, had become a patriot of late. Steadily through the summer this country of his birth and his adoption had been claiming him. It had made its demands and he had fulfilled them. In the person of Mr. Holly it had saved him and won his gratitude, through the children it had asked for service, in Stephen it had claimed his friendship and in Miss Brown his love. He had given and was one with it. He loved it. He knew now why he cared for the Castle so much, why it had always drawn him irresistibly. It was England, England, that ridiculously small country that took up so small a space in the world's landscape but, like a distant city in a Van Eyck picture, could catch its lovers in an enchantment that would never let them go; and now perhaps the enchanted city was doomed.

He stood still on the road, his chin sunk on his chest, his hands in his pockets, in the grip of that misery of dread that in those cold dark days of waiting for what the spring might bring was sometimes a visitor to stouter hearts than his, hearts that had not failed all through the clangour and danger of the summer and autumn. Could she survive? Could she? Was it possible? Twilight had come down on the woods and the sands of his faith had run out. He shivered and groaned a little.

Somewhere there was a light burning. Somewhere a lamp had been lit. It seemed to be hanging in the bare branches of that thorn tree just in front of him, a very small but very steady light. He looked at it, started, looked right through the branches of the tree and saw that it was burning in a room on the ground floor of the ruined Castle. Words that he had read somewhere flashed through his mind, by chance he would have said himself in the old days, though Stephen would have said not by chance. "Let the leaves perish, but let the tree stand, living and bare. Let the leaves fall, and many branches. But the quick of the tree must not perish." [1]

Nor would it. There was the quick of the tree, visible to his straining eyes. It was Stephen's light burning there in the Castle, Stephen to whose spirit there had gathered, like the small rivulets running through the woods to unite in the stream beside the thorn tree, the essential love and valour that the men of his blood had flung to this life before they left it. So with England. The quick of the tree was not dead. They were approaching the peak now, the height of the pain, when the texture of quality shows, and the Castle showed a living light. The end was not yet. Soon would be the time for the turning of the tide and the rising of the sap. The buds would break again and the trees be misted with the living green.

He loved the Castle as never before. He loved it with what was perhaps the most selfless love he had ever felt. When it had seemed to him like a celestial city, it had not cheated him, for within its broken battered walls it still held life, it was the house of life, and life, he suddenly knew in a flash that struck like

[1] D. H. Lawrence.

lightning, was the glorious eternal God in whom until now he had not believed. A man's life was his own, he had thought once. That was a lie. It was not his own, but God's. It *was* God. "I had rather be a doorkeeper in the house of my God. . . ."

He found that he was glowing with warmth, so warm that even the branch of the old thorn tree that he was holding seemed to have grown warm beneath his hand. What had happened to him? What had happened to him down here in this haunted valley, to *him* of all people, to Jo Isaacson, the wandering Jew, the failure, the doubter? Nothing, yet everything. What he had hitherto only accepted as a hypothesis he had suddenly seen as a fact, that was all. Seen it as though the blinds had suddenly flown up in a darkened house.

"I had rather be a doorkeeper in the house of my God. . . ."

He walked up and down beside the thorn tree, loth to leave this valley that would always be to him the holiest spot on earth. Yes, better to be a doorkeeper in that house than to dwell in the tents of exile. Those old poets of his race had known what they were talking about. . . . "Yea, the sparrow hath found her a house, and the swallow a nest where she may lay her young. . . . Blessed are they that dwell in Thy house. . . . For one day in Thy courts is better than a thousand. . . . By the waters of Babylon we sat down and wept when we remembered thee, O Sion. . . ." Exiles, when all the while the door stood open.

He stood by the thorn tree again looking up at the Castle, and quietly, gently, without diminution of his joy, without any lessening yet of the blazing vitality that was in him, he became aware once more of the pressure of material fact.

But not in relation to himself yet, only as regarded the Castle. He stood looking at it, and it hurt him intolerably to think of it left alone and uncared for in the days that were coming. A doorkeeper? There had been a doorkeeper at the Castle once, but she was dead. Mrs. Heather was dead. And the Birley treasures that once she had displayed, the old tattered flag, and the portraits, were gone too, but the stories she told of them were still alive. Who was there now to tell those stories to the weary gaping tourists, to people the old walls with living life for them and give it as their possession into their hands? Who was there now to say to them, as Mrs. Heather had said, this is yours, your own, yourself, and to send them away crowned kings, inheritors of a kingdom happy? . . . There was himself.

He gave one last look at the thorn tree where the light had shone, one last look about him at the beloved and haunted valley, and then strode up through the woods like a young man, the blood pounding in his veins and a song singing itself in his heart, and the words of the song were the words that long ago he had seen chalked upon a London wall, confronting the coming Blitz like a trumpet blast. "If in this life only we have hope. . . ." By God, *that* was true, too. This quickening divine power that he had experienced could not be confined to this world, for cruel, sordid, ugly, devilish, can be this world, and by the nature of things that power could have neither source nor ending in it; only flow through it, around it, over it, under it, gathering up the gold into its eternal shining and burning the dross in its fire.

III

Stephen, the dim ruined study lit by the light of an ancient oil lamp that belonged to Mrs. Heather, was writing a few last minute instructions for Pratt and Bob Hatchett, and making out cheques for the few remaining bills, when the wild figure of Mr. Isaacson suddenly appeared between him and the window, blocking out the grey deepening twilight. He looked up, startled. Mr. Isaacson's eyes were gleaming strangely in his dark face, and his long unbuttoned overcoat seemed in the faint light not to be of modern cut, but to hang straight from the shoulders like some dim dark garment out of the past. Stephen caught his breath, for the stench of blood and sweat was suddenly stifling him, and he heard again that cry of despair in the narrow street that was blocked at both its ends. . . . How strange it is, he thought, this persistence of events that are past. All that we do or think seems to have a double eternity, we fling it to life in this world and yet at the same time take it with us to the other country. They permeate each other, the two countries, like air the lungs, and our double responsibility is appalling. . . . It took him a minute or two to be aware of what Mr. Isaacson was saying. ". . . there must be someone to take her place."

"Whose place?" asked the bewildered Stephen.

"Mrs. Heather's," said Mr. Isaacson. "Tourists are not going to cease coming to see this Castle because it's been blown to pieces. Tourists like ruins. You need a man to live here permanently, keep his eye on the place, take them round and tell them the old tales. I shan't need much salary. I could live in Mrs. Heather's cottage."

"Miss Brown is living there with the children at the moment," said Stephen, hopelessly at sea.

Mr. Isaacson caught his breath sharply, as though yet another new hope had suddenly come to him. "I think—if you'll have me —that I could maybe arrange matters with Miss Brown," he said, and his voice was suddenly hoarser than usual, and the blazing light in his eyes turned to a desperate pleading. Stephen felt that he was not understanding quite as well as he ought. That he was not understanding at all. That he was being an utter fool.

"Would you mind saying all that again?" he asked anxiously. "I don't think I was listening properly at the start. I don't think I've quite taken it in."

Mr. Isaacson said it all again. He was stammering, incoherent, exalted, burnt-up with anxiety, devoured by longing, and at that moment utterly alien in spirit to the restrained bewildered young Englishman. . . . Stephen decided that one or both of them had gone completely mad.

"Sit down," he said weakly.

Mr. Isaacson sat down, and they faced each other across the papers that littered the table.

"But your music?" asked Stephen. "You don't want to give up your music, do you?"

"No need to," said Mr. Isaacson. "I can keep it going at the same time. I might even take pupils, you know, down in Torhaven, or get into an orchestra there. I'd be thought respectable with a home. One's not thought much use, you know, sir, unless one belongs somewhere. . . ."

He stopped, as though his voice had been suddenly torn off. He had begun the conversation in a condition of ecstatic confidence, sure that what he wanted would be given him, but now, confronted by the bewildered uncertainty of the young man across the table, he was not so sure. His hands, clasped between his knees, began to shake a little. The silence in the dim room was painful, deep and vibrating with the fate of a soul.

Stephen, drawing rather wild curls and arabesques on his blotting-paper, was doing equally wild accounts in his head. If he were once to take on Isaacson as caretaker to the Castle, the man would probably be a life-long incubus. He'd be in the cottage for life, and he'd have to be paid for life. How could he manage it? There was his war-pay. There was poor old Boulder's legacy, and there was his legacy from his mother. He supposed he could manage it somehow. The arabesques on his blotting-paper turned to figures. It had better be an annuity, or Isaacson would be flung adrift again if he himself were killed. But he did not want to do it. It would cripple him financially. It would make that far lovely future of which he dreamed, that future with Prunella, more poverty-stricken than it need have been. In the silence Mr. Issacson gave a tiny sigh.

It was scarcely more than a breath of pain, yet it seemed to Stephen an echo of that awful cry in the narrow street. What hand had the Beaulieus taken in the pogroms? Who had blocked the street at the other end? It was easy to reject that queer experience at the harbour as sheer fantasy; perhaps it was; but the English pogroms had not been fantasy, and neither had the conviction that had come to him as he flung silver pieces into Isaacson's hat. "I shall suffer, I and my race, if there is justice upon this earth."

Well, they'd suffered. Was the sin wiped out now? The Castle's sin, the sin of England?

Mr. Isaacson raised his head. He looked at the moment like a battered, moulting old eagle. "It's not only for myself I ask it, sir," he said, "it's for the Castle too. I love this place. I'd like to take care of it."

How odd, thought Stephen, that he should so love the home of the men who long ago had massacred his race. Yet not so odd, if now the sin was wiped out by the pain. It was not between them any more, and with reconcilement there comes love. "A king in Israel," had said a voice in his mind when he had first seen this man. Isaacson should have his kingdom, even if it was only the small one of a ruined castle.

"Thank-you for a first-rate suggestion," he said, stretching his hand out across the table. "I'll go away happy if I can leave you in charge. With your music to help on a bit, could you manage on what I'm managing with myself just now, three pounds a week, rent free?"

Mr. Isaacson leaped to his feet and took the outstretched hand. He nearly wrung it off but for a moment or two he could not speak. "Could I manage?" he croaked at last. "I could live like a king!"

They talked a little longer and then he went away, with trumpets sounding in his head and drums thudding in the air about him. He crossed the ruined hall with a majestic stride and went out to the terrace, where he turned back to look at the doorway of which he was to be the keeper. The actual door had been destroyed, but the porch, though battered, was still there, and the words carved over it were still decipherable.

> Come in this way, and fear no more,
> Peace in your heart, leave wide the door.

Turn not the key, nor shut the gate.
None come too soon, nor return too late.

Neither key nor door were there now, the way stood wide open to those who would come here searching for their lost inheritance within the house of life.

Then he swung round and strode off through the woods towards the lodge to fight again for something that he wanted. "Down and out," he had said to himself once within these woods, "down in the ditch outside the Castle walls," and he had not believed it possible that he could fight his way up again. But he had. He was the doorkeeper of that very Castle, and had become so by his own striving. What had come over him that he was striking these mad blows for his own happiness? "From where did I get this darned conceit of myself?" he wondered. It had come gradually, he thought, starting on that day when he had hurled his body into the train as though he flung a tool to a craftsman for his use, and flaming out into this violence of action down there in the valley of the singing stream, that blessed valley where like a lightning flash had come the knowledge of life's immensity. Yet it was not so much for himself as for life that he fought; it was not really of himself that he had this good conceit. Though he had a new respect for the tool that would never again let him sink into the inertia of the defeated, it was all but devoured in his passionate adoration of the thing that used it. . . . And God be thanked for that valley. Whatever it was that brooded there it was compassionate to man.

IV

Miss Brown pulled the curtains across the windows and put the kettle on. Then she lit a rather extravagant array of candles, for there was no gas or electricity at the cottage and Stephen had Mrs. Heather's oil lamp, and looked about her. She had already laid the table for the children's high tea and the soft mingled light of firelight and candlelight shone upon the flowery cups and saucers, the brown boiled eggs, the bread and jam and the teapot like a beehive. The ginger cat with the silver whiskers slept placidly before the fire and the glorious geraniums blazed upon the windowsill. Upstairs the children were taking off their school clothes and getting ready for tea, and as usual taking a very long time about it. Their small stumping feet went backwards and forwards, backwards and forwards, with the sturdy determination and the boundless energy of the very young who still know that living is a joyous thing, demanding all one's love. Just so must the feet of Mrs. Heather's children have sounded overhead as she put the kettle on. . . . Mrs. Heather. . . . Miss Brown thought of her with affection but no sadness. Death had struck quickly and mercifully at an old and happy woman, who like the majority had once lost her childhood's faith that life is to be loved, and unlike the majority had come full circle back and found it again before she died. Lucky Mrs. Heather that she had lived long enough for that second finding that is keeping.

Mrs. Heather, let me find it too, said Miss Brown out of the depth of her cold lifeless misery, and bent to poke up the fire that did not somehow seem to be warming her, though it was such a lovely one, made of pine logs with the resin oozing out, and sweet-scented apple wood. Silly to be living in this little homely cottage that she had always adored, together with warmth and brightness and little children, and to be so unhappy. But once, she supposed, in those days when she did not love her husband, Mrs. Heather had been just as unhappy. She would have dreaded, perhaps, as she bent to poke up the fire, to hear the clang of his boots in the stone-flagged porch and his hand at the door.

She straightened herself suddenly, startled by the footsteps, her heart beating. "Come in," she said.

But it was no ghost, it was Jo Isaacson, whom she had asked to tea. She smiled at him as he came to her, then looked up startled into his transfigured face, for she had never before seen him look so radiantly alive. There was a strange power about him at this moment, a warm and glowing power that struck right through to the heart of her lifeless misery and eased it. He looked immensely tall in the candlelight. His long dark overcoat, hanging loosely from his shoulders, gave his figure a kingly dignity that made him seem almost a stranger to her.

Yet when he spoke in his hoarse familiar voice, eagerly, and with something of the incoherence of an excited little child, she knew him again for her friend Jo Isaacson.

"Mr. Birley—Mr. Stephen—has given me a job," he told her. "Three quid a week. I'm to live here, in this cottage, and be the Castle's doorkeeper—caretaker—and take the tourists round."

Miss Brown was for a moment struck dumb with astonishment. Then she recovered herself and her eyes shone in the candlelight. "Well, I *am* glad," she said. And she was glad. This man had suffered enough.

"I'm glad, too," said Mr. Isaacson. And then he paused and gathered his strength to fight again for his own efficiency, for his happiness and hers, for the enrichment of the whole fabric of human living. He must fight now, quickly, at once, while he was still so strong. "I'm glad too," he said, "and if there could be just one more bit of luck added to this one I'd be more than glad, I'd be as happy as a man can be. I think I have loved you from the first moment that I saw you. We helped each other then. If we married, I think we could always help each other. And we could make a home for those two kids, here, in this cottage, in this shelter in the woods." He paused again, and once more he was pleading with desperation. "I love you as much as a man can love a woman. I do not ask that you should love me in that way, only that you should give me the right to love you, the chance to be of use, the chance to strike down roots and be at rest."

It was like it had been in the woods that first time. His hungry eyes devoured her face as he asked her for something that only she could give. But she was not frightened this time, for now she knew his kindness that had never hurt a human creature all the days of his life. But she was stunned, for, absorbed as she had been in her own love for the Birleys, she had not even noticed that he loved her. And she was miserable and desperate, too, for though his warmth had eased the misery in her heart, there was no response there except the old one of her liking and her sympathy. The old question came back. What was she to do? What was she to *do*?

"Miss Brown!" called Moppet down the stairs.

"What is it?" she asked, almost gasping with thankfulness for the interruption. . . . Oh, for a moment to think, to adjust herself, to find her footing in the tumbling confusion of her thoughts.

"My stocking's laddered."

"Put on the other pair," said Miss Brown.

"I can't find the other pair."

"I can!" yelled Poppet in superior tones. There was a patter of footsteps, a slither and a sudden bump, followed by shrieks of anguish.

"There! Why did I polish under that mat?" Miss Brown reproached herself. "Sit down, Jo. Take your coat off and get warm. I won't be a moment. Coming, Poppet!" And she hurried up the little winding staircase that led from the parlour to the bedroom above.

The practical duties of a mother were with her now merely a matter of mechanism. She scarcely heard Poppet's roars, she was now so used to them. As she kissed the hot red face, rubbed the bumped behind, found Moppet's stockings, picked up scattered garments from the floor and wielded a hair-brush, her stunned mind came to life again and her thoughts raced, quickly and feverishly, but with a surprising clarity, coming to her almost like a series of moving pictures.

That day when she had had tea with Mrs. Heather and realised that it was in cottages like this one that the idea of home would be kept safe. The Castles would be destroyed but the little homes hidden like Peter Rabbit's among the tree trunks would tend the flame.

That day in the woods when she had found the grief-stricken children in Mr. Isaacson's arms, being comforted by him as she had not been able to comfort them, because he knew them so well and was like another father to them. Would it not be well with them if he were to be always their father? She had been thinking that day about rehearsing scenes for the drama of living. Certainly that little scene in the woods had been like a foreshadowing of family love.

That "Enquire Within" notice in the window, that had always seemed to promise her the answer to that question as to how to achieve Mrs. Heather's "breakin' away from myself" that led to the oneness and the love "that do be man's inheritance, lost out of the world." If she married this man whom she was fond of but did not love she would have to die to herself, to batten down her old lovely memories of Mr. Birley, lest she compare one man with the other, to crush out all thought of herself at all, otherwise the thing would not be possible. If she could do that the "how" would be answered. But could she do it? Could she, God helping her, rise to a height so far beyond her own strength to attain to? Desperately she sought for the answer, searching her own character, remembering that day when she had knelt by her bed and said to herself, "I'm not a self-sufficient woman. I can't get along unless I can be indispensable to someone." Did it matter much, with a nature like hers, to whom one was indispensable? Had she not always come to love those whom she had served? Yes, she had, and in this service, because she did not want to give it, there would be, for the first time, no selfishness, and so she would dare to say, "God's help be with me," lay hold upon it and succeed.

She was astonished at this moment at the power of her own faith, remembering how once it had seemed shattered. It was Mr. Birley who had given it back to her again. He had begun the process by that talk in the train, and her unrequited love for him had done the rest. Moving step by step away from the self to which no responsive adoration turned back her thoughts she had

253

touched a reality she could not help but recognise. . . . And now here was Jo Isaacson offering her just what she had offered Mr. Birley, the best love of all, unrequited love. She, of all people, knew how to value that. And how odd it was that she should have done for Jo exactly what Mr. Birley had done for her; put him back into the pattern of things; she had not known that until he had told her that afternoon and it had immensely strengthened her tenderness for him. Could she possibly bring herself to deal him the very same blow that Mr. Birley had dealt her that afternoon? No, she could not, for she knew exactly, down to the last throb of pain, how he would suffer.

Her thoughts seemed gathering together, weaving into a pattern, catching her in the mesh, imprisoning her. For a moment she fought against it, then she yielded. The pattern had re-formed again, and it was Mrs. Heather's pattern of wife and mother. What an utter fool she had been ever to fear that life could cast one away. Yield yourself to it and it will use you to the end.

"I am going downstairs now," she said to Poppet and Moppet. "You can put on your frocks for yourselves and then come down. Put on your best frocks. Mr. Isaacson is here and it's going to be a party."

To their cries of delight she left the room and went downstairs. Jo had taken off his coat and was sitting by the fire as she had bidden him. It looked very natural to see him there. She would see him sitting by the fire like that many times, but never again, she vowed, with that look of pleading in his eyes. She smiled at him and he jumped up and held out his arms and she gave herself to them with a simplicity that was the loveliest thing he had ever known.

He could not let her go, but he held her gently, curbing his passion, trying to match the freshness of her giving with a response as clear and lovely as though it were the first of his life. And so it was, he told himself. Down there in the valley of the singing stream it was as though he had died and been born again. This was a new life and a new love, and they both of them had about them the freshness of the springtime when the buds break forth again and the trees are misted with the living green.

This woman would not go stale like the others in the old life, he thought, his arms about her; no cheat about this one. No cheat anywhere. Neither the Castle, nor his music, nor anything at all that was lovely and of good report had ever lied to him. The state of being to which the *Andante* lifted one was a state of being that existed. All true, all true, and the fear of loneliness, his own peculiar fear, destroyed for ever. What matter if she would never love him as he loved her? The glory of life did not consist in taking, and then piling up the goods about one like a prison wall.

Ten minutes later the new, happy little family sat noisily at tea. Father and Mother and children. Miss Brown, wielding the brown teapot, marvelled at the powerlessness of evil to destroy that everlasting pattern. It might strike at it, wounding and mutilating, but the severed parts only sought their complement again in a new trinity.

She smiled, then her smile faded, she set down her teapot and listened intently, for above the clamour of the children's joy came the sound of a horse's hoofs beating clearly and rhythmically in the still evening. They came up through the woods, nearer and nearer, passed the cottage, then died away into silence. It was Stephen, homeless because the light of home had shifted from Castle to cottage, riding out into exile like his fathers before him. . . . She picked up the teapot again and smiled at Mr. Isaacson, and he had no knowledge of the weeping in her heart.

v

Out through the shadows of the trees, up the hill to the main road that ran along the crest of the hill, then to the left, with the last of the sunset westward and night coming up out of the east. Don't look back. If you did you might see the old Castle through the bare trees, left desolate again after so many years, and the grey church tower rising above remembered graves, and the orchards, and the tumbled roofs of the village. Don't look back. Look forward. It was still possible to see the world about one, for the clouds had parted and a few stars shone out, while over the sea a long line of primrose light gleamed through the purple veils. There was no sound except the clop-clop of Golden Eagle's hoofs on the hard road as he trotted steadily forward, his lovely neck arched, his nostrils dilating and his body quivering with his unconquerable pride. Stephen wondered if he would eat his heart out in the new stable to which he was going. If he did no one would ever know it. He would hold his head as high as ever and give no sign.

They were on the crest of the hill, just before it dropped downwards to the valley, when they found themselves in the midst of a flock of sheep. Stephen drew rein and sat waiting, softly caressing Golden Eagle's satin neck, feeling the sensitive responsive tremor of the nerves beneath his fingers. So often he had waited like this, while the sheep went past him in the twilight. The quiet, the soft patter of the passing feet, made it a moment of deep peace.

"Good night, sir." It was Fred Weatherby, with his face like a wrinkled apple and his patient eyes, his stick in his hand and his dog at his heels.

"Good night, Fred."

The sheep passed and he rode on down the hill, and then at last dared to turn and look back, for there was no danger now that he could possibly see the Castle and the church tower above the graves.

But he could see Beacon Hill standing there like a great bastion protecting the country of his birth, and it was crowned with stars, and among the stars there moved a tall figure with a weapon in his hand and a dog at his heels. Up and down he moved, pacing the short strip of turf worn by the feet of the sentries, and then he stood quite still, immensely tall, his figure full of power, looking out over the sea.

Who was it on guard to-night? To Stephen's imagination, quickened by what Prunella had said beside the Crusader's tomb, that watcher on the hill was no man whom he knew in the flesh. He stood there dressed in steel, his helm among the stars, his great cross-handled sword drawn in his hand, looking out over the hills and woodlands that fell away below him to the sea. In his stillness there was a deep awareness. He knew of the wild things cradled in the woods and fields, and of the sheep going home over the hill. He knew about the orchards, and the farmsteads where little children were dreaming under the eaves. He knew where the dead lay sleeping and where the living wept. He knew all there was to know of this little country of his birth and he held it in the hollow of his hand. And beyond these green hills was the pulsing thunder of the workshops and the roar of cities and the strife of kings, and he knew that too, and watched it all. And he saw good and evil, light and darkness, heaven and hell, locked in combat; he saw the smoke of the battle and smelled the reek of the blood and sweat and tears, and yet he was not afraid. For he was a Man, standing on guard over his inheritance of all that lives. To him it had been given to pass through life and death to life again, and know them one; to rise to the very peak and height of agony and find himself looking into the eyes of God beneath the crown of thorns, to fall through the bottomless abyss and find himself kneeling at the feet of God pierced through with nails, to probe each way through doubting and despair and find the arms of God outstretched in love upon the cross; because he was a Man and into man has been breathed the breath of life, and life is God.